D0410435

SUPERFAN

Morris Keston dedicates this book to the memories of Philip Isaacs, his travelling companion during many of the trips with Spurs and England, and Reg Drury, who introduced him to many of his friends in football.

Nick Hawkins dedicates his efforts to his father Roland, who sadly passed away before the book was completed.

The amazing life of
MORRIS KESTON
SUPERFAN
Football fan extraordinaire & friend of the stars

By MORRIS KESTON & NICK HAWKINS

VSP

Published by Vision Sports Publishing in 2010

Vision Sports Publishing
19–23 High Street
Kingston upon Thames
Surrey
KT1 1LL

www.visionsp.co.uk

ISBN 13: 978-1905326-79-2

© Morris Keston & Nick Hawkins

All rights reserved. No part of this publication may be reproduced,
stored in a retrieval system, or transmitted in any form or by any means,
electronic, mechanical, photocopying, recording or otherwise,
without the prior permission of the publishers.

This book is sold subject to the condition that it shall not, by way of trade
or otherwise, be lent, re-sold, hired out, or otherwise, without the publisher's
prior consent in any form of binding or cover other than that in which it
is published and without a similar condition including this condition
being imposed on the subsequent purchaser.

A CIP record for this book is available from the British library

Design: Doug Cheeseman
Copy editing: Ian Turner

Typeset by Palimpsest Book Production Limited,
Grangemouth, Stirlingshire

Printed and bound in the UK by CPI Mackays,
Chatham, ME5 8TD

© **Mixed Sources**
Product group from well-managed
forests, controlled sources and
recycled wood or fibre
FSC www.fsc.org Cert no. TT-COC-002341
© 1996 Forest Stewardship Council

CONTENTS

ACKNOWLEDGEMENTS

I would first like to thank Nick Hawkins, my collaborator on this book, who had the foresight to recognise that my life in football was a story worth telling. He's done a fantastic job putting the whole thing together and made me a very proud man. Nick's father Roland, who sadly passed away a few months into the project, also deserves recognition, as without his words of wisdom and encouragement, his son may never have contacted me and my story may never have been told.

I've been blessed with many great friends in my lifetime, many of whom feature in this book, and to them all I'd like to say thanks for enriching my life. Special thanks go to Terry Venables for the foreword, Graeme Souness for his tribute and Keith Palmer for his efforts in gaining many of the quotes about me from my friends in football. I'm deeply touched by everyone's kind words.

There are many people to thank for filling in the gaps and jogging my memory during the writing process, including my wife Sylvia and former son-in-law Paul Miller. My good mates, Phil Beal, Ted Buxton, George Cohen, Monte Fresco, Sir Philip Green, Roy Hodgson, Sir Geoff Hurst, Pat Jennings, Ken Jones, Sir Stirling Moss, Alan Mullery and Dave Webb, have also helped out on that score. I'd also like to pay respects to some friends who are sadly no longer with us: George Best, Ted Croker, Reg Drury, Johnny Haynes, Philip Isaacs, Bobby Moore, Bill Nicholson, Sir Bobby Robson, Tony Waddington and Billy Weinberger. I miss them all so much.

Nick has also called upon the help of many people when researching the chapters, including Tottenham Hotspur's historian Andy Porter and Spurs fans Mark Bailey, Mike Basing and the Eldridge family. The following people have also helped out, one way or another, and I send them my sincere thanks: Graham Budd, David Convery, James Evans, John Farley, Chris Hunt, Glen Isherwood and Gary Miles. A special mention also goes to Nick's fiancée Deborah for putting up with me hogging her phone line for the last 18 months and for helping to put my memories down on to paper. Jim Drewett and Toby Trotman at Vision Sports Publishing also deserve a pat on the back, not only for backing this project, but also for their professionalism in editorial and marketing matters.

My life in football would never have been possible without the support of a very understanding wife. Sylvia certainly deserves a medal for putting up with me, and this obsession of mine. In fact, for our 21st wedding anniversary I actually bought her one! It was gold and engraved with the words: 'Awarded to Sylvia Keston for bravery above and beyond the call of duty.' She's definitely one in a million and I feel extremely fortunate to have been married to her for the last 54 years. I'd also like to thank my son Allan, daughter Shelley, nephew Lawrence, granddaughters Charlotte and Amy and my great-granddaughter Grace for keeping up the family tradition and dynasty of Spurs supporters.

And finally, to the thousands of amateur and professional footballers that have entertained me over the last 66 years. Your dedication to the sport has brought me more joy than you can ever imagine.

Morris Keston, April 2010

FOREWORD
By Terry Venables

There haven't been too many books written about football supporters, but Tottenham Hotspur's Morris Keston is anything but an ordinary football fan. Having been associated with the game for many years, I've met many diehards whose lives have been completely taken over by their love for their club. What sets Morris apart from the rest is that he's given so much more than just his loyalty to a team.

In the days when professional footballers were accessible to fans, Morris made lasting friendships with just about everyone in the game that he came into contact with. He was a good friend to so many players, managers and club officials and not just at Spurs but many other clubs besides. Back when I was playing, the money wasn't great for professional sportsmen, but Morris was always helping out players, especially those approaching the end of their careers. Whether it were organising a testimonial game or just giving them sound advice on what to do next – Morris was always the first to help the players and their families.

His life has always revolved around football, whether it's Spurs, England or just the game in general. Over the years I've travelled to many, many places with him, all over the world in fact, and usually he has gone with the team to games. He's always been extremely determined to get to Spurs matches and even temporarily sacrificed his religion for a meaningless friendly, claiming to be Christian instead of Jewish in order to gain entry to Egypt. If that's not dedication, I don't know what is!

Whenever we speak, it's nearly always about football. It's a passion that's been all consuming in his life. He's totally obsessed with it, but in the best possible way. We used to argue about football until the cows came home, but it was always in a passionate and well-meaning way and we always finished our debate with a smile on our face. I never tire of reminding him of the time he rang my office at Spurs and said, "That new signing of yours, Teddy Sheringham, he'll never play for England. You've bought a right dud there!"

In the 45 years that he's been my best friend we've had many great laughs. I remember when I took QPR to Wembley in the 1982 FA Cup Final, he was desperate to sit in the dugout with me and cheer on Spurs. I couldn't believe his cheek and told him 'No way, you can stay at home and watch it on TV.' He was there of course and loved every minute of Tottenham's victory. He's certainly a one-off, they'll never be another football supporter like him and I feel privileged to have known him and his wonderful family for all these years. Stand up Morris, finally it's your turn to take a well-deserved bow.

TRIBUTE
By Graeme Souness

I first met Morris when I came down to Tottenham Hotspur as a 15-year-old lad from Edinburgh. It would be fair to say that at the time I really needed a friend and someone to give me solid advice down in London. Morris Keston was that man. He was 'Mr Spurs' to everyone, a true fan, who was on great terms with the legends of the club. He knew all of the big-hitters like Alan Gilzean, Alan Mullery, Mike England and Martin Peters. Morris wasn't just interested in the star names though. He was just as keen to help the youngsters at the club.

At Tottenham, all of the players looked on Morris as someone they could trust and rely on for the answers to any problems or worries they might have. With Morris, you knew you could go to him and he'd sort things out, one way or another. I know from personal experience how good his advice was. He was forever trying to persuade this young chap from Edinburgh to be patient and make a go of it at Spurs. I was young and foolish at the time and thought I had all of the answers, but Morris was always someone I could turn to when I needed to be put right. He was a calming influence on me, as well as a great source for sound advice and encouragement. If you talk to any Spurs player of any generation they'll say the same. Morris has always been highly thought of and with good reason.

It's been a pleasure to have known him down the years and the best thing I can say about him is the man's still someone a 15-year-old joining Tottenham Hotspur today can turn to for the best help and advice.

INTRODUCTION

"There won't be another book like this one, as the fans don't get to know the players anymore. If you speak to any top player from his era they all know Morris Keston. When I used to go to his flat in Portman Square they were all there: Bobby Moore, Geoff Hurst, Jimmy Greaves, you name them, they were there. The players love him, not only because he is genuine, but because he's a wonderful man. If he were a woman, I'd marry him!"
Monte Fresco MBE (sports photographer, SJA award winner)

Morris Keston is widely acclaimed to be Tottenham Hotspur's most fanatical fan. He was brought to the attention of the football world in 1972 when he was featured in Hunter Davies's seminal book about Spurs, *The Glory Game*. In the chapter entitled 'The Hangers-on', Morris's obsession with the club and his friendships with the players he'd pay good money to watch was dissected in detail; the picture painted of him was one of a successful businessman desperate to burn his company profits on Tottenham's star players. "Every big club has a fan like Morris Keston, but few have them as big as Morris," Davies said. However, dig a little deeper, and it quickly becomes clear that it was actually the players who used to 'hang on' to him. Being part of Spurs' most fanatical fan's inner circle and getting invited to his legendary parties was as beneficial to players such as Jimmy Greaves, Geoff Hurst and Bobby Moore as they were an ego-trip for Morris.

Such parties compounded a falling-out with the directors of Tottenham in 1967, when the FA Cup-winning side abandoned the party laid on for them at the Savoy for Morris's livelier affair at the Hilton. However, they also enabled him to develop friendships with sportsmen that opened doors into a whole other incredible world: a seat on Frank Sinatra's private plane, a meal with Muhammad Ali, an invite to Zsa Zsa Gabor's wedding reception, guest of honour at Caesars Palace in Las Vegas. Morris's love of shoulder-rubbing went on to be fed by friendships with Hollywood royalty that would never have seemed possible to Morris when he worked as a 'lather boy' at 14 in an East End barbers.

For a generation of football legends, however, Morris Keston was more than a friend of celebrities and honorary club social secretary. His victory celebrations and fundraising testimonial matches and dinners for the likes of Bobby Moore, Gordon Banks and Alan Mullery pale into insignificance when compared to his role as an unofficial adviser to the footballers he had befriended, who, in the days before agents and magazine deals, had to look out for their own affairs. Morris acted as an unofficial football agent before there were football agents, and all of his introductions, advice and inside knowledge were given for free. Geoff Hurst signed for Stoke City in a secret meeting organised by Morris in his West London flat and unknown by many, Tottenham's Pat Jennings was signed up for a lucrative tour of Indonesia on loan to another club on Morris's recommendation.

At the very heart of Morris Keston's story is his 66-year love affair with football. He is firstly a fanatical fan and the statistics, meticulously noted down by him since 1952 in well-thumbed journals, speak for themselves. Since dodging Hitler's doodlebugs as a boy stood on the terraces at White Hart Lane, Morris has attended over 4,500 matches; almost 3,000 involving his beloved Spurs, of whose games he has only ever missed two home games since 1951. That equates to over 400,000 minutes of live action, and in that time Morris has seen the ball hit the back of the net more than 13,500 times! He has followed Tottenham from Belgrade to Bratislava, from Connecticut to Cairo, all during an era when such foreign travel was not the norm. The 1,500 other games Morris has watched include many of England's biggest moments, from the 1966 World Cup win at Wembley to the penalty defeats at Italia '90 and Euro '96. He has attended the majority of FA Cup finals played since 1952 and travelled all over Britain watching lower division and non-League encounters. He also witnessed many of George Best's comebacks and Pele's stint in US soccer.

When Spurs had a week off, Morris usually ended up in the directors' box as an honoured guest of a multitude of other top clubs whose officials he had befriended. These very clubs saw the potential value of such dedication to football, and often tried to turn his head from Tottenham, even offering him directorships of clubs such as Derby, Fulham and Stoke City. Morris was never tempted, and the only board he ever wanted to sit on was that of Tottenham Hotspur. He came within a whisker of that very boardroom, but was pipped at the post by Alan Sugar, who linked up with then manager Terry Venables to take over the club in 1991. Ironically, it was Morris who had introduced Sugar to Venables several years earlier.

Morris Keston's obsessive following of Spurs and the national team and his deep involvement with football has had a constant effect on his family. In 35 years, he only went on one family holiday, as there was simply never a week when there wasn't a match to attend, a celebration party to organise or a player who needed his help. Morris's holidays were spent following Spurs on pre-season tours. The very conception of his children was meticulously planned around his football commitments, and the most important of family social events were not enough for him to sacrifice even the most insignificant of matches for. Morris earned no money from football, and his trips, parties and tickets were financed by his family's only income: his clothing warehouse in Bethnal Green. In dealing with objections from the family, Morris soon found himself an ally from within: in 1981 his daughter, Shelley, married Tottenham's defensive rock Paul Miller after meeting him at her 'uncle' Terry Venables's pub in East London.

Friendships with football greats such as Venables have proved deep and long-lasting, and they are friendships that the football fan of today would find it impossible to make. Morris Keston grew to love football in an era when its stars were anything but 'starry': he remembers giving lifts to the players in the fifties, and forged relationships with players in the days when he used to take home the same wage working in a factory as they did playing professional football. Today, Morris retains his super-fan status but seldom gets anywhere near the players of the modern game. This reflects the enormous change that money has brought about in football. Getting through the legions of agents, bodyguards, publicists, pop-star wives and, indeed, hangers-on, is impossible for today's fans, and means that there really will never be another supporter who could take a similar path as Morris Keston and gain access to the heart of the game. For Morris, however, his links with the players of yesteryear mean that he still has his finger on the pulse of the modern game. He counts many of today's Premier League managers as personal friends, and his thoughts and opinions are still heard and respected by the people grappling with today's billionaire owners and multi-million pound contracts. As fans go, there's never been one quite like Morris and there probably never will be again. There really is, only one Morris Keston.

PREFACE

"We're talking about the most dedicated individual you could ever wish to meet; to his team, their players, wherever they played or celebrated, and most of all, to Spurs and football. His functions for various cup-winning sides were legendary and typical of an incredibly generous and thoughtful man."
Ken Jones (sports journalist, former chairman of the Football Writers' Association)

"Morris was, and always will be, a true and revered friend amongst three generations of Spurs. He is a very genuine and decent man, who won respect and admiration for the great support, generosity and friendship that emanated throughout our playing years, and beyond."
Steve Perryman MBE (Spurs and England, FWA Player of the Year 1982)

I must give credit to the older boys who lived in my street for first introducing me to football. My mother said I often watched them playing from the living-room window, trans-fixed, as they kicked a well-worn tennis ball around our potholed street, just off Commercial Road in London's East End. One afternoon, she urged me to go and join them. She was probably keen to get me out of the house so she could tidy up before my father, a tailor, returned from the factory where he worked. I always did as my mother said and went outside and asked one of the boys if I could play. "Do you know the rules?" he asked. I admitted that I didn't and listened intently as the eight-year-old explained them to me.

"This lot are shooting into this goal and our lot are shooting into that goal. Remember, it's football, not rugby – you're not allowed to pick the ball up."

After that brief explanation, I rushed from the pavement into the road and joined the game. After chasing the ball for five minutes and getting nowhere, I was told it was my turn to go in goal. Within seconds of taking up my position in between a pile of coats, the first scuffed shot trickled slowly towards me. I excitedly rushed from my imaginary goal line and took a wild swing and connected – with fresh air. I quickly turned round and watched in horror as the ball crept into the goal. Half of the boys cheered in delight and my teammates glared at me in disbelief. At that moment, I wished those holes in the road would swallow me up.

"You idiot! You're the goalkeeper! Why didn't you just pick the ball up?" screamed one irate boy. Fighting back the tears, I replied: "But you told me I couldn't use my hands!" As the sound of laughter echoed in my ears, I ran back inside the shelter of my home and slammed the door behind me.

That humiliating introduction to the national game took place in 1939, roughly about the time that Germany invaded Poland and the Second World War began. It must have brought back bad memories for my parents, who had both fled Poland to escape anti-Jewish riots when they were children. My mother Jeannie was just a toddler when she arrived in England in 1907 and my father Sidney Kasten was 14. He hitchhiked all the way from Poland to escape the pogroms and joined his brother Joe in England. When he arrived on a boat from France, immigration officials incorrectly registered his surname as Keston and it has remained our family name ever since.

Life was hard growing up in war-torn London, although as kids, my sister Betty and I were oblivious to the hardships. Despite being classed as a foreigner, my father still served in the Army with the Pioneer Corps. He was stationed in Aldershot and then Cheshire and did what he called "the dirty work", cleaning out the messes and barracks. I remember him telling me when he returned on leave that England footballer Stan Cullis was his PT instructor. It didn't mean too much to me at the time, but I told the boys in our street and they were impressed enough to promote me from ballboy to defender.

In 1939, Betty and I were evacuated from our Stepney home to Egham in Surrey, where we stayed with an old couple.

Their house was very nice and clean, but they hardly ever fed us. When my mother found us in an emaciated state she insisted that the authorities moved us to a more caring family in the town. After four months with a new family, my mother visited again and after finding us living in a filthy house and infested with head lice she took us back to East London. "You're better off risking the Blitz with me," she said and it certainly was a risk! We would have to rush down to the underground shelter at Aldgate Station when Hermann Goring came knocking. One night our house was destroyed in one of the German Luftwaffe's bombing raids. After salvaging what we could from the remains of where our home once stood, my mother took us to Leeds and the safety of my uncle's home. We returned to London after the Blitz in May 1941 and I won a scholarship to a very good grammar school called Grocers in Hackney Downs. Harold Pinter, the playwright and Nobel Prize winner, was in my class. Unlike Pinter, I never paid much attention to the teachers and couldn't wait to leave when I was 14.

I wasn't particularly into football before the age of 12, preferring to go to the cinema on a Saturday afternoon. I did have two friends at school though, called David Fisher and David Abrahams, who were both mad about it. They were cousins and one supported Arsenal and the other Tottenham. They argued constantly about which team was best, or whether George Ludford of Spurs or Ted Drake of Arsenal was the better player. In the summer of 1943, I finally cracked after being nagged for months by my friends to join them at a Saturday afternoon match. However, I insisted that I had to be back in time for the early evening film at the Clapton flicks. As it happened, on 23rd August, 1943, the opening day of the 1943/44 season in the Football League South, Arsenal were playing away at Chelsea, whereas Tottenham were at home to Crystal Palace. It was easier to get the train from my home in Hackney to White Hart Lane Station than travel across London to Chelsea, so we went to the Spurs game. I think it was sixpence to get in and we stood in the enclosure, which was in front of what is now the West Stand. My friends insisted that we arrived two hours before kick-off to get a good spot. We gave a guy an extra penny to be lifted over the turnstile into the second part of the ground, where we could watch the game from the halfway line. The ground was quite basic then. There were no tea bars and no corporate boxes and both ends were uncovered.

During wartime football, clubs could field guest players in their sides. For my first game, the whole of the defence were Spurs players, and Ludford was the only forward not a guest player that day. Percy Hooper played in goal and deputised for Ted Ditchburn. The right back was a guy called Ralph Ward, who my friends called 'the Butcher', because he used to make mincemeat of all forwards, and the left back was a Welsh international called Bill Whatley. The half back line included Roy White, an Army sergeant who had been evacuated from Dunkirk after his boat was torpedoed. He temporarily lost his sight during that incident, but eventually recovered it and continued to play for Spurs and became an Army major. Jack Chisholm, with his neatly trimmed beard, played at centre half and Vic Buckingham, who won two Wartime caps for England, played at right half.

A crowd of 8,189 witnessed a 1–1 draw that day, with Stan Clayton, a Notts County player at inside right, scoring Tottenham's goal. I doubt many of the spectators who hurried out of the ground at the end felt inspired by what they had seen, although I certainly had been. I loved every second of those 90 minutes and queued for an hour after the game at the players' entrance to get George Ludford's autograph. I was immediately hooked and returned to White Hart Lane the following week, this time to see Arsenal, who shared Tottenham's ground during the war while their Highbury home was used as an air raid precautions stronghold. I enjoyed watching the Arsenal team just as much, but it was one week too late for me; my allegiance was already with Spurs.

I left school aged 14 in 1945. My mother and father weren't too pleased with my decision to leave school early, especially when they were ordered to pay back some of the grant money that had helped to buy my books and school uniform. They were equally unimpressed when I took a job as a lather boy in a barber's shop in Euston Road, near King's Cross Station, although I reasoned that it was to help pay them back the money. I worked all day, Monday to Friday, and Saturday mornings, lathering faces and sweeping up hair for 37 pence a week. Our busiest days would be Fridays and Saturdays, as soldiers who were stationed in the Midlands and up North would come down by train for a weekend in London. They'd pop in for a haircut and a shave before a night on the tiles. However, this proved problematic for me, as I insisted that my boss let me leave early on Saturday to go and watch Spurs. He would soon get the hump when I downed my broom and shaving stick and walked out on the stroke of midday. One Saturday, the shop was packed solid and men were even queuing outside for their short back and sides, and when I walked out, the barber pleaded with me to stay. When I refused, he told me not to bother coming back! It was a shame as I enjoyed working there. I could have been the next Vidal Sassoon, but Spurs got in the way!

I suppose that was the beginning of my Spurs obsession. I continued to go to every home match during my youth and apart from an 18-month period from 1950 to 1951 when I was stationed in Egypt during National Service, I've watched all but two of Tottenham's home matches since 1952. A triple-heart bypass operation forced me to miss a match against West Ham in April 1994. I begged the surgeon to allow me to go, telling him: "I don't want to lose my home record!" He said: "If I let you go we'll lose YOU!" I also missed the visit of Manchester United in September 2004, after tripping on the pavement and badly injuring my shoulder. Spurs lost both games, so at least I can still say I've seen every Spurs victory at White Hart Lane since 1952.

After receiving my demob papers, I immediately threw myself into football again. I took a job as a commercial traveller with a firm called Lekissa and would spend two weeks at a time on the road delivering suits and dresses to department stores all over the country. I'd leave straight after the Spurs game on a Saturday and head west with a packed van. I usually stayed at a guest house in Bournemouth overnight and after delivering some stock, I'd drive to Plymouth and watch a second division game, before making my way to Exeter St David's Railway Station to collect more stock that the firm had sent down on the overnight train. From there, I'd often drive to Bristol and see a midweek reserve game at either

Eastville or Ashton Gate, before heading north and watching Worksop play in the Midland League. I'd then drive to Leeds and after making another drop-off, I'd watch a match at Elland Road, before heading back to London with an empty van in time to see my beloved Spurs. After a week's rest, watching whatever matches I could find in London, I'd stock the van up and start all over again.

In 1952, I was going to as many as four games a week and began recording details of each match that I saw in a journal. I've still got that journal and have completed two more since. Back in the fifties, the only way to see a game was to part with two shillings and go through the turnstile. The only football shown on TV in those days was the FA Cup Final and occasionally the England versus Scotland international. That was it! If you wanted to see the best players in action you had to make the effort. In 1957, I read a newspaper article about a player from Argentina called Omar Sivori. The reporter reckoned this chap was the best player he'd seen in 30 years, and so I made it my mission to see Sivori in the flesh at the earliest opportunity. By chance, the playmaking forward moved from River Plate to Juventus that year and when the Italians fixed up a Thursday night floodlit friendly against Sheffield Wednesday at Hillsborough, I made sure that I was there to see it. I finished work early and caught the train to Sheffield and was there to see Sivori orchestrate a 4–3 win for the Italians. He was a classy player who loved to nutmeg a defender and then go back and nutmeg him again. He was wonderful to watch, a real entertainer, although I can imagine he'd have his teammates tearing their hair out. That night, Juve's forwards kept straying into offside positions waiting for Sivori to pass. Four years later, the player I'd been so keen to see won the Ballon d'Or, gaining three times more votes than the great Hungarian, Ferenc Puskas. The result surprised many people, but not me: I already knew he was a great player and worthy of the accolade.

When ITV signed a deal in 1960 to bring live league football to the nation, I steadfastly refused to take the easy option and instead of watching the first televised game between Blackpool and Bolton from the comfort of my armchair, I travelled up from London to see it. I stopped at Bury on the way and saw their 3pm kick-off against Swindon in the Third Division, before rushing to Bloomfield Road for the 6.50pm start and witnessed history being made as Blackpool, without the injured Stanley Matthews, lost 1–0. Two days later, I was at the Den to watch a Fourth Division clash between Millwall and Barrow and two days after that I was back at White Hart Lane to see Spurs beat Bolton 3–1. I know because my journal says so!

I suppose the sixties marked the beginning of my metamorphosis from super-fan to something more of an 'insider', and it is from this decade onwards that the stories described in this book all took place. It's hard to pinpoint the moment things changed, but I was just around so much; yelling from the sidelines at every game, staying in the same hotels as players on away trips and sharing train carriages home that I just naturally became friends with them. One day I was giving Tommy Harmer a lift to White Hart Lane, the next Bobby Moore was popping over for tea to discuss England's chances in the upcoming World Cup – I never deliberately set out to befriend these superstars, it just happened quite organically. That said, I loved the glamour of it all.

When sports writer Nick Hawkins suggested we write a book about my life in football, the fact that I still had my old journals tucked away made me confident of getting the job done. We've flicked through them hundreds of times over the last 18 months and the matches and dates recorded inside have helped trigger memories and piece together many of the stories contained in this book. Without my journals, I'm sure many of the experiences would have lain dormant in my head. My 50-year-old scribble has even proved more accurate than the Internet! For example, during the 1966 World Cup finals, I recorded watching three games in two days. I remembered it well, as footballers Johnny Haynes and Terry Venables came to all three matches with me. We drove from London to Liverpool on 15th July and watched Hungary beat Brazil at Goodison Park. The next day, we drove to Villa Park to see Argentina versus West Germany, which kicked off at 3pm. After that goalless draw, Terry put his foot to the floor and we arrived at Wembley in time to see England beat Mexico in the evening. "Impossible!" said Nick. "Every website and even the 1966 World Cup tournament programme say both games kicked-off at the same time – 3 o'clock!" It wasn't until I pulled out my 43-year-old match ticket stub and showed him the words "kick-off 7.30pm" that he believed me!

The journals have certainly served me well in writing this book. However, I must admit that I can't remember all of the people present during some of the events described; that would be impossible, even for someone with a good memory! The conversations I've had though have remained surprisingly vivid considering many were over 40 years ago, and the ones that aren't so memorable have been portrayed as accurately as possible after consulting friends who were present to help fill in the blanks.

I've been lucky and count many of football's legendary players from the past 50 years as friends. No supporter today will ever get as close to football's top stars as I did, during a time when the game's elite were relatively accessible to a fanatic like me who wished to socialise with the players I watched from the terraces each week. Nowadays, a supporter who spends thousands of pounds following his team all over the world, will be lucky to have exchanged more than a few words with his footballing idols.

I honestly believe that I am the last man who will ever have the sort of relationship with his heroes that I have had. Footballers have gone from quite ordinary, working-class lads whose careers never stopped them taking the number 149 bus to matches on a Saturday afternoon to global superstars who are chauffeured around in armour-plated cars! The stars of today are totally untouchable and inaccessible, and the game itself has gone from everyman's weekend hobby to a multi-billion pound empire and a pursuit barred to many due to the exorbitant cost of watching a match and wearing your favourite team's shirt. It's sad, and it makes me even more appreciative of the experiences I have had. It also, I hope, will make my stories all the more fascinating and surprising to read about. When I told him about this book, Terry Venables asked me whether it was to be my autobiography. "No," I replied, "it will just be a collection of stories about my football memories and obsession with Spurs!" Terry laughed, "So it is your life story then! Your life IS football!"

THE MILLION-POUND CHEQUE

"A brilliant supporter, who travelled everywhere with the team. Morris loves the club and was equally loved by the players. He should have been offered a place on the board years ago!"
Terry Dyson (Spurs, Double winner 1960/61)

"I was totally gutted after losing to West Germany in the 1970 World Cup finals, but a trip in Morris's company helped relieve the stress and I thank him for that."
Martin Peters MBE (Tottenham and England, World Cup winner 1966)

When I look back over the 66 years that I've supported Spurs, two events during that time stand out above the rest. The first happened on the pitch at exactly 4.30pm on 6th May, 1961. Time stood still, as I watched diminutive Spurs winger Terry Dyson, the son of a jockey, leap high into the air and plant a header past goalkeeper Gordon Banks. That goal in the FA Cup final gave Tottenham a 2–0 lead and with just 15 minutes of the match remaining, and Leicester City one man down due to an injury to defender Len Chalmers, the 'impossible' double was on the brink of being achieved by my beloved club.

Fifteen minutes later, the referee Mr Kelly gave a final loud blast on his whistle and I punched the air in ecstatic jubilation. From my viewpoint, close to the Royal Box at Wembley, I then watched with great pride as our captain Danny Blanchflower collected the gleaming silver trophy from Her Royal Highness the Duchess of Kent. He then hoisted it high in the air and paraded it around Wembley, along with the rest of the team, Bill Brown, Peter Baker, Ron Henry, Maurice

Norman, Dave Mackay, Cliff Jones, John White, Bobby Smith, Les Allen and Terry Dyson. The best side in England for many a long year. It was a dream come true to see Bill Nicholson's side win the FA Cup and achieve the double, having won the league a few weeks earlier. It was, without doubt, the most significant and enjoyable moment of my life as a Spurs fan.

The other most memorable event in my life with Spurs actually happened off the pitch, 30 years after the double, in another significant year for the club. It was a Friday afternoon, the day before the 1991 FA Cup final against Nottingham Forest and I was at home when I received a phone call from a long-standing Spurs-supporting friend, Philip Green

"Hello Morris. Stop whatever you are doing and come to my office."

"What's it about?" I asked.

"No time for questions. I'm about to go into a meeting that will be of great interest to you and I want you here to witness it. I'll fill you in when you arrive."

I'd known Philip for many years through business. At the time, I had my own ladies' fashion showroom and wholesalers in Bethnal Green in London's East End, while Philip in 1991 was Chairman and Chief Executive of publicly listed fashion group Amber Day. As I made my way to his office in Baker Street from my home in St John's Wood, I chuckled to myself, remembering the fun that I'd had ten months earlier with him, when he took me to Turin to see Bobby Robson's side play West Germany in the semi-finals of Italia '90. Despite England's exit on penalties, I was grateful to Philip for taking me along to witness one of England's great games. After Chris Waddle blasted his penalty over the bar, Philip jumped out of his seat and said to his guests, who included journalist Jeff Randall and businessman Ian Grabiner.

"Come on you lot, no time to watch grown men cry. We've got a plane to catch!" As Paul Gascoigne and Stuart Pearce sobbed on the field, we hurriedly made our way outside the Stadio delle Alpi, where Philip had organised a taxi to meet us and take us to the airport to catch a private plane back to London. After waiting for 15 minutes at the agreed pick up point, Philip started to panic,

"We'd better start asking aroud to see if someone will give us a lift to the airport. It closes at midnight and I've got to get home tonight or I'll miss my meeting tomorrow." Philip began frantically stopping supporters walking past us to ask for a lift. He managed to stop two Irishmen and they asked, "Where yer going?"

"The airport," replied Philip in hope.

"Sorry. It's a bit out of my way."

"There's four of us and I'll make it worth your while," he replied and flashed a huge wad of notes in their faces.

"Jeez, it'll be a squeeze, but I'll fit you in alright." They did fit us in, but I wouldn't say I was 'alright', lying on the back seat of a tiny Fiat Uno stretched out across Philip, Jeff and Ian's lap! We arrived just in time for the small private jet to take off before the airport closed. On the flight home I said to Philip, "You could have bought that rusty Fiat with the money you gave those two students for the lift."

Philip smiled and replied: "True, but we'd still have the problem of where to park it at the airport!"

Now here I was, almost a year later, wondering what he had in store for me. I arrived at Amber Day's offices and was quickly ushered from the reception into the boardroom, where Philip greeted me.

"Ah, Morris. That was quick. I think you know most people here. Take a seat and I'll tell you what's going on."

My eyes circled the room and I immediately clocked my good friend Terry Venables, then the manager of Spurs, sitting on one side of a large circular table. Sitting to Terry's right was Tony Berry, a director of Tottenham. Also in the room were a couple of other club officials, whom I knew by sight and another chap I didn't know. Terry looked over and grinned as Philip introduced all of the suited gentlemen sitting around the table, including the mystery man.

"And this is Peter Robinson, Irving Scholar's solicitor," Philip said, unravelling the mystery.

It didn't take Einstein to realise that for Terry to be away from the Spurs squad on the eve of a Wembley final, some important business was under discussion.

Philip, who was still standing, then held a piece of paper

in the air and proceeded to fill me in with what exactly was going on.

"Morris, I have in my hand a cheque which I am about to make payable to Irving Scholar for his shares in Tottenham. This will enable Terry to finally buy him out and help save our beloved club from extinction.

"As Tottenham's most loyal fan, I've asked you to come along and witness this momentous event in the club's history, as well as inform you that if Scholar accepts the deal you will immediately be installed as the club's acting chairman."

I gulped, a large gulp, trying to take in the enormity of what Philip had just said.

"You could be sitting next to Princess Diana in the Royal Box tomorrow!" Terry declared with a big smile across his face.

"I'd better call Sylvia and ask her to collect my best suit from the dry cleaners before it shuts," I quipped back at him.

Terry and I had been good friends for 25 years and the possibility of me becoming chairman thrilled him as much as it did me. We had spoken a fair bit over the previous six months, discussing the progress in his quest to form a consortium to buy the controlling shareholding in Tottenham, held by Scholar and fellow director Paul Bobroff.

I must admit that I had long admired the guile at the way in which Scholar had gained control of the club in 1982. The previous chairman, Arthur Richardson, actually called me at home one afternoon and asked me if "I knew a chap called Scholar." I told him I did; the players often sorted me out with complimentary tickets and Scholar had been the recipient of some of these.

I told Richardson, "Irving Scholar is a true fan. He loves the club and travels all over to see our matches. Why do you ask?"

"He has been contacting the shareholders and offering them £250 for every share they own and I believe quite a few have taken him up on the offer."

I found Richardson's revelation very interesting and could tell Arthur was quite put out by Scholar's sheer audacity. At the time, I probably thought Scholar had little chance of ousting Arthur or his son Geoffrey Richardson, who was vice-chairman. I was wrong though, and Scholar managed to purchase 1,500 of the 4,892 shares in issue at the time, including 700 from the largest shareholder, Sidney Wale, who was chairman before Richardson ousted him in 1980 when Wale refused to authorise the proposed rebuilding of the West Stand.

After initially staying in the shadows, Scholar took over as chairman of the football club in 1984. During his tenure, Tottenham Hotspur plc amassed debts of over £10 million during a period when the club attempted to diversify its business after becoming the first football club to float on the London Stock Exchange. The result was a catalogue of business failures through a variety of ventures ranging from sportswear distribution, ticketing and women's fashion! Under the Scholar regime, the redevelopment of the East Stand in 1988 also went £3.9 million over budget and by 1991 the club faced the possibility of going into receivership. Scholar's time was certainly up and Terry had spent the last six months trying to get a deal together to save the club. Through the boxing promoter Frank Warren, he'd been introduced to a businessman called Larry Gillick and the pair, along with Tottenham director Tony Berry, tried to strike a deal to buy Scholar's shares. After three fruitless months of Gillick trying to secure a realistic package from Middle Eastern backers, Terry was forced to drop him. Rather than walk away, Terry continued to talk to businessmen, hopeful that he could save the club he had supported as a boy. The path now led to Philip Green's door and I found myself joining Terry on his rollercoaster ride.

Philip pointed to a telephone on the table next to Peter Robinson and asked him to call Scholar.

"Now Morris is here, let's get this deal done."

Robinson got through to Scholar and after exchanging pleasantries told him who was present at the meeting before passing the phone over to Philip.

"Hello Irving. I'm delighted to say that Terry finally has the money to buy your shares in Spurs. I am staring at a big fat cheque with your name on it and was hoping to hand it over to you in person. Why aren't you here?"

Scholar told Philip that he had been at a meeting with Mel Stein, Paul Gascoigne's agent, and Nat Solomon, the chairman of Tottenham Hotspur plc. He said that he had hoped to present an acceptable offer to Stein that would prevent Paul Gascoigne signing for Italian club Lazio in a £7.9 million transfer deal.

For the past year, Tottenham's bankers, the Midland Bank, had been insisting that the club cut its huge overdraft by selling some of its assets and without doubt, Gascoigne was its prime one. England's 1990 World Cup hero had almost single-handedly got Spurs to Wembley with some amazing performances during the team's run to the FA Cup final. Gazza had scored six goals *en route* to the final, including an amazing free kick from 30 yards out that whizzed past Arsenal goalkeeper David Seaman and set Spurs on their way to a famous victory over their North London rivals at Wembley in the semi-final.

Scholar told Philip that Stein had said that it would cost Tottenham £2 million, plus a large annual salary on top of that to keep Gascoigne at the club for the next season. He then told Philip that Terry, as the team manager, might have a better chance of persuading Gazza to stay.

"I'm quite prepared to do a deal, and Terry can have my shares for 80 pence. But if he manages to keep Gascoigne at Spurs, then he can have them for 70 pence. That's a discount of £270,000, if he can pull it off," Scholar said.

Peter Robinson kept the phone line to Scholar's office open as Terry discussed the proposal with Philip and the others sitting around the table. Terry was unimpressed with Scholar's 'Gazza discount'.

"As far as I know, Gazza's signing for Lazio," he said. "I met his advisers myself earlier today and told them that I'd make Gazza the best paid player in the country if my takeover of Tottenham went ahead. I told Stein and Len Lazarus that I could build a team around him and win the League title and make much more money for Gazza in the long run. They weren't interested in what I had to say. "Mark my words, Gazza will be tucking into spaghetti bolognese and cornettos by Wednesday." My heart sank. Like most Spurs fans, I knew that our superstar's future at the club was in doubt, but to hear that tomorrow's final was now certain to be his last in a lilywhite shirt was still a shock. Terry caught my eye; we had discussed his hopes to keep Gazza and I knew he would be gutted.

Philip then proceeded to make the cheque out for £1 million. My eyes bulged. He turned to Peter Robinson and said, "Tell Irving that I have written out a cheque for the amount without the 'Gazza discount'. I expect that as soon as the Midland Bank approves me as the new guarantor to Tottenham's debts the deal will be done, probably sometime next week."

Mr Robinson conveyed this to Scholar on the phone, but his reply wasn't one Philip expected to hear.

"Gentlemen. Irving accepts the offer on the understanding that the deal is closed today."

"Hang on a minute," said Philip. "Peter, Let me talk to Irving."

"Irving. My understanding is that it will take the Midland Bank more than one phone call for them to agree with our refinancing plans for the club. Firstly, we need to ascertain the bank's position, before signing a contract with you. Your solicitor has our cheque, the deal will be done as soon as the Midland Bank gives the green light."

For the next two hours, Philip sat around the table trying to get through to the Midland Bank's 'intensive care' unit, who had been put in charge of solving the club's financial mess. With their working week over, calls to his advisers and lawyers became more and more frantic as he tried to assess the risk of taking over a club that could go into receivership at any time. As the clock ticked into the early evening, Terry could take no more. My dreams of a cozy half-time chat with Princess Di were fading.

"This is ridiculous. I can't stay here any longer. The team will be at the Royal Lancaster Hotel by now and probably wondering where I am. We've got a Cup final to win tomorrow and if I don't get back soon the players, especially Gazza, will start to worry. Call me as soon as there's any news."

With the clock in Philip's office showing 7.45pm, Terry stood up and made for the door, but before exiting the room everyone wished him good luck for the final. I felt for him,

Spurs were in their first final for almost a decade and he had the added pressure of trying to save the club.

For the next two hours, I sat in my chair sipping cups of coffee and listening to bankers, businessmen and lawyers bashing their heads together trying to keep my dream alive, or so I fancied. A life spent fanatically supporting Spurs flashed before my eyes. I remembered those days just after the War when I would follow the players on their journey home. It was so easy then: I would hop on the bus, brandishing my autograph book. As soon as I had obtained the precious scribble, I would jump off and run back to the bus stop, ready for the next player to begin their bus ride home. I soon became a familiar face and many would greet me by name, chuckling as they listened to me telling yet another member of the squad that he was my favourite. How had that young boy got here? I had never made it as a player, a manager or, indeed, forged any sort of career in football. It was purely my fanatical support over the years which had gained me notoriety and saw me now sitting around this table. We were all at Scholar's mercy and I chuckled as I recalled how many times he had been at mine before he took over the club, desperate for my help in securing tickets for away matches. He and I were of the same breed, Spurs devotees whose money, in his case, and personality, in mine, had allowed us to become part of our beloved club.

The clock was ticking and I hoped the imminent loss of Gascoigne would be too heavy a blow for Scholar's pride.

"Please ask Irving to be reasonable," Philip urged Robinson, when it became clear at 10pm that Philip, having weighed up the risks, couldn't close a deal that night.

"It will be financial suicide if we hand over the money as the club could still end up being put into receivership on Monday morning."

"Sorry Philip. Irving wants an unconditional deal and he wants it closed today," replied Robinson.

"Then the deal is dead," said Philip, who picked the cheque up off the table and tore it up. I watched as the pieces fell from his fingers and onto the floor. The dream was over. I hauled myself out of the chair and shook Philip's hand.

"Thanks for thinking of me," I said, as everyone began to leave the room.

Philip consoled me saying, "I'm sorry for wasting your time. You deserve to be chairman. Maybe one day."

That day was never to come. My one and only chance had eluded me. I shook myself. There was still the FA Cup Final to think about.

At Wembley the next day, I sat just a few metres from the Royal Box. I glanced over before the kick-off and could see Irving Scholar sitting next to John Major, the prime minister. "That's a godsend," I thought. "I know bugger all about cricket."

As soon as the match began, I became what I always am when sitting in the stands, a Spurs fan. I no longer cared about boardrooms, lawyers and bankers; I just wanted to see my team lift the Cup. Anyway, there was enough happening on the pitch to keep my mind off what might have been. Paul Gascoigne was determined to make his final game in a Spurs shirt a memorable one. From the off, it was clear that the star man was wound up too tightly for the occasion, and I could understand why Terry had been in such a hurry to get to him the previous evening. Gascoigne needed Terry's calming influence before the biggest match of his club career, but Terry had been busy trying to save the club. Referee Roger Milford should have booked Gascoigne for a bad foul. Ten minutes later, he lunged at fullback Gary Charles and scythed him down. From the resulting free-kick, Stuart Pearce rifled home a bullet shot to give Brian Clough's side the lead. With Forest cheers still echoing around Wembley, Gascoigne collapsed in a heap, having shattered the cruciate ligament in his right knee. My heart sank watching Terry walk on to the pitch to re-organise his team as Tottenham's prize asset was stretchered off the field. I hoped for a miracle. The optimist in me was rewarded as, despite their loss, Spurs took control of the game. We howled as Gary Lineker had a perfectly good goal ruled out for offside and then failed to convert a penalty before half-time. I spent the break trying to convince myself that all wasn't lost and my positive vibes must have helped as Paul Stewart soon equalised with a low shot into the corner. There were few clear-cut chances for either side for the rest of the half and Wembley had to wait until extra time for a winning goal. It came from Forest defender Des Walker when he headed into his own net. Spurs had a priceless victory, a lucrative place in Europe and I was over the moon.

As Spurs captain Gary Mabbutt climbed the 39 steps of the old Wembley to the Royal Box, I could see Irving Scholar standing next to Princess Diana applauding the players. At that moment, I didn't feel any jealousy or bitterness towards him, as I knew how much Tottenham Hotspur meant to him. I remembered when he took me for a walk around the East Stand when it was being redeveloped. Standing amongst the rubble, we climbed endless stairs and then a ladder towards the TV gantry, where *Big Match* football commentator Brian Moore was getting accustomed to the new TV camera position. After giving Brian a wave, Scholar turned to me and said, "Up here in the gods is my favourite view of the ground." We both looked across the freshly mowed pitch to the West Stand opposite.

Scholar added, "It makes me proud to know this is all mine." I bit my lip, thinking, "It belongs to the fans, not you Irving". I guess at that moment he was bursting with pride having improved the stadium, albeit way over budget.

Looking back on Scholar's reign as chairman, it's obvious that the club's directors bit off more than they could chew after floating the club on the Stock Exchange. The pressure from the suits in the City to boost profits by diversifying Tottenham into a leisure company resulted in too many bad business decisions. There is no question in my mind that Philip Green, or Sir Philip, as I should call him now, would have been an ideal partner for Terry in taking the club forward. If only Scholar had not taken the stance he did the night before the '91 FA Cup final. If only he had been more reasonable and allowed Philip a few more days to complete the deal. I've often wondered how I would have reacted if I'd been Scholar. Maybe, like him, I would have held on to power for as long I could, although that would have been a wrong decision. Of course, Philip Green in 1991 wasn't the Sir Philip Green that he is today. At that time, Philip had only recently made his first million cleverly buying and turning around failing retailer Jean Jeanie. He wasn't in a position where he could risk losing £1 million on a football club that could go into receivership. Today, he is the billionaire owner of high street chains Top Shop, BHS, Burton and many more besides. He is reputedly the sixth richest man in Britain and worth an estimated £3.83 billion according to the 2009 *Sunday Times* Rich List. How my beloved Spurs could do with him at the helm today. Terry Venables and Philip Green would have been the dream ticket for Tottenham, but Philip soon lost interest in reviving a takeover deal.

Terry didn't throw the towel in quite so easily, although today I guess he probably wished he had. Desperate to keep his dream alive, he cast his net one final time in the hope of landing a big fish to partner him. Soon after the FA Cup was sitting pretty in the White Hart Lane trophy cabinet, we met for lunch and Terry revealed, "Remember that chap Alan Sugar, who you introduced me to all those years ago? He wants to team up with me and take over Tottenham." I probably choked on my dinner in surprise at hearing that news. In the late seventies, when Sugar was building up his electronics business, he contacted me asking if I could "provide a bit of celebrity glamour" for an Amstrad party that he was throwing for some buyers. I got in touch with my comedian friend Jimmy Tarbuck, who had been the star act at many of the testimonial dinners that I'd organised over the years. Jimmy was happy to help Sugar out, and Terry agreed to join Tarby and also took Malcom Allison along for the company. At the time, Terry was assistant manager at Crystal Palace, where Malcolm was the manager. With his flamboyant image, complete with fedora and cigar, Malcolm certainly provided "a bit of celebrity glamour". I too went along to the event, held at the White Elephant on the river in Pimlico. The four of us sat around tables and chatted to buyers from various electrical retailers and had a decent enough evening. Terry though, seemed to take an instant dislike to Sugar, and it surprised me to hear that he was considering joining forces with him. I reminded him that he had reiterated his dislike for the Amstrad owner a few years after that first meeting, when he again worked for Sugar. Terry, then manager of QPR, was the face of an Amstrad advertisement on the back of London buses. 'The best player I ever signed' was the strapline used to plug Sugar's stereos. It was certainly an inventive slogan, but Terry wasn't happy with that advertising job for reasons he preferred to keep to himself.

Despite Terry's reservations, Team Sugar–Venables saw off a late bid by *Daily Mirror* owner Robert Maxwell and bought Scholar and Bobroff's stake in Spurs, to the immense delight of Tottenham supporters worldwide. As a result of the takeover, Alan Sugar became chairman of the plc and Terry became a director and chief executive of the company. Terry's first job was to appoint Peter Shreeve as team manager for the 1991/92 season. A great tactician, Shreeve had almost secured the league title for Spurs in 1985. However, this time around he struggled to get the best out of the players and the club finished 15th, only guaranteeing safety from the drop with a 3–2 win over Wimbledon with three games to go. At the end of the season, I met up with Terry to tell him where I thought it had all gone wrong for Shreeve and Spurs. I'd always been keen to express my views about Tottenham to Terry and now that he was the club's chief executive I was even keener. At times we disagreed on players' abilities and such like, but he certainly valued my opinion and often invited me along to board meetings to give a fan's perspective on the club.

It was clear to me that Terry needed to take more of an active role in team affairs and I helped convince him a few days after the curtain fell on his first season as the chief executive.

"What are you going to do about the manager?" I asked him.

"Peter's only on a one-year contract and I won't be renewing it," he told me.

"Who are you going to get in?" I asked.

"Not sure Morris. Got any suggestions?"

"Yeah," I said. "I'm looking at him."

Terry smiled and proceeded to tell me that he had his work cut out trying to get the business side of the club back on an even keel after the Scholar regime. Paul Gascoigne had by now regained full fitness after his cruciate knee ligament injury and was finally heading for Lazio, albeit at a reduced price of £5.5 million. Gary Lineker, the club's ace striker, was also on his way out of White Hart Lane, saying 'sayonara' to Spurs and agreeing to join Japanese club Nagoya Grampus Eight. I now feared for Tottenham's future on the pitch and was desperate for Terry to take a more hands-on role with the team.

"It's no good you spending all your time sorting out the club's problems off the pitch, if we are relegated from this new Premier League in its first season," I said. "You've got to manage the team or at least work more closely with your next manager."

Over lunch, Terry acknowledged that he had actually already been thinking along the same lines. Hearing my views helped confirm in his own mind that he should oversee team affairs.

"I've been thinking of promoting Peter's assistant Doug Livermore," he said. "I wanted him to take the job last year, but he felt it was too big a job for him. I think he'll take it if I also help him out on the training field.

"Do it Terry," I urged.

The following season, with Terry chipping in considerably on team selection, Spurs faired a lot better on the pitch. The club finished eighth in the league table, on the same points as sixth-placed Liverpool. In the FA Cup, once again Spurs faced Arsenal at Wembley in a semi-final clash. This time around we lost 1–0, when I felt we deserved better. Off the pitch though, as I'd feared, Terry and Alan Sugar were at loggerheads. From conversations I had with Terry, it seemed that the pair's personalities constantly clashed and he frequently cursed me for having introduced him to Sugar in the first place. I often lightened the moment telling him, "You didn't have to get into bed with him."

In the final league game of the season, Spurs gained revenge over the Gunners with a 3–1 victory on 11th May, 1993, a match I watched from the directors' box at Highbury as a guest of Arsenal manager George Graham, who like Terry, is another long-time friend of mine. George sought me out after the match and told me not to get too excited, as we "had only beaten Arsenal's reserves" and "his best players had been rested for the Cup final in four days' time".

"Don't you remember Morris? It was only one month ago that we beat you in the FA Cup semi-final," he quipped.

After enjoying the post-match banter with George, I met up with Terry, who had offered to give me a lift home. Terry's lawyer friend Jonathan Crystal, a non-executive director of the club, also joined us for the ride. I expected to find Terry in a jovial mood, having just beaten the enemy on their own territory. Instead, I found a very troubled man. A few minutes into the journey I asked him what was on his mind.

"Sugar's fired me," he said.

"What! Why?" I exclaimed.

"I'm damned if I know," he said. "He wants me out and it will be made official in a couple of days."

I couldn't believe what I was hearing. I was lost for words at first, although the anger soon built during the drive home.

"Sugar's going to wreck the club without you. We're on the verge of something big. Teddy Sheringham's just scored 30 goals in his first season and we've got some of the best young players in the country. Anderton and Barmby are the best prospects I've seen for a long time. Without you nurturing them, they'll never reach their full potential."

"I make you right Morris," Terry said forlornly.

I was desperately sad for him. He had helped save Spurs from extinction and deserved a medal, but all he'd received was loads of grief.

Three days later, at a board meeting convened by the plc, Sugar officially declared to Terry "You're fired", a phrase he would later learn to love as the boss in the BBC reality TV series *The Apprentice*.

For the many Spurs fans outside White Hart Lane that fateful evening, Terry's dismissal was no joke and they left Sugar in no doubt about the strength of their feelings. The players too rallied behind Terry, with Neil Ruddock and Teddy Sheringham leading the support in the dressing room. After gaining a temporary injunction and being reinstated, Terry eventually lost a three-day High Court hearing and was ordered to pay costs. It was the end of the road for him at Spurs, but around the corner the England job awaited. And for me, I was left to rue Irving Scholar's decision not to sell the club to Philip Green in the first place. Almost 20 years on, and I'm still waiting for Tottenham to win the FA Cup again. It's also nearly 50 years since the club won the league title! I'm certain that if the club had Sir Philip Green's millions in the bank and Terry Venables at the helm, another side capable of matching Bill Nicholson's double side of the sixties would have been assembled. I certainly would have been a very proud chairman!

2   1966

"*In all my lifetime I've never met a more rabid football fan. Morris's first love may have been Spurs, but he also followed the fortunes of many other clubs, as well as the national side. He's a good friend to many of the Boys of '66.*"
George Cohen MBE (Fulham and England, World Cup winner 1966)

"*We've been friends since that terrible year of 1966. In that time we've been on opposite sides more often that not, but we've always remained the very best of friends.*"
George Graham (Arsenal and Scotland, Double winner 1970/71, Manager of Arsenal 1986/1995)

O n the cold January morning of the day that the draw for the 1966 World Cup finals took place, I found myself sitting next to England skipper Bobby Moore on the 10am train from Liverpool to London. I'd stayed the night at the Adelphi Hotel, having spent the evening watching England scrape a 1–1 draw against Poland at Goodison Park, and bumped into the London contingent of the squad as they boarded the same train heading home.

"You've got no chance of winning the World Cup if you can't beat Poland," I said, as I plonked myself down on a seat next to Mooro.

"Hello Morris. Fancy seeing you here."

Before offering up some sort of defence for the poor result, Moore introduced me to the other players in the first class carriage. They included his West Ham teammate Geoff Hurst, Fulham's George Cohen and Arsenal pair George

Eastham and Joe Baker. Hurst was the only one of the party not to have played against the Poles. He was on his first trip with the England senior squad and Alf Ramsey had chosen not to award him his first cap just yet. It was probably for the best, going by the inept team performance I'd witnessed. In fact for Baker it proved to be the last time he ever played for the national side.

"We should have won, but at least I finally scored for England," said Mooro.

"It's about time. After all, you've only got forty-odd caps."

"You're nearly right Morris. I've got thirty-six."

"OK. I stand corrected. I won't mention the fact that you gifted them their goal."

Mooro held his hands up. "Yeah, must admit I was a bit casual with that pass on the muddy surface."

I grimaced. "You lot aren't feeding me with much confidence. Didn't Italy put six past Poland a few months ago?"

"Yeah, but we don't want to peak too early," said Moore.

"Good point Robert. We've still got six months before the Finals get underway," chipped in George Cohen.

We then discussed the draw, which was to take place at Kensington's Royal Garden Hotel that evening. I asked the group who they most wanted to avoid.

"Italy," laughed Moore.

"You will," I said. "They're seeded along with Brazil, Germany and you timewasters."

"We're seeded? That's nice of 'em," said George Cohen. Eastham's face then popped up from behind a *Daily Mirror*, "Says here Italy are 8/1 at Joe Coral."

"I might have a few quid on 'em," laughed Moore. "What are we?"

"9/2 second favourites," replied Eastham, before retreating back behind his newspaper.

"I wouldn't waste your money," I said. "Personally, I can't see past Brazil."

"Brazil. 5/2 favourites," Eastham helpfully added.

Privately, I felt we might have a chance of winning if Jimmy Greaves managed to recover from hepatitis. Without him I couldn't see who was going to score the goals. The Spurs and

England hotshot had been sidelined for two months with the debilitating virus, having been taken ill after Tottenham's 2–1 home win over West Brom in late October. It was as if Mooro had read my mind:

"I spoke to Greavsie the other day," he said. "He reckons he'll be back playing by February. He'll be scoring for fun come July when we need him."

"Yeah. Greavsie will do the business," added Geoff Hurst, before stealing my pen to do the crossword.

I chatted to Mooro and George Cohen for most of the journey to London. It was the first time I'd ever met George and we went on to become good friends.

On arriving at Euston Station, I said my goodbyes before making my way home to Hendon. At 6.25pm, I switched on my black-and-white TV and tuned into BBC1 to watch the draw live. I cheered as Uruguay, Mexico and France were drawn in England's group. Sylvia studiously ignored my elation as she plonked a steak and kidney pie in front of me.

"Are we going to get a bloody holiday this year?"

"Yes my love," I said. "Don't worry. I'll be making myself available when the season ends, but I'll need to be back by the time England kick-off against Uruguay on the 11th July."

"I'm truly honoured," she replied.

Jimmy Greaves made his Spurs comeback at the end of January, scoring in a 4–0 win over Blackburn. I watched him intently over the remainder of the domestic season, searching for signs that he was back to his best. He scored five more times before Tottenham's trophyless season ended. On the train home from one disappointing result, an FA Cup defeat at the hands of Second Division Preston, I sat opposite him and we chatted for most of the journey.

"You're sick we've lost, aren't you Morris?"

"Of course I am, it's bloody Preston. They're not exactly Liverpool or Leeds are they? Aren't you sick Jim?"

"Nah. There's another game next week." His response shocked me a bit. He'd scored in the game and played well, but I still expected him to be peeved about going out of the Cup to an average side at the fifth-round stage.

He reasoned, "As one player in a team, there's only so

much you can do to affect the outcome. We've got a decent side here at Spurs and we might still win something with the players we've got. But remember, Danny's hung up his boots, Smithy's gone and Maurice has broken his leg. We've also lost dear Johnny White, God rest his soul. We're a team in transition Morris and things can take time. Hopefully, Bill will open up his cheque book soon and bring in some new faces."

We discussed his recovery. Greavsie said he had been slogging his guts out in training, and I wondered aloud whether he thought he'd be included in Ramsey's World Cup line-up.

"Don't see why not. Hopefully, it'll be yours truly scoring the winning goal in the final!"

His hard work on the training field was rewarded, and on 4th May, Greavsie made an eagerly anticipated return to the England side after a five-game absence. Ramsey's World Cup hopefuls won 2–0 against Yugoslavia in what was the national side's last match at Wembley before the finals. Greavsie marked his return by scoring one of the goals and five days later he was on target again, only this time for Spurs in the last game of the league season – a 1–0 victory over already relegated Blackburn at Ewood Park. As nothing was riding on the game, the FA allowed the new signing Greavsie and I had hoped for, namely Terry Venables, to make his debut. The 23-year-old £80,000 midfielder had been in England's 40-man squad for the World Cup, but had learned three days before the trip to Blackburn that he hadn't made the 28 selected to take part in an 18-day World Cup training camp at Lilleshall. Terry managed to cast aside the disappointment and put in a good performance that day.

I hadn't met Terry before he joined Spurs, but Bobby Moore had often spoken about Chelsea's talented young captain. The pair were good friends and lived just a few miles apart, Terry in Gants Hill and Mooro in leafy Chigwell in Essex. Before Terry signed for Chelsea as a 15-year-old amateur, Mooro had taken him under his wing when he trained at West Ham. Mooro had told me that he'd tried to persuade the youngster to join the Hammers, but a confident Terry believed he'd be able to force his way into Chelsea's first team more quickly. He was probably right and played his first senior game at Stamford Bridge a few days after his 17th birthday. I was certainly keen to meet the man Mooro had enthusiastically spoken about and that May I got my chance.

I'd heard that Tottenham's assistant manager Eddie Baily was taking the team on a four-week long end-of-season tour of North America and Terry would of course be on the trip. I told Sylvia that her summer holiday would be "a lovely week in New York", although I forgot to mention that we'd be watching Spurs during the break!

"I know New York is lovely at this time of year, but the guidebook says Hartford in Connecticut is even better," I grinned, as we arrived at John F Kennedy International Airport.

"What you got planned Morris?"

I read out the blurb in my guidebook: "Mark Twain was a resident of Hartford when he wrote *The Adventures of Tom Sawyer*, and said of the town: 'You don't know what beauty is if you haven't been there.'" She knew me too well.

"What's the catch?" she asked.

"We're going to a Spurs match."

"For God's sake Morris, can't we have a holiday without football taking over?"

"Look, I promise you'll still get a full day in Bloomingdale's, with my wallet for company."

"What do you mean for company?"

"Er. I won't be with you as I'm going to the Spurs versus Bologna game in New Jersey."

To her horror, I went on to explain that I actually had three games to watch: in addition to the Hartford and Bologna matches, I also wanted to catch Celtic play the Italians at the Roosevelt Stadium. Sylvia's face looked like thunder, but after lengthy negotiations that the United Nations would have been proud of, she agreed to let me go for the price of a pair of white go-go boots and a trip to the south of France when the World Cup was over.

We made our way to the hotel (where the Spurs touring party happened to be staying!) and before long we were sipping cocktails around the hotel bar with Alan Mullery, Pat Jennings and new recruit Terry Venables.

"Hello Morris. Good to put a face to the name. Bobby

has told me all about you and your obsession with Spurs."

"Glad to hear it. Are you settling in well at the club?"

Terry raised his vodka martini, smiled and replied, "Yeah. The lads are making me feel most welcome." Terry gave me a blow-by-blow account of the team's 3–2 win over Bermuda, proudly claiming one of the goals. They'd been unlucky against Celtic in Toronto, conceding a last minute winner, but this seemed not to have dampened his enthusiasm for his new club or for America's second city.

"We've been in New York for a couple of days. We went sightseeing yesterday morning and raced up the Empire State Building and in the afternoon a crowd of us went to the base-ball to see the Yankees take on the California Angels. I tell you what Morris, baseball's a boring game. We left before the end!"

Sylvia and I spent a boozy evening with the lads in the bar and didn't rise from our bed until midday. We enjoyed a big American breakfast before bumping into the players as they boarded a coach to take them to Hartford. As I attempted to hail a taxi for the two-hour journey, Spurs director Charles Cox came over and asked me if I was going to the game.

"Look Mr Keston. Don't bother with a taxi. Why don't you come on our coach? The chairman and his son won't be joining us for a few more days. I can bend the rules a bit when they're not here."

"Well, that's very good of you. My wife is with me though."

"That's not a problem. There's plenty of seats at the back."

In all the years I'd been following Spurs, the club's officials had always turned their noses up at me. It seemed, finally, at least one of them was giving me the respect my loyalty deserved.

"You must be a lucky omen," I said to Terry as Sylvia and I sat down next to him. "It's the first time the Mafia have allowed me a seat on the bus." Terry raised his eyebrows,

"Do they see you as a threat then?"

"God knows. It's not just me, they don't like anyone who gets too close to the players or their own inner circle." Terry laughed incredulously,

"Are they scared you'll take over the club or something?"

"Maybe. I have no plans to! I'm just in love with Spurs! Anyway Terry, I bet you'd rather be preparing with the England squad than stuck on a bus in the Big Apple?" Terry nodded. I asked if he was planning to go to any of the games.

"Yeah, but I haven't decided which ones yet. I'll sort out some tickets when I get back, probably off Mooro or Peter Bonetti. How about you?"

"Yeah. I've bought one of those ten-game packages, which includes all the Wembley matches and the one at White City."

"I quite fancy seeing Brazil play Hungary at Goodison Park. If I can get some tickets, do you want to come?"

"Count me in. I haven't seen Pele in the flesh yet."

A large crowd of women, many waving Union Jack flags, greeted us on our arrival at the Dillon Stadium in Hartford.

"Blimey. Look at this merry lot," Terry said on spotting the hordes.

"I read in *Woman's Own* that American women like soccer," chipped in Sylvia, who was clearly enjoying the envious looks from the waiting ladies. She snuggled up to Terry and gave her best royal wave. We disembarked to the sound of high-pitched screams. It turned out that many of the teenage girls there welcoming us were the daughters of GI brides who had set up home in Hartford after the Second World War. Sylvia and I chatted to a few of them inside the stadium, and their mothers too, who were happy to get the opportunity to talk to some Brits for a change. A large group of them stayed behind after the match and made a real fuss of the players. They were great hosts.

Two days later on 27th May, I travelled with the team to Jersey City to watch Celtic play Bologna. I remember the evening well for a conversation I had with Terry about Bobby Moore, in which he pulled me in to a plan he'd been hatching to try to persuade the Hammer to join Spurs. Terry told me that Mooro was unhappy at Upton Park and that his contract was to expire at the end of June.

"That gives us a month to work on him," I said.

"The thing is Morris, this tour doesn't finish until 22nd June which doesn't really give me anytime to work on him. It's down to you mate."

As soon as I arrived home a few days later I picked up the phone and called Mooro. After a bit of small talk, I told him of the rumour I'd heard about his possible departure from West Ham.

"I might have known you'd be the first to the grapevine. Yes I am. It's been on my mind for a few months. I suppose you're calling me up to try and persuade me to join Spurs?" Mooro laughed.

"Come on Bobby, think about it. We're just one world-class player short of producing another double-winning side. You're that man. You'll be amongst your friends at Spurs and you won't even have to move house."

"Morris. You really don't need to convince me. I'm itching to join your mob and I've already told Ron Greenwood that, but he's having none of it. He's adamant that I'm staying at West Ham."

"What about Bill Nicholson? He's good pals with Ron. Can't he persuade him to sell you?

"I can't see it happening. Ron can be a stubborn old mule if he wants to be. Basically, I've got no power and no say in anything. All I can do is let my contract expire at the end of June and refuse to sign another one."

That's exactly what Mooro did, until the World Cup rulebook forced his hand a few days before England's opening match against Uruguay. It stated that only players registered with clubs affiliated to the FA were allowed to play for England. It meant Mooro was technically ineligible under FIFA regulations to play in the World Cup finals. England coach Alf Ramsey acted quickly, and summoned Greenwood to the team hotel in Hendon with the appropriate forms. Under pressure from an impatient Ramsey, Mooro signed a one-month contract with West Ham that covered the length of the tournament. England had their skipper and Spurs it seemed would have to wait for their man until the tournament was over.

I was amongst the crowd of 87,000 who witnessed England's frustrating opening match. The South Americans packed out their defence with eight men and not even Greavsie could find a way past that lot. It was the first time England had been goalless at Wembley since 1938. The next game that I attended two days later wasn't much better, with England's group rivals France and Mexico drawing 1–1 in a poor match.

As part of my £25 World Cup package, I also had a ticket for the Uruguay versus France encounter at White City. The match was played there as Wembley's owners had refused to cancel their regular greyhound race meeting. To be honest, I was thinking of giving my ticket away after watching their awful first matches and was pleased to receive a phone call from Terry the day before the game, wondering if I wanted to join him at the Brazil versus Hungary clash at Goodison Park instead. I delightedly agreed.

"Good. I've also got tickets for Argentina versus West Germany. I was thinking we could stay at a hotel overnight and then travel to Villa Park the next day to watch it. George Graham is going to meet us there for that one. It kicks off at three o'clock."

"What about England versus Mexico? I've got a ticket for that one."

"Me too. If we get our skates on we should be able to get to Wembley in time for the 7.30 kick-off as long as we don't get caught in heavy traffic. It's only 100 miles. I'll be driving and the Maestro will be navigating, so we can blame him if we are late."

"The Maestro?"

"Yeah, Johnny Haynes is coming along."

I tried to take this news with nonchalance, but inside my head was spinning with the thought that I would soon be breathing the same air as one of the best footballers England had ever produced. He was the David Beckham of his day, the first player to be paid £100 a week and the best passer of a ball I'd ever seen. When Terry said goodbye I put down the receiver and immediately felt giddy with excitement.

Brazil, who were aiming for the third successive World Cup victory and their star player Pele, were the hot topic of discussion during the drive from London to Liverpool.

"Did you see Pele's 'banana shot' against Bulgaria?" asked Dave Underwood, the former Watford goalkeeper, who made up our foursome for the journey from London to Liverpool.

"What a free-kick that was," mused Terry.

"I'm really looking forward to seeing Brazil tonight. Hungary are no mugs, but I can't see them turning them over," I offered.

"I wouldn't be so sure Morris. The Hungarians will get at Pele, like the Bulgarians did. The poor fella's in for a difficult night if you ask me," reckoned Johnny.

Pele's bruising night never materialised after Brazil's selectors decided to rest him and played Tostao in his place. It was a big mistake and although Tostao scored, the Hungarians won the game 3–1. It was the first time in 12 years that Brazil had lost a match in the World Cup finals. The following day we met George Graham, a friend of Terry's from his days at Chelsea, as planned at Villa Park for the West Germany versus Argentina match. It was the first time I'd met George and we were to become good mates. His first wife Marie later worked for me in my ladies' fashion business.

"Will you be cheering on England tonight?" I asked him, as we hurried out of Villa Park following another goalless draw.

"Yee joking?" he said. "I'll be cheering for the wee Mexicans. I hope they stuff ya."

Enter Bobby Charlton. With half-time approaching against the Mexicans, he collected the ball inside his own half and surged forward before hitting a thunderbolt of a shot from 30 yards into the net. Liverpool's Roger Hunt scored a second for England in the second half and we had the win that we wanted and George and five million other Scots desperately didn't. It was a difficult journey home for George that night, especially after he became the butt of our jokes when Terry revealed that George moved to North London believing that Stamford Hill was a short walk to Stamford Bridge in Chelsea! I don't think I've ever laughed so much. Looking back, it's interesting to note that both Terry and George would go on to manage my beloved Spurs, both winning trophies, Terry the FA Cup in 1991 and George the League Cup in 1999.

The back pages the next day were sceptical of England's chances of winning the tournament, but said Ramsey's inclusion of Martin Peters in the side at least gave England more creative imagination in midfield. As I was sat in the living room of my Hendon home reading the opinions in the press there was a knock at the front door. I was expecting to be greeted by an eager salesman selling carpet sweepers or the

Encyclopaedia Britannica, but instead I got Jimmy Greaves, Bobby Moore and George Eastham.

"Any chance of a brew Morris?" asked Greavsie. They walked into the living room and sat down. Sylvia's face lit up.

"You're in luck boys. I've just made an apple crumble," she said.

"It's handy you being around the corner from the Hendon Hall. Now we know where to come for our elevenses," said Greavsie, as he balanced a cup of tea in his lap and pawed a large helping of crumble. I smiled.

"You know you're welcome anytime,"

"I've got those shirts you asked for," said George, before opening a bag and handing over four international jerseys he'd purchased on England's tour of Scandinavia and Eastern Europe in the lead up to the finals. I'd asked him to get me one during the tour for my growing collection of international jerseys, but I didn't expect one from each game!

"Here you go. Finland, Norway, Denmark and Poland."

"They look a bit crumpled," said Mooro, who was always immaculately turned out. "Have you washed them?"

"There's still grass stains on this one," cried Greavsie.

"Don't worry about that," I said. "How much do I owe you?"

"Nah. It's OK Morris. I didn't even pay for them, just walked into the dressing rooms and the players handed them over."

"Don't you want to keep the Denmark one?" I asked, knowing George had scored one of the goals in the 2–0 victory in what turned out to be his final cap.

"Nah, you have 'em. I've got my England ones." Our conversation turned to last night's match. The boys were amused by Jack Charlton's belief that he deserved the glory for his brother's cracking finish.

"Says he hit the two-yard pass that sent Bobby on his way to goal," laughed Mooro. We dissected each player's performance and agreed that Martin Peters had been an excellent addition to midfield. Greavsie told me that Alan Ball had reacted badly to being dropped, and was even talking about going home.

"Blimey. That's a bit rash," I said.

"I know, but I think we've talked him round," replied Greavsie. Mooro weighed in,

"He might get another chance. It all depends whether Alf changes his mind about playing with wingers. When we played without them against Spain last year it worked well and then again against Poland when Ball and Peters supported the attacks from midfield. The thing is, Alf prefers a winger in the side, that's why he's got three in the squad."

He was right. Ramsey preferred wingers and Ball failed to reclaim his place for the final group game against France, with Liverpool winger Ian Callaghan coming in to replace Terry Paine on the right wing, who had been ineffective against the Mexicans, possibly due to a bang on the head he received in the first half. Peters retained his position on the left side of midfield. England played poorly on a slippery Wembley pitch, but still won 2–0 thanks to two well-taken goals by Roger Hunt. His clubmate Ian Callaghan was no more effective on the wing than Paine had been against Mexico or John Connelly against Uruguay. The talking point in the papers the next day wasn't the winger issue but how Nobby Stiles had heaped embarrassment on the country with a terrible tackle during the game on Frenchman Jacques Simon. As I digested the comments in the press, many saying Stiles should be banished from the competition, Bobby Moore once again arrived on my doorstep looking for some light refreshments.

"I see Nobby's grabbing the headlines," I said as he walked into the living room.

"Yeah, but they've missed the big story," he said.

"Oh yeah, what's that?" I asked.

"Greavsie's out."

"What? Injured?"

"Yeah. He'll miss the Argentina game and the semi-final if we get there," he said forlornly.

"Bloody hell. I saw the trainer treat him after a knock, but he seemed to play on alright."

"I know, but his shin has opened up right down to the bone," revealed Mooro.

"Crikey. I didn't realise it was that bad."

"Neither does the rest of the world," he said.

"How's Jimmy taken it?"

"He's devastated, as you'd expect."

"Where is he?"

"Back at the hotel. I think he wants to be left alone for a bit, to get his head around it."

"It's gonna be at least a week before he can play again."

"So that means he could be OK if we get to the final?"

"Yeah in theory, but I can't see Alf changing a winning side if we get there."

"But it is Jimmy Greaves. He may do."

"Possibly, who knows?"

I wondered how England would have a hope of reaching the World Cup final without Greavsie. He was to England what Pele was to Brazil, but Mooro was optimistic,

"At least we're keeping clean sheets. That's the important thing." He was right, but I was nonetheless worried about England's lack of creativity in the side. Mooro wondered whether Ramsey might now forget about wingers, re-call Alan Ball, and go with a 4-3-3 formation.

"Well, Alf's got to do something. If only Stanley Matthews was a little younger," I mused.

As Moore predicted, Ball returned to the side at the expense of Callaghan for the Argentina clash, with Ramsey, indeed naming a wingerless team. Ball put in a good performance, shackling the dangerous Argentine attacking full back Silvio Marzolini, as England won 1–0 with Greavsie's replacement Geoff Hurst scoring the goal. The match itself was bathed in controversy with Argentina skipper Antonio Rattin taking eight minutes to leave the field after being sent off by German referee Rudolf Kreitlein for 'violence of the tongue'. Watching on from my seat in Block 81 at Wembley, I felt like charging down to the pitch-side, running on to the field and dragging him off myself!

I discussed Rattin's behaviour, amongst other things, when Moore visited me at home for a final time during the '66 World Cup, the day before England's semi-final against Portugal.

"You can't keep away can you?" I said on opening the door.

"Nah and I hope you don't mind, I've brought a few more along this time." Standing with Mooro were Geoff Hurst, Martin Peters and a dejected-looking Greavsie.

Mooro took his usual place on our three-seater sofa in front of the TV, and I invited the others to make themselves at home.

"What did you think of Argentina?" asked Moore.

"I didn't think they were as dirty as the Portuguese against Brazil."

"We didn't see that one," said Martin.

"Alf made us watch Argentina versus Switzerland," said Geoff.

"Well, they gave Pele a good kicking, so you'd better be prepared for them to show their studs," I warned. Geoff grimaced,

"They can't be any worse than the Argies. They were a disgrace," he said. "Twice Albrecht kicked me in the ankle when I was nowhere near the ball."

Martin agreed and shook his head in disbelief when Geoff described the state of a FIFA official after the game, who he said was "covered in spit". Mooro believed the culprit to be Onega, who had apparently given Nobby Stiles some of the same treatment during the match.

"Animals," I said, before handing over the plates of cheese and pickle sandwiches Sylvia had speedily prepared.

"A few of 'em were spoiling for a fight afterwards," said Geoff, as I passed him the sugar for his tea. "Jack and Nobby were ready to take 'em on, and would have done, if the Old Bill hadn't stopped the Argies from getting into our dressing room."

Greavsie changed the subject to the food – he was delighted with the sandwiches, which he said made a change from the daily sides of roast beef with all the trimmings for lunch at Roehampton every day after training.

"Are you more bored of the lunches or John Wayne westerns?" asked Mooro.

"It's a tough call, but I reckon if Alf makes us sit through another western this summer, I'll dress up as Sitting Bull in protest," replied Greavsie, showing that his humour was still intact in spite of his badly timed injury. I passed him a leather pouffe and told him to put his leg up, before handing him a tin of biscuits. He didn't say anything, just gave me a wink and nod of thanks as the conversation turned to the upcoming semi-final against Portugal.

"I couldn't believe it when I read on the scoreboard at Wembley that Korea were 3–0 up against Portugal," said Mooro.

"Me neither. Five-three, must have been a cracking game," added Geoff.

"The Koreans certainly shocked a few people, me included," said Mooro.

"Not me," I said. "I backed them to beat Italy and won a few quid. I knew they'd give Portugal a game."

"I read in the paper that 700 angry Italians greeted the team with a barrage of tomatoes on their arrival at Genoa Airport," said Geoff.

"I wonder if they had saved enough for their bolognaise," laughed Greavsie.

"How are you going to stop Eusebio then Mooro?" I asked.

"I think Alf will put Nobby man-to-man on him. He won't let England down. Tonight, we'll be watching Germany versus Russia on the TV back at Hendon Hall. I don't know about you lot, but I'm confident it will be us and not Portugal playing the Germans in the final," he added.

"I make you right skipper," said Martin confidently. Geoff also nodded an approval and Greavsie slowly sipped his tea before adding: "I bloody hope so. It will be good to beat the Germans in the final."

I felt for Greavsie. Despite doing his best to appear upbeat, I could tell he was desperately disappointed. I'm sure at that point he still harboured dreams of playing in the final, but in reality I don't think anyone in the room believed he would be in the starting line-up if England got there. Indeed, the injury was the beginning of the end of his international career, as Geoff was to become England's first-choice striker. In my mind, Jimmy Greaves was the most naturally gifted goal scorer of his generation, and Geoff agrees with me on that.

Alf Ramsey stuck with the same team and formation of 'wingless wonders' for the semi-final against Portugal. Stiles, as Mooro expected, was handed the job of man-marking Eusebio and he did it superbly in an entertaining match devoid of any more ugly incidents. Bobby Charlton produced possibly his best game in an England shirt, scoring the two goals that earned England the final we'd all wanted.

The question on everyone's lips in the days before 30th July was whether a fit-again Jimmy Greaves would get back in the team. The answer, as history now shows, was no. Most people to this day believe Geoff Hurst, who as everyone knows scored a hat-trick in the final, was selected by Ramsey instead of Greavsie. It's a natural assumption to make, as Hurst had replaced the injured Greaves against Argentina and retained his place in an unchanged starting line-up from then until the final. However, my friend Ken Jones, who was the *Daily Mirror*'s chief football writer and one of Alf Ramsey's most loyal advocates in the press at the time, revealed to me soon afterwards that England's coach had in fact agonised over whether to re-call Greavsie and drop Roger Hunt for the final. Geoff, it appears, had done enough in two matches to convince Ramsey that the team needed a big target man, an old-fashioned centre forward in the mould of Bobby Smith, Nat Lofthouse and Dixie Dean. He had held the ball up superbly against Argentina and Portugal and enabled the midfield to push forward and join the attacks. The burning question for Ramsey was whether he should sacrifice hard-running forward Roger Hunt for the mercurial unpredictability of Jimmy Greaves. According to Ken, Ramsey believed Hunt deserved the place more. He had played very well against France, scored three goals to Greavsie's none in the group stage and the team itself had played better during the competition without the Tottenham striker in the line-up. It was a brave decision, but one that can't really be questioned due to the glorious outcome.

On the day of the final, I invited a few friends for a pre-match lunch at my Hendon home. My guests included a large party from South Africa's Highlands Park Football Club who had flown over especially for the game. Amongst their officials was former Israeli international player and manager Joe Mirmovich who became a good friend of mine. Highlands Park were celebrating doing the treble in South Africa and we were all three sheets to the wind by the time we arrived at Wembley. I sat in my usual seat in Block 81, an area mainly reserved for FA dignitaries. It was a great spot that allowed me to gain access to an area known as the Long Bar, where refreshments and sandwiches were available for VIPs. At half-time, and with the score tied at 1–1, I was heading off in search of a stiff drink to calm my nerves when I bumped into Greavsie in the narrow corridor leading to the Long Bar.

"Hi Jim. Where are you sitting?"

"I'm on the bench, with a good pitch side view."

"I'm sorry you're not playing. I guess it's just one of those things."

"Yeah. Thanks Morris."

"I don't know about you, but I'm a bundle of nerves. I reckon it might go to a replay." I said.

"Maybe, although who knows, Geoff may get another and win it for us."

"Yeah. Bobby Charlton hasn't seen much of the ball, has he?"

"Alf's got him man-marking Beckenbauer."

"You must be hoping it goes to a replay? Alf might pick you for that."

"If it goes to one, I won't be here. I'm off on holiday tomorrow."

"But surely you'll cancel it Jim?"

"Nah. The flights are booked and I've packed my bags. Irene and the kids, and myself come to think of it, are really looking forward to it. I won't be around for any replay."

"Oh, right." I said in disbelief.

To say I was shocked to hear that was an understatement. I'm sure Greavsie was hurting at having not been picked for the final, but would he really have chosen to miss a replay? I can only say that at that moment, I totally believed him and relayed his words to my friends when I arrived back at my seat for the start of the second-half.

Like every England fan that watched the rest of the match, either from inside the stadium or on their TV sets at home, I was beside myself with joy after Geoff slammed home England's fourth goal just as some people were on the pitch thinking it was all over. After watching Ramsey's men parade the Jules Rimet trophy around Wembley, I made the short journey back to my home in Hendon where champagne corks were soon flying. The party was well and truly swinging when my wife called me in from the garden to say my friend Reg Drury, the sports reporter, was on the phone.

"Morris. I need a favour. Can you get down to the Hendon Hall Hotel and tell Geoff Hurst that the *News of the World* has voted him the Man of the Match. We've got a huge trophy for him and Tom Finney is going to present it to him tomorrow. Also, get a quote off him if you can."

As I hurried down to the hotel, I wondered whether the players would even be there as Moore had turned down an invite to my World Cup party, saying the players had to attend a banquet at the Royal Garden Hotel whether they won or lost. However, as I approached the Hendon Hall I saw a throng of flag-waving supporters crammed together by the team bus cheering the players as they queued up to get on. I quickly spotted Geoff standing with Martin Peters and managed to reach him before he boarded.

"How does it feel to be the first man to score a hat-trick in a World Cup final?" I asked in my best reporter's yell.

"Amazing. I wasn't a hundred per cent sure that the third one had counted, as the ref blew the final whistle immediately after I struck the ball."

"It counted alright. You got the match ball?"

"No. It's the first I've thought of it."

"I'm sure someone will retrieve it for you." (Someone did – thirty years later – when the *Daily Mirror* and Richard Branson agreed to pay £80,000 for its return from Germany's Helmut Haller.)

"Anyway, Reg Drury told me to tell you that the *News of the World* has voted you the Man of the Match. They'll be presenting you with a trophy tomorrow."

"That's great. Thanks for letting me know Morris."

"Enjoy the party."

"We will."

Geoff may have been the best player in the final but over the whole tournament three players stood out from the rest: Eusebio, who had scored nine goals and helped Portugal claim third place, England's Bobby Charlton, who had been brilliant in the tournament's best match against Portugal, and of course the winning captain, Bobby Moore, who hadn't put a foot wrong in any of England's six games. For me, Mooro just shaded it. I called Terry Venables the next day, after reading the *News of the World* and its match report under the headline, 'Hurst is the Hammer'.

"So, the papers are going for Geoff as man of the final, but who do you reckon was the best over the whole tournament?" Terry agreed with me,

"I'd have to say Mooro. There's no chance of him coming to Spurs now though".

"Yeah. West Ham will never let him go. We may as well forget about that idea".

We were right. West Ham soon agreed to almost double Mooro's earnings, offering him a three-year contract on £150 a week with an option to retain him for a further three years after that. I'm sure Spurs or any other club would have been happy to have matched it, but there was no way the Hammers were going to sell their World Cup-winning captain. For the remainder of the summer I was left wondering what could have been.

By the beginning of August, Spurs still hadn't signed a new defender and as the press were full of stories saying that Greavsie might never be the same player after his World Cup heartbreak. I was concerned enough to have an irritated Sylvia make her own way home with the kids from the south of France at the end of our summer holiday. I was desperate to find out what was going on with my friend, and the prospect of catching a few matches in the Costa del Sol, where Spurs were ending their pre-season, was more inviting than coping with bored kids in the last weeks of their school holidays. The tournament featured Malaga, Atlètico Madrid and Benfica, who included Eusebio in their ranks. After waving goodbye to my disgruntled family, I called Terry at his hotel and delightedly told him that I was on my way. He promised to meet me at the airport. However, when I got to Nice I found that the plane I was due to catch to take me to Malaga had been severely delayed and wouldn't arrive in time for me to go to the first match. After some frantic negotiations, I managed to get to Barcelona Airport, where I hoped to then get a flight to Malaga. Unfortunately, with it being the height of summer and packed with holidaymakers I couldn't get a fight from there either and ended up flying straight back to London. Two days later, Terry phoned me at home.

"What happened to you Morris? Me and Phil Beal waited for three hours at Malaga Airport for you."

"I'm so sorry, but it was beyond my control. My flight was delayed. I got to Barcelona but couldn't get a flight to Malaga."

"That's too bad. It didn't matter to us though, as we got pissed in the bar waiting for you."

"How's Greavsie? Does he seem OK after his disappointing summer?"

"He's alright, full of jokes as usual. He scored when we beat Benfica 2–1 in the tournament final and looked every bit as good as Eusebio. Don't worry, he'll get over it."

"What about the defence?"

"Ron Henry played as a makeshift centre-half in Spain. He did well, but Bill Nick's gonna sign Mike England from Blackburn. He may not be Bobby Moore, but he's the next best thing."

"Really? That's brilliant news."

"Don't you worry Morris, your Spurs are in good shape for the season ahead."

Terry was right of course. Greavsie bagged 25 league goals during the 1966/67 campaign and top-scored in the FA Cup, as Spurs secured the trophy, beating Chelsea in the final. Ten months after England's World Cup triumph, I reckon there was only one man happier than me to see Greavsie collect a winners' medal at Wembley – and that was Jimmy Greaves himself.

3 MAKING FRIENDS AND AVOIDING THE ENEMY

"Morris is a truly endearing and genuine character, and the best supporter Tottenham Hotspur have ever had. I really don't think they ever knew what they had in their midst such was the man's intelligence, warmth and ability to generate friendships."
Eddie Baily (Spurs and England, League Championship winner 1951 and Spurs assistant manager 1963–1974)

"When I was managing Southend, Morris recommended I take a look at the Heybridge Swifts goalkeeper. I knew it was a good tip as soon as I spotted Harry Redknapp in the crowd watching the same player. Simon Royce signed for Southend, played 150 games, and I got one over on Harry. Thanks Morris."
Dave Webb (Chelsea, FA Cup winner 1970)

The goalkeeper and French philosopher Albert Camus once said, "Don't walk in front of me, I may not follow; don't walk behind me, I may not lead. Just walk beside me and be my friend." I've spent my life following Albert's advice on friendship and have made many friends as a result, especially in football.

The first great friendship of my life was forged at a youth club near where I lived in Clapton, East London. It was there that I met a football-mad 16-year-old called Reg Drury. He was two years older than me, but despite the gap in our ages we clicked and hung around together. We played football on Hackney Marshes with the other lads in the area. Reg was a really good player, much better than me. He scored a hat-trick in a trial match at Enfield, then a leading amateur club, and they tried to sign him up. Reg turned them down though and opted instead to join the local Tottenham newspaper. He'd been writing match reports for *Sports Weekly* since leaving school at the age of 14 and was keen to get a proper foot on the ladder. It proved a great decision on his part, as it was the beginning of a 50-year career during which time he spent 30 years as football correspondent with the *News of the World*.

It was with Reg in November 1948 that I made one of my first away trips up North to see Spurs. Blundell Park was the venue for a Second Division clash against Grimsby. We left at midnight on a George Ewer coach from North London and arrived in Cleethorpes seven hours later: there were no motorways in those days! It was bloody freezing that November morning and I remember getting off the coach and being struck by a blast of cold air.

"Where do we go now? I asked Reg, thinking my hotshot reporter mate would have a plan for the next eight hours before the game got underway.

"Dunno," was his useless reply. Back in those days away fans didn't exist and we walked around for hours waiting for a café to open to get a hot drink. There was absolutely nothing to do and it wasn't until the home supporters started to arrive that the place livened up. We ended up sitting outside Blundell Park for three hours waiting for the ground to open. I vowed that day never to return and it took me 43 years to break that resolution. Terry Venables persuaded me to make the journey with him in 1991 for a League Cup game.

Reg may not have been the best planner as a teenager, but his enthusiasm for football certainly rubbed off on me. We'd chat about the game for hours on end, giving opinions on the players and teams that visited White Hart Lane. As a young reporter, Reg was always telling me how important it was in his profession to make good contacts. In those days, there were no mass media press conferences; a reporter had to cultivate strong relationships with players and managers to produce his stories. Reg would often point to his bulging contacts book and say: "Without this, I wouldn't survive." He was particularly good at spotting up-and-coming managers. He knew Bill Shankly very well long before he became a legend at Liverpool and Brian Clough, the greatest English manager never to manage the England team, was giving Reg his forthright opinions in the early days at Fourth Division Hartlepools. He was also a confidant of England manager Alf Ramsey, whom he'd known since Ramsey's playing days at Southampton. When the Boys of '66 were dropping in at mine for tea and biscuits, Ramsey was at Reg's home in Finchley, North London, sipping a brew and dunking rich tea. Bob Paisley and Joe Fagan from the Anfield boot room and Terry Venables were other top managers who put their trust in him. They knew if they wanted something kept private and off the record, that's the way it stayed. They showed their appreciation by giving Reg the exclusive story when they landed new jobs or signed star players. Like Reg, I've never underestimated the importance of having a bulging book of contacts, whether on a social level or in business: you can never have too many contacts or too many friends.

The first professional footballer to become a good friend of mine was the late Tommy Harmer. We met by chance in 1952, when I was driving my work's van through Hackney on the way to a Spurs match. Tommy was waiting for a bus to take him to Tottenham when I spotted him standing by the kerb. Instinctively, I slammed on the brakes and pulled over.

"Do you want a lift?"

"Can you fit me in?" he asked, looking at my mate Dave inside who was already sitting in the passenger seat.

"Yeah. I've got room, just so long as you don't mind going in the back."

"Beats waiting for the bus!" With the van's engine still running, I jumped out and opened the rear doors.

"It's gonna be a tight squeeze," said Tommy, looking at the rails of dresses hanging up in the back. Undeterred, he threw his kit bag and boots into a corner and jumped in, parking his nine-stone frame cosily into the limited space available. Twenty minutes later, I parked up near the ground and opened the back doors to find him looking like he'd been dragged through a hedge backwards.

"I had to hold on to those rails for dear life every time you went around a corner!" he said with a forced smile.

"Sorry Tom. Dave said he'd go in the back next time."

"Thanks. At least I'm here in one piece!" It was the first of many lifts that I gave to the player, known affectionately as 'Harmer the Charmer'. On a subsequent trip to White Hart Lane, I was surprised to learn that as well as living in the same area, we both shared similar experiences growing up in the East End. He too had been evacuated to Norfolk during the Second World War, and like me, had returned to find his school playground turned to rubble by Adolf Hitler. Reg Drury also became a friend of Tommy's and admired him both on and off the field. He was undoubtedly one of the most skilful players that I've ever seen on a football pitch. He was a magician with the ball at his feet and would have me, and opposing defences, mesmerised with his silky skills. He was deadly in dead-ball situations, especially from the penalty spot, when he would run up and then suddenly stop, before sending the goal-keeper the wrong way.

Annoyingly for Tommy, his slight frame and style of play didn't suit Arthur Rowe's 'push-and-run' football, and he was overlooked in favour of the stronger and better one-touch passer Eddie Baily. Rowe's successor, Jimmy Anderson, made Tommy the first-choice inside right and he proved his worth in a creative midfield alongside Danny Blanchflower, when Spurs finished runners-up to Manchester United in the 1956/57 season. Tommy was man of the match in Bill Nicholson's first game in charge – the famous 10–4 win over Everton – when he netted a screamer from outside the box. He remained in the side for another season, but with the signing of John White the writing was on the wall and he left for Watford in 1960. Like most Spurs fans, I was very sad to see him go, but enjoyed seeing him socially for many years afterwards.

About the time that Tommy Harmer left, I struck up another friendship with a Spurs player – exhilarating right-winger Terry Medwin. I had engaged in polite conversation with him on a few away trips during the 1960/61 season, but it was our wives that became good friends before we did. Terry had told me during one trip that his wife was down in the dumps, as she didn't feel she had anything suitably glamorous to wear to a party. When I told Sylvia, she got in touch with

Joyce and offered to lend her a mink stole for the occasion. I think Terry ended up buying his wife one anyway, but the sentiment was there and the girls became good friends from that day onwards. Through their friendship, I got to know Terry better and he introduced me to his teammates in Tottenham's double-winning side.

A few weeks into the 1962/63 season, I invited the Medwins and the rest of the players and their wives to a party at my home. I arranged it for the day that Spurs played West Ham at Upton Park, although Sylvia warned, "They won't feel like partying if they lose." I guess it would have been safer bet if I'd picked a day when Spurs faced Orient or Fulham, but it mattered not as the lads hammered West Ham 6–1! After the victory, the entire forward line of Jimmy Greaves, Terry Medwin, Cliff Jones, John White and Bobby Smith turned up for a celebratory drink. Amazingly, all of those players, except Smithy, who was injured and didn't play, scored that afternoon. The party definitely benefitted from that great result earlier in the day. It wasn't often that Spurs beat West Ham that comprehensively, even back then with that great forward line!

In the summer that year, Sylvia and Joyce took the kids to the Butlin's holiday camp in Clacton, Essex. They were having a great time participating in the round-the-clock activities laid on by the redcoats, until word reached them that Terry had broken his leg playing in Tottenham's end-of-season tour of South Africa. Sadly for him, the break forced him to retire at the age of 30. Terry later returned to the professional game, coaching at Fulham and then serving as assistant manager to John Toshack at Swansea in the early eighties. We are still in touch with the Medwins, who live in Swansea.

Having established firm friendships with the Spurs players in the early sixties, it wasn't long before those friendships snowballed and I became friends with their friends. Jimmy Greaves introduced me to his England colleague Bobby Moore, who in turn introduced me to his clubmates at West Ham. Soon, players from other London clubs like Fulham, Chelsea and Arsenal were also in my social network. Before I knew it, my address book was as impressive as Reg Drury's!

Bobby Moore and I became trusted friends and went into business together in 1968, selling men's suede and leather jackets. Our mutual friend Freddie Harrison was also a partner in the venture. These were the days when professional footballers didn't earn big wages and tried to supplement their incomes by making a few extra quid elsewhere. The business attracted some great publicity, but unfortunately that didn't transfer into the sales we'd hoped for. At a fashion show staged at the Hilton Hotel in London, I spotted an opportunity when I noticed boxing legend Sugar Ray Robinson walk through the door with his entourage. I grabbed my photographer mate Monte Fresco and threw a tape measure at Mooro.

"Sugar Ray! Sugar Ray! Over here! I've got England's greatest footballer with me and he wants to measure you up for a new coat."

"My man. I'll be straight over!" The world's greatest ever pound-for-pound fighter and England's World Cup-winning captain laughed and joked as Mooro took Sugar Ray's measurements. I love that picture, it's one of Monte's best. In hindsight, I wish I'd asked them all to sign it, as it would be worth more money than we ever made in that venture!

Following England's success in 1966, Bobby became a national icon overnight. His popularity should have opened many doors to him in the advertising world, but he didn't get the amount of jobs you'd expect. I couldn't understand it, as he was the epitome of a British athlete: tall, blond, good-looking and with a clean-cut image. The only TV commercial I can remember him doing was for the pub industry, when he played darts with his wife Tina and urged everyone to "look in at the local". One night in Annabel's nightclub in the West End, a few months before the World Cup finals in Mexico, I spoke to him about his lack of success and discussed the merits of having Mark McCormack as his agent. McCormack was the top man in the US, with golf's 'Big Three' – Arnold Palmer, Gary Player and Jack Nicklaus – all on his books, as well as Australian tennis ace Rod Laver. He had recognised sport as a way for companies to communicate with consumers and had told Bobby that he wanted him to be the first footballer on his books in Britain.

"Listen Bobby. This is Mark McCormack we're talking about. He's not some fly-by-night. He is 'the man' in the sports marketing business."

"That may be the case, but he also wants a percentage of my current earnings. I don't mind him having a large chunk of what he brings in, but I can't let him have a percentage of my West Ham salary."

"He'll make you so much more, before long you won't even care about what West Ham pay you!"

"I just can't see it Morris. Jack Turner takes ten per cent of what he brings in. Others have wanted 15 and 20, but ten percent is fair in my book. I can't let McCormack have a percentage of my salary when there's no guarantee he'll bring in enough from off-the-field activities!" I spent three hours that night trying to persuade Bobby to sign on the dotted line with McCormack, but to no avail. It was a shame, as I believe he missed out on becoming a very wealthy man. McCormack went on to represent the likes of Pele, Martina Navratilova, John McEnroe, Greg Norman, Nick Faldo, Pete Sampras and Michael Schumacher – all of whom, by all accounts, bene-fitted greatly financially from working with the man *Sports Illustrated* later called "the most powerful man in sport".

Not long after Bobby told McCormack, 'thanks, but no thanks' he asked me to chair his 1970 testimonial committee. It was the first time that I'd taken the chairman's role, although I had some experience, having sat on the committee for George Cohen's. For Bobby's, I organised a dinner and dance at the Hilton Hotel and also a gentlemen's evening, when comedian Freddie Starr, then relatively unknown away from the Northern clubs, provided the entertainment. Freddie had everyone in stitches with his high jinks that night, although I remember Bobby laughed even louder when I told him about the joke the comedian played on me one night at the Sportsman Club in central London. Back in the seventies, the restaurant and casino was situated on Tottenham Court Road and was a favourite hangout for sports stars and showbiz celebrities. In the foyer they had a board, on which they'd put up the names of every sports star that was inside that night. Jimmy Hill acted as the club's PR man and brought in many of the sporting greats that came through its doors. Bobby Moore, Jimmy Greaves, Dennis Compton, Henry Cooper, Jimmy Connors, Muhammad Ali and Mark Spitz were just a few of the sporting legends that frequented the place. One night, they jokingly put my name up with the words, 'Morris Keston – Winning Race-horse Owner'. I was sitting down with some friends having dinner and laughing about discovering my name on the board under 'sporting legend' when Freddie Starr walked in and came over to see me.

"Hello Morris. Sorry to interrupt you as you're eating, but can you do me favour?"

"Of course Freddie. What is it?"

"I'm due to meet some friends in the next five minutes for dinner. As you know, I'm new on the London scene, but I really want to impress the people I'm having dinner with. If you don't mind, would you give me a wave and say hello when you see me walking through into the restaurant with my friends?"

"I can do that. No problem."

"Thanks." For the next five minutes, I slowly ate my starter and kept my eyes fixed on the restaurant entrance. Freddie soon walked in with his friends and I called out and gave him a wave.

"Yoo-hoo, Freddie!" To my surprise he looked straight through me, said something to his friends and sat at a table as far away from mine as he could find. I thought to myself, "that's strange, maybe I did something wrong." I continued my meal and didn't think any more of it. As it happened, Freddie's group finished their meal before mine and when he got up to leave, I gave him another wave and tried again.

"Yoo-hoo, Freddie. It's me, Morris." One again he ignored me, grabbed the arm of one of the people with him, hid behind them and hurried out into the bar. Five minutes later, I got up and went to find him, and found him in hysterics. When he finally managed to control himself he revealed:

"I told my friends before walking into the restaurant that there's a gay chap inside, who has developed a crush on me and is following me all over London."

"You didn't!"

"And I told them, 'I'd bet he gives me a wave and tries to

talk to me, but I'm going to steer clear and ignore him.'" I don't know who laughed more, him or Bobby Moore!

I frequented the Sportsman a lot in the seventies. During one Gala Dinner there I was introduced to world heavyweight boxing champion Muhammad Ali. After shaking his hand, I asked him, "I know you're 'the Greatest' but tell me, are you scared of anything?"

"Yes," he replied. "Flying. I'd rather get in the ring and fight George Foreman and Joe Frazier at the same time than get on a plane."

"We have something in common then," I said. "I also hate flying, but I'd rather have a few stiff drinks before take-off than get in the ring with anyone, even my wife!" He laughed and then taunted me as a photographer prepared to take our picture. "Go on sissy, punch me. Show me you're a man. Go on sissy, you can do it!" Ali then clenched his fists and put his hands up. I reached out and grabbed one. It was as hard as a rock. I then put my hands up and playfully connected in slow motion with his jaw as the photographer's flash went off. "Now it's my turn," grinned Ali. Needless to say, I bid a hasty retreat!

As well as mixing with the likes of Muhammad Ali at the Sportsman, I'd often meet Terry Venables there when he was after a second opinion on a footballing matter. In the summer of 1976, he called me at home late one night and asked if I'd join him for a drink to discuss a job offer he'd received.

"I thought you'd taken the Crystal Palace job?" I said, as we sipped our pints.

"Not yet. I haven't signed a contract."

"What's stopping you?"

"Arsenal. They want me." I was gobsmacked. I'd read that Arsenal's long-serving manager Bertie Mee had resigned, but expected the Gunners to turn to an experienced manager as his replacement. Terry was untried and untested at the time and had only just been offered the chance to make the step up from coach to manager at Third Division Crystal Palace following the sacking of Malcolm Allison.

"I know what you're thinking," said Terry.

"I'm thinking it's too good an opportunity to turn down?" I replied.

"I agree with you," he said. "But I've told Ray Bloye [Palace chairman] that I'll take over at Selhurst Park."

"But as you said Terry, you haven't signed anything yet."

"I know Morris. I told Ray about the Arsenal offer last night, but he said he's not willing to release me. He says if I join the Gunners, then I've broken my word."

"That's true. The question is, 'Will you be able to live with the guilt if you join the Arsenal?'"

Terry laughed. "Maybe you're not the best person to speak to," implying that I might not take an impartial stand, knowing my feelings towards Tottenham's local rivals.

"If you go to Highbury, you'll also lose me as a friend," I joked.

"You're not making this easy for me Morris."

"Truthfully Terry, however much it pains me to say it, I think you should take the Arsenal job. You might never get another chance."

"I just don't know Morris. Part of me thinks it's come too soon. Don't get me wrong, I believe I'm good enough, but at the same time I've got no managerial experience."

"True, but they've spotted your potential."

"I'm flattered that they have, but I think I'm better off learning my trade at Palace."

I nodded. "I must admit, when you first mentioned Arsenal, that was my immediate thought. If you're good enough, the Arsenals of this world will come knocking again." Our conversation had taken a remarkable U-turn, "You should do what feels right for you," I said.

The next morning, Terry phoned Arsenal chairman Denis Hill-Wood and told them that Ray Bloye wouldn't allow him to leave Crystal Palace and therefore he'd be declining their offer. It was a brave decision on Terry's part and one that I hoped that he wouldn't live to regret. I must admit that I breathed a huge sigh of relief. I knew Terry was the best young coach around and didn't want to see him on the wrong side of North London. Arsenal then turned to Terry Neill, who had just resigned at Spurs, and appointed him to step into Bertie Mee's shoes.

Terry Venables's first season in management was a huge

success, with Palace gaining promotion to the Second Division. At Tottenham, that 1976/77 season was a different matter. Following Neill's departure, Keith Burkinshaw was promoted from first-team coach to manager, but he failed to prevent the team's downward spiral and Spurs were relegated for the first time in over 25 years. During that wretched season, I was invited by the directors of Derby County to watch the game against Spurs from the directors' box at the Baseball Ground. By then, I'd taken a leaf out of Reg Drury's book, and my contacts in the game had moved on from friendships with the players to include the directors of many top clubs. I had a fantastic view that day, sitting next to Derby's vice-chairman George Hardy. It was just a shame that I had to sit through Spurs getting thrashed 8–2!

Somewhat surprisingly, Derby boss Dave Mackay lost his job a few weeks after that impressive victory over his former club. George Hardy unsuccessfully tried to persuade Brian Clough to leave Nottingham Forest and return to Derby, whom he'd led to their first league title in 1972. After failing to land Cloughie, George asked me whom I'd recommend for the job.

"Terry Venables. He's the best young manager around." Terry's Palace side had just taken Liverpool to a replay in the FA Cup and George, who had by now replaced Sam Longson as chairman, gave my recommendation some serious thought. However, in the end, he believed Terry wasn't high profile enough for Derby and eventually gave Tommy Docherty the job. You couldn't get more high profile than the Doc. He'd just won the FA Cup with Manchester United and been sacked a few weeks later after the tabloids revealed that he had been conducting an extramarital affair with the wife of United's physiotherapist Laurie Brown. Docherty stayed at Derby for two seasons, only just avoiding relegation in 1979 before resigning and moving to Queens Park Rangers. Terry replaced the Doc at QPR in October 1980 and took Rangers to the FA Cup final in 1982 before leading them to a fifth place finish in the First Division. I often wonder whether George Hardy regretted not acting on my recommendation and handing Terry the job. Sadly for the Rams, they were relegated to the Second Division in 1980 and then again to the Third

Division in 1984. It took three more years before they returned to the top flight.

The friendships that I made with the directors extended to many clubs besides Derby, and included Fulham, Liverpool, Stoke and Chelsea, where I got on brilliantly with their chairman, the late Brian Mears. With his fur coat, sunglasses and Rolls-Royce sporting the private plate CFC II, Brian symbolised Chelsea in the Swinging Sixties. He certainly enjoyed the lifestyle and raised the profile of the club with his celebrity friends like Raquel Welch, John Mills, Laurence Olivier and Dickie Attenborough, whom he invited to Stamford Bridge. He was a lovely guy and the hospitality that I received at the Bridge took some beating. They were fabulous times and Brian certainly enjoyed the glitz, if not the responsibility of following in his father's footsteps at the club. Joe Mears was a key figure during England's preparations to host the 1966 World Cup, but died of a heart attack in Oslo one month before the finals got underway. He was certainly a hard act to follow, but Brian managed it with the help of his trusted secretary, Christine Matthews. In truth, Chris pretty much ran Chelsea back then. She organised everything at the club and was totally indispensible, not just to Brian, but also to the players as she was the first port of call for any problems they had. With Chris's help, I organised three testimonial matches for players at Chelsea during the seventies. They were great times. Unfortunately, my relationship with the directors at Tottenham during the sixties, and much of seventies, was never as harmonious as the ones I shared with the directors at other clubs.

In the early sixties, when I began mixing with the players at Spurs, Fred Wale was the club's chairman and his son, Sidney, was its vice-chairman. The pair rarely spoke to me, preferring to ignore me whenever I mixed socially with the players in hotels during away trips. Sidney, especially, would go out of his way to make me feel uncomfortable. On one occasion before a European Cup Winners' Cup clash with Manchester United in December 1963, Jimmy Greaves was left fuming by Wale's attitude towards me. I had checked into the same Manchester hotel as the players and club officials and was sitting on my own in the hotel lounge when Jimmy Greaves, Cliff Jones, John White and Bobby Smith came over and sat down beside me for a chat. Sidney Wale then walked into the room, followed by a photographer from the *Manchester Evening News* who wanted to take a picture of the players relaxing at the hotel. I could see what was happening and began to move my chair out of the way, so the photographer wouldn't have an unknown face in the photo. Wale could see what I was doing, yet still walked over and said to the photographer, "This gentlemen isn't a player or official of Tottenham Hotspur, so please ask him to move out of the photograph." He then turned around and began to walk out of the lounge. I was lost for words.

"Hang on a minute," said Greavsie, before turning towards me and saying: "Why don't you tell Wale that it was us who came over and interfered with you. You didn't interfere with us. You shouldn't have to move anywhere. What a bloody cheek."

It was typical of Sidney Wale's attitude towards me. It wasn't just me that was treated in this way, but anyone who tried to get too close to the inner circle at Tottenham. For whatever reason, Wale saw me as a threat and treated me like an enemy. Maybe he feared that I'd befriend the other directors and prevent him from following in his father's footsteps as chairman? Things came to head in 1967, when the players got bored with the speeches at the club's FA Cup celebrations at the Savoy and left the party early to come to mine at the Hilton. Sidney Wale was livid by all accounts and I was shunned by all of the club's directors after that. Two years later, Sidney replaced his late father as chairman, but that didn't bring about a change in the way he acted towards me. Maybe he still saw me as a threat to his position. I certainly would have been a popular choice amongst the players to have filled some sort of role at the club, if I'd been offered one. I'd helped organise quite a few fund-raising benefit nights and testimonials for the players at Tottenham. The fact is, for whatever reason, Sidney misread my intentions and oblivious to the truth made up his mind to keep me at arm's length. I never had any sort of grand plan to push for a seat on the board, although, if

I'm honest, I certainly wouldn't have turned one down! My only interest was to offer the club I loved my full support.

During the early seventies, I continued to organise parties for the players, although I specifically told them to come to mine after the official one held by the club. I organised one in 1971 to take place after the League Cup final against Aston Villa. A few days before the match, manager Bill Nicholson called me up out of the blue at home. I rarely spoke to Bill, as he was totally dedicated to his job of winning football matches and wasn't the type to celebrate after achieving one.

"Mr Keston?"

"Speaking."

"This is Bill Nicholson from Tottenham Hotspur. I'd like to inform you that the party you're throwing for my players ..." I interjected.

"Mr Nicholson, with respect, I'd like to tell you that I'm not throwing a party for your players. It's a party for my friends in football. If your players choose to come along they're very welcome. If they don't, my party will still go on."

"I see, but Mr Keston, all I was going to say is don't expect them early, as they will be spending some time at the club's one."

"That's fine, and if you'd like to extend your evening on Saturday, then you are more than welcome to join the players."

"Thank you for the invitation, but I don't want to jump the gun. We may not have anything to celebrate."

"I have every confidence in you and the team Mr Nicholson. Good luck." Needless to say, Bill Nicholson didn't come to my party. He preferred to stay at the club's with the directors. They didn't come either, although I did invite them!

My first party in 1967 was open to the public, but after that one I decided just to invite my 'friends in football'. I had more than enough to fill the Coronation Suite at the Hilton Hotel on Park Lane. I missed a great photo opportunity at the do in 1971 after Spurs beat Villa in the League Cup final. Denis Howell, who had only just relinquished his position as Minister for Sport under Harold Wilson's Labour government, was walking around socialising arm-in-arm with notorious ticket tout Stan Flashman. They were both great friends of mine and even though they were on opposite sides of the spectrum got on famously together that night. It's a shame Monte Fresco wasn't there to snap that one!

Sidney Wale's attitude towards me changed in the mid-seventies, and I had George Hardy, then vice-chairman at Derby, to thank for that. I had got to know Hardy through Labour politician Tom Pendry, now of course Lord Pendry and a former Shadow Minister for Sport. He is an avid Derby fan and at the time was my neighbour. He introduced me to Derby's club secretary, Stuart Webb, who in turn invited me for tea and sandwiches with the Derby directors before a game, where I struck up an instant friendship with George. The season after Derby had won the league title with Dave Mackay at the helm, George invited me to sit with him in the directors' box at White Hart Lane. I turned down the offer, citing Sidney Wale's dislike for me and saying that I didn't want to antagonise him or the other Tottenham directors. George understood and instead asked me to join him for the return fixture at the Baseball Ground later that season. On the day of that match in January 1976, I was in the boardroom chatting to Derby chairman Sam Longson before the game when I spied George in conversation with Wale. Just before we took our seats, Sidney approached me with his hand outstretched.

"Hello Mr Keston. Let's shake hands. I want to let bygones be bygones." I shook his hand and we shared some small talk about the game ahead. I later discovered that George had told Wale, "If Derby had a fan like Morris Keston, I'd have him on my board immediately." Maybe the penny finally dropped on hearing George's view. Perhaps Wale realised that he'd been stupid not to embrace my enthusiasm for the club. It certainly felt strange watching the game just a few seats away from the man who'd been my nemesis for 20 years. The strange thing was, we'd never had an argument. I just couldn't understand why he ever disliked me so much and I never really found out. Things were different between Wale and I after that shaking of hands. In 1981, he accepted an invite to my daughter's wedding and I sat him next to George Hardy at the reception. We never did become best buddies or anything like that, but we shared polite conversation whenever in each other's company. I never did manage to break into the inner circle at the club and Wale never did invite me to watch a game from the directors' box at White Hart Lane.

Terry Venables also came to my daughter Shelley's wedding. Shelley began dating Tottenham's central defender Paul Miller in 1979, not long after he had broken into the first team. I can remember the evening they first met, as Shelley had spent much of the early evening in the doldrums as she fancied a night out, yet her friends all wanted a night in. I suggested that she call her 'uncle' Terry Venables and go for a drink at the pub he owned in the East End. She took my advice and got a cab there. Paul also happened to be at Terry's pub that night, along with his good mate Jerry Murphy, himself a talented young footballer at the time with Crystal Palace. After spending the night chatting, Paul asked Shelley if she fancied going somewhere for a late drink. Shelley told him, "I'll have to ask my uncle Terry." Terry told young Miller, "Behave yourself son, Shelley's dad is one of my best friends, so you look after her and make sure she gets home safely." My new son-in-law had him in stitches during the speeches when he announced, "This is a very emotional moment for Shelley's father, people used to know him as Morris Keston, Tottenham Hotspur's number one fan. Now that I've married Shelley, he's going to be known as Morris Keston, Paul Miller's father-in-law." People used to say to me that I must have been thrilled at having a Spurs player in the family. "You must have fulfilled a lifetime's ambition," said one journalist friend of mine. In truth, it was quite the opposite. I could no longer relax watching matches, as I was desperate for defender 'Maxie Miller' not to make a mistake at the back. I hated listening to supporters slag him off during games when he put a foot wrong or was at fault for a goal. Thankfully, it didn't happy too often as he was a superb footballer and the team was extremely successful with him in it, winning three major honours. However, I certainly didn't shed any tears when David Pleat sold him to Charlton in 1987. It felt like a huge weight had finally been lifted off my shoulders and I started to enjoy my match-day experiences again.

The same year that Paul left Spurs, Terry Venables took

the manager's job at White Hart Lane. He had spent three seasons at Barcelona during which time he led the Catalans to their first league title in 11 years and to within a whisker of clinching the European Cup, losing to Steaua Bucharest on penalties in the final. Terry's reputation soared after that successful stint abroad. When he left QPR for Barcelona in April 1984, most pundits at home and in Spain predicted 'El Tel', as he was now known, would be sacked before Christmas. I knew he'd prove them wrong, as he never shirks when it comes to making tough decisions. A few weeks after taking the Barcelona job he told the president to sell their best player, Diego Maradona. The Argentine was due to miss the first three months of the season after receiving a ban for his part in clashes on the pitch following Athletic Bilbao's win over Barça in the 1984 Copa del Rey. Maradona's huge entourage were also racking up enormous bills all over Barcelona and Terry thought it best to get rid of him. When Maradona was sold to Napoli, Terry called me at home when trying to decide whom to buy to fill the number 10 shirt.

"Morris, you know the players at Spurs. What's Steve Archibald like? Does he like a drink? Does he mix well with the players?"

"Maxie's the social secretary at Spurs and he says Archie's a bit aloof and chooses not to go on many of the nights out that he arranges. The players tell me he's a loner."

"Brilliant! That's exactly what I need him to be. I want a loner, someone who won't miss his mates and get homesick after a few weeks. He sounds like the single-minded type and I'm sure he'll do a good job for me. The president wants Hugo Sanchez, but you've helped convince me, Archie's my man." Stevie Archibald jumped at the chance and was an instant hit at the Nou Camp. The Spanish Press christened him 'Archigoles', after he notched twice in a pre-season friendly. He then scored and had a hand in two others when Barcelona won 3–0 at Real Madrid in Terry's first competitive match in charge. He was certainly one of Terry's best ever signings.

Before returning to England to manage Spurs, Terry had actually signed a contract to become Arsenal's new manager. He had intended to leave Barcelona after two seasons, but having been such a success the Catalans weren't in their usual hurry to bring in someone else. He was actually their 11th manager in ten years! In the end, Arsenal allowed him to break the agreement and appointed George Graham, Terry's best mate, instead. George had turned around Millwall's fortunes in a very short space of time, helping them to avoid relegation to the Fourth Division in his first season and getting them promoted to the Second Division in the next. As everyone knows, at Arsenal, George was a revelation. He won six major trophies in nine years, including two league titles, an FA Cup and the European Cup Winners' Cup. He's still a great friend of mine, despite his achievements at the enemy, although I must admit that I used to detest the very sight of him. It seemed that every time I met George, usually before derby games, his Arsenal side would beat Spurs. He started to believe that I was his lucky talisman, and so made sure that he saw me before every North London clash. He'd go out of his way to keep up the ritual and follow his superstition, whereas I did everything in my power to avoid him. On one occasion, I'd managed to avoid him for a month before the derby and on the eve of the big game the doorbell rang.

"Can you get that Morris?" asked Sylvia.

"No, I can't. It might be George."

"For God's sake Morris. It won't be George at this time of night."

"No. Don't answer."

"This is ridiculous. It could be family or friends."

"If you answer that door and it's George and he sees me, then Spurs will lose tomorrow."

"I'm answering it: you'd better go and hide." I ran to the toilet and hid in there. Meanwhile, Sylvia answered the door and was greeted by a grinning George.

"Where is he Sylvia? He's been avoiding me, but he can't any longer."

"He's not here George; he's out with Terry."

"That's a lie and you know it." He barged his way past through the front door and started to search the flat for me and eventually found the toilet door bolted.

"Got ya Morris. Come out!"

"If I come out, you'll see me and Spurs will lose tomorrow." Outside the door, I could hear George walking away. I thought, "what's he up to now?" The answer soon arrived when I looked up and saw him peering through the glass above the door. He'd got a chair from the living room and was standing on it and tapping the window in joy.

"That's it, I've seen yer. I'll sleep tonight and we'll beat you tomorrow." He left as quickly as he'd arrived, and was gone before I even had time to open the toilet door to curse him. The next day, Arsenal beat Spurs at White Hart Lane. George was over the moon.

"See you again before the rematch at Highbury. You know you can't avoid the enemy Morris."

MY LOVE AFFAIR WITH THE FA CUP

"The man is football through and through and a world away from the extremes of today's sometimes extreme tribalism. Morris is, and has been, a true and valued friend, whose company I have enjoyed over many decades. In fact, I've never heard a detrimental word about a man who is ably backed up by his supportive and equally giving wife, Sylvia. A great team!"
Cliff Jones (Spurs and Wales, FA Cup winner 1961, 1962 and 1967)

"Morris is responsible for many of the first things I did. He provided me with my first Wimbledon tennis tickets, my first evening at the Ritz and a visit to my first strip club when I was injured and couldn't play in a UEFA Cup tie. I can say without fear of contradiction that my life with Morris has never been dull and I'm a better person for having spent a small portion of my life with him. Thanks Morris."
Garth Crooks OBE (Spurs, FA Cup winner 1981 and 1982)

I've had two great love affairs in my lifetime: one with my wife Sylvia, which has lasted over 50 years, and the other with the FA Cup – and I like to remind her that it's lasted even longer!

My first encounter with the FA Cup came in 1948, when as a 16-year-old boy I followed Tottenham's journey all the way to the semi-final. At the time, I was working as a showroom assistant at a trendy fashion store in London's Oxford Street. On the day of Tottenham's third-round trip to Bolton, I persuaded my boss to give me the Saturday off so I could catch the early train up North to see the game. Spurs had been stuck in the Second Division for 13 years and weren't expected to trouble the mighty Bolton Wanderers on their own patch.

However, the team, managed back then by Joe Hulme, defied the odds that day, winning 2–0 in extra time with centre forward Len Duquemin scoring both goals. My passion for the world's oldest football cup competiton was born on that cold January afternoon. I can still remember the joyful train journey home like it was yesterday.

After beating West Brom and then Leicester at home in the next rounds, I travelled to Southampton for the quarter-final. I can't remember much about the game, although the record books say that Spurs won it 1–0 and Les Bennett scored. I can, however, vividly recall what happened after the match. As we left the Dell ground and walked towards the station, a huge number of local people came onto the street so they could clap and cheer us as we walked the mile-long route to the railway station. Well-wishers leaned out of windows, waved rattles and called out, "Good luck in the next round!" and "Hope you win it Spurs!" Can you imagine that happening today!

I could barely sleep in the weeks leading up to the Villa Park semi-final against Blackpool, who had 'the Wizard of the Dribble', Stanley Matthews, in their ranks. Spurs hadn't reached an FA Cup semi-final for 26 years, so you can imagine the excitement in North London leading up to the game. Len 'the Duke' Duquemin gave Spurs the lead midway through the second half and I was convinced our name was on the trophy. Sadly, it wasn't to be. Stan Mortensen equalised in the dying moments for the Seasiders after beating four defenders and goalkeeper Ted Ditchburn and slotting home from an impossible angle. Blackpool went on to win the match 3–1 in extra time. I was absolutely devastated and cried most of the train journey home. I remember being as pleased as punch when Manchester United beat Matthews, Mortensen and Co in the final. It was payback for the trauma they'd caused me.

The next year, Spurs were drawn against neighbours Arsenal in the third round, who were the reigning league champions. It was the first time that the two clubs had faced each other in the FA Cup, and the clamour for tickets was immense. I was so keen to get one that I joined a small queue outside Highbury just before midnight, nine hours before they went on sale. At 11.30pm, there were only six people in front of me, but by the morning there were about 150 in front of me, all of them claiming their place in the queue had been saved. I wasn't in the best of moods after spending a freezing night wrapped in jumpers. I remember at about 6am a guy turned up pushing a wheelbarrow full of hot water shouting "Penny a wash". I took him up on the offer, but felt cheated when he failed to supply some soap! Typical Arsenal! I really shouldn't have bothered queuing for a ticket for the game, firstly because it wasn't an all-ticket match and secondly because the Gunners thrashed Spurs 3–0! Only 47,000 turned up in the end, 17,000 below the capacity, with many supporters staying away fearing a crush.

In October 1949, aged 18 years and four months, National Service call-up papers landed on the doormat, and the British Army ended two years of watching FA Cup football. The first six weeks of my Army life was spent getting fit at the training camp in Aldershot. I hated every minute of it. During the training period, we weren't allowed out of the barracks as we weren't deemed fit enough to be seen wearing the uniform. After that, we were allowed the occasional weekend pass to go home. Despite this rule, I managed to upset our troop's Sergeant by beating the system and getting more than my fair share of weekends away. My extended stays away from camp were solely down to my friendship with Reg Drury, the former *News of the World* football reporter who passed away in 2003. In 1949, Reg had just started making waves in the world of football reporting and freelanced for the *Enfield Gazette*, writing match reports under the pseudonym 'The Watcher'. Every other weekend, he would send a letter to the Army's office at Aldershot requesting my release to cover a football match in London. Reg was always in great demand, even in his early days as a reporter. The *Daily Express* would often give him a call and ask him to cover a match. Reg, being Reg, wouldn't like to say no, even if he was already covering a game for the *Enfield Gazette*. That's when I stepped in. The Army would usually give me a 36-hour pass from Friday lunchtime. I'd thumb a lift down to London, pop in to see Mum and Dad, and then watch a game, write the report, and meet up with

Reg for a night out. Sundays were spent making my way back to Aldershot. They were great times, but my sergeant put an end to my fun one afternoon when I was polishing my boots.

"Keston, I'm sending you to the furthest part of the world that I'm allowed. You're off to Egypt. Try writing your match reports from there!" I had to laugh though when I arrived at the Army base on the banks of the Suez Canal and my new seargent said, "Keston, I understand you're a football reporter. We'd like you to start covering all the Army's football matches in the *Egyptian Gazette!*" There were 10,000 troops stationed in Egypt at the time, so the paper had a large circulation. Each regiment would play one game a week and I'd report on all of them from a shady spot beside the pitch. It was certainly the highlight of my week, as I hated my Army days and missed going to watch my team.

I was only supposed to stay in Egypt for 11 months, but in response to the Korean War, National Service period was increased from 18 months to two years. It was like a prison sentence. I did general office duties during the day, which included monitoring British troop movements. The only action I saw was on guard duty, when occasionally the locals would jump over the fence and try to steal our food rations and blankets. Back home, Spurs secured promotion to the First Division in 1950, playing their entertaining 'push and run' football under new manager Arthur Rowe. I was still in bloody Egypt for the entire 1950/51 season, when Spurs won the First Division title! I was gutted, although I did manage to follow their fortunes during Saturday film nights in the desert. We would take it in turns to listen to the football results on the BBC World Service at 7pm, before running to the open-air theatre to relay the scores to the others before the film started at 7.15pm. I was most upset one evening, when I heard that lowly Huddersfield Town had knocked Spurs out of the FA Cup. I'd told all my mates in the 15th Battalion Royal Army Ordnance Corps that we were going to do the double.

In August 1951, I finished my stint in the land of the pharaohs and was discharged from the Army three months later. Thankfully, the only wound I suffered in the two years came when the Army surgeon removed my appendix. I returned to my old job in Oxford Street, where I'd pack coats, dresses and jackets into parcels before taking them to the railway station for distribution to other stores around the country. I'd usually hop into a taxi with the boxes piled high on the back seat, although on the occasions when I could carry them all, I'd get the bus instead, pocketing the extra money that I'd been given for a taxi. It was a nice scam that helped pay for the luxuries that post-War ration books couldn't provide.

My love affair with the FA Cup continued and I attended my first-ever Wembley Cup final in 1952. Reg Drury managed to get me a ticket for the match between Arsenal and Newcastle. At the time, Reg was working for *Sport Magazine* and the editor there exchanged his own ticket for a nice pin-striped shirt. Newcastle's Chilean inside left George Robledo, whose brother Ted also played for the Magpies at left half, scored the only goal of the game. I can't say that I was too unhappy watching Arsenal lose the final. The following year, I should have been at Wembley cheering on my own team, but Blackpool ended the dream once again at Villa Park in the semi-final. Alf Ramsey, who had played 25 consecutive matches at right back for England, played a dodgy back pass in the 89th minute that failed to reach my hero, goalkeeper Ted Ditchburn. Jackie Maudie nipped in for Blackpool to win the game 2–1. I barely spoke to anyone on the train ride back to London, my dream of seeing Spurs at the Twin Towers over for another year. When I got off the train at Euston, I went straight to a dance hall near Russell Square, where a friend's wife had arranged for me to meet a girl on a blind date. I didn't feel like going, but went away.

"Hello Morris. I'm Sylvia, your blind date."

I forced a smile towards the pretty brunette, but in my head all I could think about was Alf Ramsey's shocking pass.

"Hello."

"What's up with you? You couldn't look anymore miserable if you tried." she said.

"You'd better get used to it," I replied. "I support Spurs."

Sylvia's been getting used to it for over 50 years now. We dated for two years and were married on 22nd May, 1955 – the day England played Portugal in a friendly game in Oporto.

Reg Drury was one of our 200 guests at the wedding cere-mony. As I walked past his table with my lovely bride on my arm, I stopped.

"What's the score?" I asked.

"Is that all you can think of?" said Reg.

"Almost," I replied with a wink. "Are you going to tell me or should I ask someone else?"

"Sorry Sylvia," said Reg, "Roy Bentley scored early on, but Portugal have scored three since then."

I cursed, before leading my gorgeous wife to the top table.

Despite Tottenham's depressing FA Cup exit, I still tried to get a ticket for the 1953 final, but they were like gold dust: even Reg couldn't get me one. Instead, I watched Stan Mortensen's famous hat-trick in the 'Matthews Final' on a nine-inch black-and-white TV set at home. I may have missed 38-year-old Stanley Matthews collecting his winner's medal at Wembley, but I did get to meet him in person eight months later. Reg asked me to cover for him when he'd double-booked his match-reporting services during FA Cup weekend. While Reg was at Highbury reporting on Arsenal's shock exit against Norwich, I was at Upton Park for West Ham's fourth-round clash against the Cup holders. The Hammers were a Second Division club at the time, but earned a replay that day with a 1–1 draw against their First Division opponents. West Ham outside right Harry Hooper, whose father was a trainer at the club, scored that day. After the match, I followed a few hacks into Blackpool's dressing room in the hope of getting a quote from one of the players. I quickly spotted the great Stanley Matthews, who was standing up in a corner, looking into a mirror and adjusting his tie.

"Excuse me Stan. What did you think of Harry Hooper's performance today?"

Matthews turned towards me and with a puzzled look on his face said: "Who's Harry Hooper?"

"The winger who scored West Ham's goal," I said.

"Oh him, yes, Hooper did alright." And with that Matthews picked up his kit bag and walked out of the dressing room door. I thought, "Thanks for nothing Mr. Matthews".

Blackpool won the replay at Bloomfield Road, but exited

the competition in the next round. Spurs were knocked out by the eventual winners, West Brom, in 1954, who beat them 3–0 at the Hawthorns. I went to that game and the final, when the Baggies beat Preston 3–2 in an exciting match in which the lead changed hands three times.

By the mid-fifties, I had built a large network of contacts in the game and managed to get a Cup final ticket every year from 1954 to 1985. The 34-year run ended when I had to go into hospital in 1986 to have my gallbladder removed. In 1956, Spurs lost a semi-final at Villa Park for the third time in eight years, this time following a 1–0 defeat against Manchester City. Before the match, I was beginning to think that a gypsy curse might be hanging over Tottenham at that ground. I was convinced of it when Spurs were denied a late penalty after City keeper Bert Trautmann grabbed George Robb's leg just when he was about to shoot into an empty net. The referee just waved play on! Trautmann collected his winner's medal that year with a noticeably crooked neck following a collision with Birmingham's Peter Murphy. An X-ray later revealed it to be broken!

Around this time, I moved to Kingsbury in North London with my new wife. Sylvia set up a lovely home and in 1957 my daughter Shelley was born. Allan came along two years later, a few days before Tottenham's FA Cup clash with Norwich. I had somewhat reluctantly decided to miss the match at Carrow Road, so I could pick my wife and new baby up from the hospital. Although Sylvia had said that I could go to the game, it didn't seem worth taking the risk of upsetting a hormonal new mum. Two days before I was due to collect her, she caught a virus in hospital, and they kept her in. I got to go to Norwich after all and Sylvia swears today that I poisoned her hospital food; she had the last laugh as Spurs were beaten 1–0.

With two hungry mouths to feed, I worked as many hours as I could. From 8 am until 6 pm, I cut cloth at a clothing factory that my father part-owned in Old Spitalfields. When my shift was finished there, I'd quickly grab a bite to eat before walking the half mile to Sneider & Snick, another clothing factory where I worked from 7pm to 10pm. I'd get a train back to Kingsbury, before doing it all again the next day. It was hard work, but times were hard for everyone in the fifties. To make a few extra quid, I'd also do a bit of part-time buying and selling. Most coats that we made in the factory would go to the stores, but we'd always have a few left over which I'd sell. I could always sell more than I had, so I went around my work colleagues, bought their surplus, and sold theirs too. It wasn't long before I started up my own wholesale clothes business.

One of my first regular customers was based in Blackpool, and I'd often travel up to see him. The chap was a big fan of his local club and friendly with the Seasiders' centre half Roy Gratrix. A couple of weeks before the 1959 FA Cup final between Nottingham Forest and Luton Town, the chap called me and asked if I'd like to meet up with him and Roy before the match.

"OK. But why don't you meet me at my home in Kingsbury? Sylvia will make us some lunch and we'll go to the game from here. I'm one train stop after Wembley, so you'll miss all the crowds that way."

That year was the beginning of my FA Cup Final luncheons. The next year, I invited about a dozen people and it became a ritual that ran for over 20 years. By the mid-seventies, I had over one hundred of my friends in football turning up, some even arrived at 9am wanting breakfast as well! They were great social occasions and regular attendees included Bobby Moore, Geoff Hurst, Malcolm Allison, Terry Venables, Allan Harris, John Hollins, George Graham, John Bond, Tony Waddington and the Stoke City directors. Every year Sylvia would prepare a smashing buffet for our guests and we'd all have a great time drinking champagne whilst looking forward to the afternoon match. Mike Kelly, the former England goalkeeping coach, was always the first to arrive and the last to leave.

The most memorable of all the FA Cup finals I have attended was 1961's, the first I was to see my side win. I was beside myself with joy. I had seen Spurs lose three semi-finals over a 13-year period, but now we had a chance of getting our hands on the trophy. Bill Nicholson's side were also on the threshold of becoming the first club to win the Double in the 20th century. As I walked down Wembley Way towards the famous Twin Towers that day, I could barley contain my excitement. By then, I had watched countless games at Wembley, including eight FA Cup finals, but this time it felt different. This time, it was Tottenham Hotspur at Wembley, and knowing that somehow made me feel more aware of the spectacle being played out around me. The wooden rattles being shaken by children seemed louder, the call of "souvenir programme one shilling" more exciting.

During the game, every time Leicester got close to Spurs goalkeeper Bill Brown I could barely watch. The Foxes frustrated Spurs in the opening exchanges and it seemed the weight of expectation was heavy on Tottenham's players. Midway through the first half, Leicester full-back Len Chalmers got injured, and I knew from that moment that my team would be victorious. With no substitutes allowed in those days, Leicester were a sitting duck. Cliff Jones was unfortunate to have a goal disallowed for offside before half-time, but it only delayed the inevitable. Bobby Smith broke the deadlock in the 66th minute, latching onto a pass from Terry Dyson and smashing the ball past Gordon Banks. The double was sealed when Smith returned the compliment and crossed to Dyson who headed a second. Watching Danny Blanchflower lift the trophy aloft that day was the best feeling I've ever had at Wembley, greater even than when Bobby Moore collected the Jules Rimet trophy from Her Majesty the Queen in 1966.

Sylvia and I moved to the West End in 1967, which kind of defeated the point of having a party as we were no longer on Wembley's doorstep. Despite the logistics, the same old crowd insisted on making their way to my flat in Portman Square for the Kestons' Cup final luncheons, before jumping into taxis at 1.30 pm to take them to Wembley. I blame Sylvia for making those buffets too good to turn down!

That year, Tottenham and Chelsea met in the first ever all-London Cup final. It was a massive occasion and one which I thought merited having a 'celebration' party after the match. I floated the idea with Alan Mullery and Terry Venables when we met at the Colony Club in London, a few hours after they'd played their part in beating Nottingham Forest in the semi-final at Hillsborough.

"Go for it Morris, but we'll be at the Savoy at the club's celebration evening," they said.

"If you get bored, then come to mine. It's bound to be better!"

Of course, I was taking a bit of a gamble by even organising a 'celebration evening', when it could just as easily have been a 'commiseration evening'. However, I hedged my bets somewhat, by also inviting the Chelsea players. Terry helped with this, as he had skippered the Blues before joining Spurs at the end of the 1965/66 season. My first job was to find a suitable venue. I went to a few hotels in London, but settled on the Coronation Suite at the Hilton on Park Lane. The manager there offered me an all-inclusive evening, whereby I could charge people £15 a ticket. For that everyone got a buffet, drinks and a small band provided the entertainment. Word quickly spread and I was soon getting calls from people I didn't even know wanting to buy tickets.

The party proved a real success, helped by the fact that Spurs won the Cockney Cup final. Goals from Jimmy Robertson and Frank Saul proved too much for the Blues, who stole a late consolation goal through Bobby Tambling. My party kicked off at 10 pm, which gave the lads enough time to get home from Wembley and the ladies plenty of time to get dolled up. The staff at the Hilton gave the room a Spurs theme, with navy blue and white balloons and streamers. A huge cockerel carved out of ice was the room's centrepiece. It all looked great and went down a treat with the partygoers. The celebration had just got going when I spotted Alan Mullery and his wife June walk into the room.

"Mullers, so glad you made it, but how come you're not at the Savoy?"

"The evening's winding down there, although to be truthful it never really wound up. We left when the waltzing started."

"Anyone else coming?"

"Everyone! Greavsie and Big Pat were in a taxi behind me and the rest are following in a fleet of black cabs."

"Blimey, the club's party must have been bad."

"Bill Nick's in one of his moods. He stood up and told us all to be quiet when the champagne corks started popping."

"Really? That's a shame. Well, you know me, the more champagne corks popping the better. Congratulations and get busy celebrating!"

Not only did the entire Spurs team turn up that night, but so did Allan Harris, John Hollins and a few more of the Chelsea boys. I'm sure those with losers' medals in their pockets enjoyed the occasion almost as much as those with winners'.

The next day, I joined the thousands of supporters who lined the streets of N17 to watch the players parade the FA Cup from an open-top bus. I had a terrible hangover from the night before but that didn't bother me, standing as I was on cloud nine. That evening, I took a few phone calls at home from players wanting to thank me for inviting them to my party. Goalkeeper Pat Jennings was one of them.

"Great party Morris. The lads were saying today how pleased they were that we made the collective decision to swap venues. Mind you, the chairman wasn't too happy. We left him with a celebration party which didn't contain the reason for the celebration."

"I bet my name's mud with Sidney Wale and the rest of the directors."

"It probably is Morris, but I wouldn't worry about that." I didn't worry – he'd ignored me for years anyway.

Twelve days after my party at the Hilton, Wale and I were on the same flight from Berne to London. We had been to see Spurs play two end-of-season tour games in Switzerland. I walked over to where he sat on the plane to say hello but on seeing me, he turned away and looked out of the window. He even ignored me when I said, "Good afternoon Mr Wale". It seemed Pat Jennings was spot on when he said that my party had gone down like a lead balloon with him. If we had spoken on the plane, I would have told him to allow the players to bring more than just one guest to club functions. The players enjoyed my parties because they could also bring their friends, as well as their wife or girlfriend.

The last Cup final luncheon I held took place in 1981, the Chinese Year of the Cockerel. It was also the year of the 100th FA Cup Final and pitted Spurs against Manchester City. John Bond, a regular attendee at my previous luncheons, missed this one. I'm sure I invited him, but I guess he was too busy: he was Man City's manager! My daughter Shelley came, but her fiancé didn't, although like John he had a decent excuse: he was playing for Spurs!

I only just made it to my seat in time to see referee Keith Hackett blow his whistle to start the game. My luncheon guests had somewhat overstayed their welcome, and by the time I'd got them into taxis, I was cursing the whole lot of them. I hate missing any of the action, and can never understand people who choose to arrive late or leave early at matches. The game ended 1–1 that day, with City's Tommy Hutchison scoring for both sides.

The replay five days later, the first one ever at Wembley, was one of the best finals I'd ever seen, certainly the most exciting one involving Spurs. Ricky Villa, who had cut a forlorn figure when substituted in the first game, put Spurs 1–0 up after eight minutes. City keeper Joe Corrigan blocked Steve Archibald's close range effort but Villa followed up to score with ease. City levelled in spectacular fashion three minutes later, Steve Mackenzie's sweetly struck volley beat Milija Aleksic. City took the lead five minutes after the break, when my future son-in-law was judged to have brought down Dave Bennett in the box and Kevin Reeves scored from the spot. The penalty, the first to be awarded in a final since 1962, was a ridiculous decision by Hackett. Bennett ran into the penalty area to chase a through-ball but collapsed to the floor as Paul shepherded him away from goal. Jackie Charlton called the decision "total nonsense" during his BBC TV commentary. It would have been sickening if that had cost Spurs the trophy. As it turned out, the last 20 minutes belonged to Tottenham, with Glenn Hoddle at his brilliant best in midfield. Garth Crooks made it 2–2 following a neat lofted pass from Hoddle, and Villa dribbled his way through the City defence before turning the ball past Corrigan for the winner. The Argentinian's strike that night is consistently voted one of the best goals ever scored at Wembley, although I think it's a bit overrated. City defenders Kevin Reeves and Tommy Caton should have got closer to Villa during his weaving run into the box!

I joined Paul and the rest of the team at the Chanticleer

restaurant in Tottenham for the party of all parties after the match. Cockney duo Chas & Dave, who penned the team's Top Ten record *Ossie's Dream*, were also there, but I'll always remember the occasion for it being the night I met my hero, goalkeeper Ted Ditchburn. As a youngster, I had always pretended to be him when playing football with my friends during the war years. In fact, World War II cost Ditchburn seven years of top-flight football, but when normal football returned in 1946, Tottenham's fearless number one missed just two games over the next eight years. He was without doubt the most outstanding goalkeeper in England during the 1940s and 50s, and probably the most influential player during Tottenham's 1950/51 championship winning season. Now, 30 years on, Ditchburn and I were celebrating the club's latest achievement in the same restaurant. I can honestly say that I've never been as nervous about meeting anyone.

"Just walk over and introduce yourself," urged Sylvia.

"I can't. It's Ted Ditchburn."

"Oh, for God's sake Morris. You're a 49-year-old man, not a nine-year-old boy." Sylvia confidently strode over to him.

"Excuse me Mr Ditchburn, would you mind having your picture taken with my husband? You're his hero."

"Of course. I'd be glad to."

Sylvia took the photo and I chatted to Ted for a few minutes about Ricky Villa's 'wonder goal', before shaking his hand and thanking him for his time. It was one of the highlights of a lifetime following Spurs. Ted passed away on Boxing Day 2005, aged 84. I took a phone call from a radio station the next day, asking if I would say a few words about Ted's life.

"Would I? It would be an absolute honour and a privilege."

I recorded a five-minute obituary which was broadcast at six the following morning. I managed to get a few copies of the interview and sent one to Ted's son Robin, whom I traced through contacts at the club. I've been told that Robin used to play the tape on his car stereo on his journey to work. You'd be hard pushed to find a better goalkeeper than his Dad.

Shelley and Paul Miller got married in September 1981. Eight months later, Paul was back at Wembley when Spurs reached the FA Cup final for the second year running. However, this time he wasn't the only one in our family who got on to the Wembley pitch. His father-in-law did too! On the day of the final, broadcaster Peter Lorenzo, who I'd known for years through Bobby Moore, accosted me on my way into the stadium and asked if I'd do an interview live on the radio. "You'll get to walk on the pitch," he said. "Where's the mike?" I asked. Peter then handed me a security pass, which gained us access to the stadium through the tunnel and out on to Wembley's hallowed turf. It was a dream come true, as I walked out on to the freshly mowed lush green grass. Stanley Matthews, Bobby Moore and Bobby Charlton had all had their finest moments here and I felt like I was now having mine. Just before Peter and I went live to the nation, both sets of players joined us on the pitch for the traditional suited pre-match stroll to soak in the atmosphere and wave to family and friends sitting beneath the Twin Towers.

"Morris, you must be really proud of your son-in-law Paul Miller, who is here for the second year running playing at the heart of Tottenham's defence."

"Well, I'm a bit upset with him actually, as he's just got my daughter pregnant."

Peter didn't quite know what to say to that, and to be honest I'm not sure why I said it in the first place. I think it was a classic case of stage fright and I just said the first thing that came into my head, thinking it would be funny. Of course, I was over the moon when I became a granddad for the first time.

"I understand that despite being a Spurs fan, you were invited to watch the game from QPR's dugout today."

"That's right. Terry Venables and I go back a long way. A few years ago we made a deal that if he ever managed a side that reached Wembley, I could sit on the bench with him. Terry kept his promise and invited me onto QPR's bench for today's match, but asked what I'd do if Spurs scored. When I told him I'd jump off my seat and celebrate, we agreed that I'd better sit somewhere else!"

Terry also invited me to attend QPR's 'celebration party' after the final. But I told him, "Thanks for the invite, but when Spurs win I'll be gloating and that wouldn't go down well with your partygoers. And in the unlikely event that QPR win, then your party is the last place that I'd want to be!"

Terry certainly believed his Second Division outfit had a chance of upsetting the odds against Tottenham. QPR had only just missed out on promotion to the top flight by two points, whereas Spurs were looking jaded after a long campaign. They had looked like claiming some early silverware in the League Cup final at Wembley, but threw away a 1–0 lead against Liverpool in the 87th minute and lost 3–1 in extra time. A semi-final exit against Barcelona in the European Cup Winners' Cup followed soon afterwards and a host of injuries, coupled with a mammoth fixture pile-up ended any hopes of winning the league title. Off the field, British troops were preparing for the first land battle against Argentine soldiers in the Falklands. Manager Keith Burkinshaw had lost midfield maestro Ossie Ardiles, who had returned to his homeland to prepare for the World Cup. His countryman Ricky Villa had stayed in England, but faced a barrage of abuse every time he played. Despite coping well and having the full support of his teammates, the situation 8,000 miles away in the Falklands was deemed too sensitive for him to play in the final.

The match at Wembley that day was a dull, tense affair, with few chances for either side. The game was goalless after 90 minutes but Spurs broke the deadlock with 10 minutes of extra time remaining. Glenn Hoddle hit a low shot from 20 yards, which took a slight deflection before beating goalkeeper Peter Hucker. In my mind I was preparing a commiseration speech to Terry when Rangers hit back with five minutes left on the clock, scoring from a set piece. A long throw was back-headed by defender Bob Hazell and nodded in by the unmarked Terry Fenwick, who was to become Terry's first signing when he took charge of Spurs in 1987. The replay, five days later, was a better match than the first. Spurs took the lead early on through a Glenn Hoddle spot kick. Terry urged his side on and they played well, but weren't good enough to prevent Steve Perryman lifting the trophy for the second successive year. I think the Spurs players went to the Savoy that year to celebrate, but I didn't go. I called Terry and tried to lift his spirits, telling him that his lads had put up a good fight. He was despondent; I guess there was little I could say to a manager whose side had just lost an FA Cup final.

The thing is, Terry Venables, like me, grew up in an era when the FA Cup final was *the* highlight of the football calendar. The match was traditionally always the last fixture of the season and the most important one. The league championship always played second fiddle to the FA Cup. Supporters all over the country were united in that view and like me shared the same dream of seeing their club reach Wembley. If your club was lucky enough to make it there, you were just one step from heaven. The build-up to every final seemed to last for weeks, with newspapers providing special one-off colour editions that focused on the players contesting the season's finale.

I'm often asked, "What was the best FA Cup Final you've ever seen?" In terms of pure football, I'd have to say the match between Spurs and Burnley in 1962 would take some beating. Both sides played the match like a game of chess, and it became a battle of wills and tactics. Jimmy Greaves, who had signed from AC Milan five months earlier, opened the scoring after three minutes with a quick swivel and shot past Burnley keeper Adam Blacklaw. The Clarets equalised shortly after the interval through Jimmy Robson, who in doing so notched the 100th FA Cup final goal at Wembley. However, Bobby Smith turned in the box and fired Spurs back in front within a minute. With 10 minutes remaining, Burnley defender Tommy Cummings handled the ball on the goalline and Danny Blanchflower sealed the victory from the spot. It was a fantastic match, real end-to-end stuff. The 'Matthews final' of 1953 was probably even better than that one, but as I said earlier, I only watched it on TV.

In terms of excitement, I don't like to admit it, but Arsenal's 3–2 victory over Manchester United in 1979 would come top of the pile. For over 85 minutes, the match was anything but a classic. The Gunners took a 2–0 half-time lead following goals by Brian Talbot and Frank Stapleton. With 85 minutes gone, the thought of seeing Arsenal skipper Pat Rice lift the Cup turned my stomach so against my principles, I made for the exit. Just as I reached it, I heard the crowd cheer a goal. I rushed back up the stairs, as I was sure United had pulled one back from the direction of the cheers. By the time I got back into my seat, Sammy McIlroy had dribbled past two Arsenal defenders and equalised. I was ecstatic and cheered the goal like Spurs had scored it. With the game poised for extra time, Arsenal's brilliant Liam Brady made a run forward and fed teammate Graham Rix, who crossed to the far post for Alan Sunderland to score with only seconds remaining. I threw my match programme on the floor and hurried away from the scene of the crime.

Thirty years on from that amazing final of 1979, English football has changed beyond recognition. With the formation of the Premier League in 1992, and the subsequent sale of television rights and signing of lucrative sponsorship deals, mind-boggling sums of money have come into the game. As a result, chairmen of today's top clubs have done their best to devalue the FA Cup, stopping at nothing to ensure their Premier League status is retained. Many of today's top-flight managers have been forced to allow the FA Cup to slip off their radar. Given a choice of reaching an FA Cup final or avoiding relegatation from the Premier League, they'd choose staying up every time. It makes my blood boil to see the world's oldest Cup competition devalued. The trouble is, the game's all about money these days, and the way it dictates what's worthy and what's not makes me sick. Whatever happened to tradition? The FA Cup is steeped in a history of David versus Goliath battles and marvellous memories of giant-killing acts. It's a competition that was cherished by our fathers and their fathers before, and deserves to be treated with respect, rather than being considered an unwelcome distraction for those riding the Premier League gravy train. What reason, other than fear of losing millions, can relegation-threatened Premier League sides have for playing fringe players in FA Cup matches? Ask any ex-pro who played the game before the nineties and the majority will tell you the FA Cup was the trophy they wanted to win. Many players back then valued an FA Cup winner's medal above a Championship-winning one. Tottenham's 1981 FA Cup winner Ricky Villa values his medal more than the World Cup medal he won playing for Argentina in 1978! He told me, "My big moment in football was 1981, when I scored twice in the final at Wembley. People in Argentina say to me, 'But you won the World Cup!' But I only played a small part in those games. At Wembley, at least for one day, I was the king. It was the biggest moment of my career."

I believe the only way the FA Cup can regain the importance it deserves is through the only language that football chairmen understand: money. If a sponsor were to offer a £20 million bounty to the FA Cup winner, rather than the £3.4 million currently accumulated during the winner's journey, certain clubs and their managers might begin taking it more seriously. Another idea would be to give the FA Cup winners automatic qualification to the UEFA Champions League. Whatever plan can be devised to help restore its significance in the football calendar I'm all for it. Whatever the future holds for the FA Cup, I'm one man who will never tire of the romance of it. Like my feelings for my long-suffering wife, it's a love affair that will never end.

FOLLOWING SPURS IN EUROPE

"If Spurs were playing, Morris would be there. A more genuine, honest and welcoming character you couldn't wish to meet. A true friend..."
Bobby Smith (Spurs and England, European Cup Winners' Cup winner 1963)

"Morris has made so many friends in football, and all of them of the highest calibre. As football fans go, he is unique. There will probably never be another supporter like him and Tottenham Hotspur have been lucky to have had him."
Paul Miller (Spurs, UEFA Cup winner 1984)

European Cup 1961/62

When Tottenham won the league championship in 1961, it opened up a whole new world for fans like me who followed the team wherever they played. The thought of taking a trip into Europe to see Spurs compete in the European Cup was an exciting prospect, one that really caught my imagination. Up until then, only three English clubs, Manchester United, Wolves and Burnley, had competed against the rest of the continent's champions in the European Cup and the trophy itself had only ever been won by Real Madrid (four times) and Benfica (once). At that point, the furthest I'd travelled to watch the team was Sunderland, so a journey into Europe was a trip into the unknown. Back then, ordinary people rarely left their own backyards and if they did, it was once a year on their annual summer jaunt to a British seaside town. This was a time before mass-market package holidays to the Costa del Sol, as back in 1961 flying was almost exclusively for the rich and famous.

73

They really were primitive times compared to today's modern age of budget airlines and low-cost flights to just about every small city in Europe.

When I heard that Spurs had been drawn to play Polish club Gornik Zabrze in the preliminary round, I bought a huge map of Europe and spent ten minutes with a magnifying glass trying to find Gòrnik. It wasn't until my wife suggested that I look for Zabrze that I found it, a pinprick near Katowice. I wondered how on earth I'd get there and contacted the supporters' club for advice. They told me they didn't know of any company organising travel for fans to Poland. Undeterred, I made some more enquiries with travel agents in London. I was told that Katowice didn't have an airport and my only option was to fly to Warsaw and then catch a train for the four-hour 160-mile journey to Katowice. It all seemed like too much hard work and I reluctantly gave up on the idea. A few weeks later, I read in my morning newspaper that Spurs had lost 4–2 in Poland, although it could have been worse as they trailed 4–0 after 47 minutes. Cliff Jones and Terry Dyson notched late goals to give Spurs a lifeline. I was pleased that I'd talked myself out of going, as the trip home would have been bloody miserable. Tottenham got their act together in the return match and hammered the Poles 8–1 in the club's first 'Glory, Glory Night' at White Hart Lane.

The next round paired Spurs with Dutch champions Feyenoord. I knew getting to the Holland would be a much easier proposition and this time I had no excuses for missing out. When enquiring about travel to the game in Rotterdam, I was introduced to a chap named Basil Graham who worked for a travel company called Riviera Holidays. He told me that a Spurs supporter called Aubrey Morris had set up Riviera in the mid-fifties. They had a fledgling business selling package holidays to resorts in Europe for working-class families. Graham said, "We've spotted another gap in the market. We're now catering for Spurs fans who want to follow the team in Europe." I couldn't believe my luck as it saved me the time and hassle of organising the trip myself. I bought a ticket for the flight to Rotterdam and used Riviera for most of my subsequent trips into Europe until Thomson Holidays bought them out in 1965.

Spurs beat the Dutch 3–1 in Rotterdam, with Frank Saul scoring twice and Terry Dyson bagging the other. Cliff Jones later told me that Bill Nicholson had a right go at the players in the dressing room after the game, saying they made too many errors and didn't deserve the victory. It's staggering to think Nicholson was disappointed when the team had just won and notched three away goals in Europe! In the second leg, Dave Mackay was carried from the field on a stretcher after being knocked unconscious. He returned to the pitch ten minutes before the interval to huge cheers from the White Hart Lane faithful. There were no substitutes in those days and there was no way that Mackay was going to leave his team-mates a man down! They don't make them like him any more. Spurs drew 1–1 on the night to set up a quarter-final meeting with Dukla Prague on Valentine's Day.

The general topic of conversation on the plane over to Prague was the depressing sights we were likely to witness on our adventure behind the Iron Curtain of a communist country like Czechoslovakia. I expected Prague to be smog-filled and dominated by grey, ugly buildings with streets full of starving people. I was quite taken aback when I discovered it was actually the most charming and beautiful city I'd ever visited, with its countless church spires, gold-tipped towers, medieval castles and scenic bridges lined with statues. And the people certainly didn't look like they were starving either. The only food queue I saw was outside a patisserie where people were buying cakes.

Fewer than one hundred Spurs fans watched the side lose 1–0 in Prague, but we weren't too downhearted on the journey home as the general feeling was that we'd stuff the Czechs in the second leg. We were right. Bill Nicholson's men won 4–1 on a freezing night in London, when John White's amazing balance and ball control on an icy pitch covered in snow made me think I was actually watching an elegant ice-skater rather than a footballer. Interestingly, before the game in Prague about a dozen of us had our picture taken standing on the pitch holding a banner that read, 'Come On You Spurs'. *Daily Mirror* photographer Monte Fresco gave me a copy of the photograph and years later I was showing it to my friend Philip Isaacs, when he pointed to a face in the background and declared, "That's me!" Funny to think we had both been at the same place years before we became friends.

Tottenham's £99,999 record signing Jimmy Greaves was eligible to play in the semi-final against the holders, Benfica. I was convinced that with England's best forward in the side, Spurs would go one better than Hibs (1956), Manchester United (1957 and 1958) and Rangers (1960) and reach the European Cup final. A couple of hours before the first leg got underway at the Stadium of Light in Lisbon, Greavsie saw me waiting outside the players' entrance and came over for a chat. I was with a group of Spurs fans, none of whom I knew personally. We all stood round in a small circle and chatted about the game ahead. Greavsie said the players were feeling relaxed and confident of getting a good result ahead of the second leg a fortnight later. He then asked the group about their trip over to Portugal and if we'd bought any souvenirs during the day to take home.

"I've bought a ring for the wife," I said.

"Blimey Morris. I was thinking more along the lines of a match programme, scarf or a bottle of port."

"I got myself in the doghouse after Prague. I forgot to get the missus a Valentine's Day card." I then pulled the ring out of my pocket and showed the group.

"Eighteen carat gold. Cost me sixty pounds."

"That's an expensive mistake. I bet you won't forget to buy the wife a card next year?" smiled Greavsie.

"How much duty will you have to pay on it?" asked one of the supporters standing in our small group.

"I'm not gonna declare it. It's cost me enough already." On saying that, Greavsie pulled a face in a manner to attract my attention. He then raised his eyebrows and stretched his neck muscles before moving his head to the side as if he was about to head an imaginary football into the corner of the net. I looked at him baffled and continued with my conversation about my golden purchase.

"I bet there's nobody here who can honestly say that they would declare the ring at customs?"

"You might look a bit stupid trying to explain why you've got a small woman's diamond and sapphire ring in your possession," said one smiling chap on my right.

"Yeah. I doubt it will even fit on your little finger," said another. I then tried it on my little pinky and it wouldn't go past the knuckle.

"Maybe you'd better declare it," said Greavsie, bizarrely heading yet another imaginary goal.

"Are you alright, Jim?

"Couldn't be better," he smiled, before changing the subject and revealing that Bill Nicholson was going to play him on the right wing. We wished him luck before finding our seats amongst the few hundred Spurs fans in a crowd of 86,000. Greavsie later asked me if I had declared the ring to Customs.

"Nah. I smuggled it through."

"I was trying to warn you to keep quiet, as one of the supporters who was standing with us works as a customs official!" We laughed about that for quite sometime afterwards. Can you imagine players of today chatting to fans outside the ground an hour before one of the biggest games of their careers?

The two matches against Benfica were probably two of the most frustrating I've ever had to watch as a Spurs fan. In both ties the referees made some extremely questionable decisions and I lay the blame squarely on their shoulders for Tottenham's exit from the competition. I would go as far to say that it wouldn't surprise me if other forces were working to ensure Spurs didn't reach the final. I have no evidence to confirm this, other than the shocking decisions I witnessed by the Swiss and Danish officials who took charge in Lisbon and London respectively. In Portugal, Greavsie had a perfectly good goal ruled offside which was ludicrous as he'd run between two Benfica defenders and Bobby Smith had the ball over the line in the last five minutes, but again the referee called it offside even though Benfica had two of their players standing on the goal line! Greavsie, who was obviously much nearer the action than me, told me after the 3–1 defeat that he was just as dumbfounded as to why it hadn't counted. In the return leg, Benfica's captain and centre forward Jose Aguas

scored in the 15th minute to give the visitors a 4–1 aggregate
lead. It stung Spurs into action and eight minutes later Greavsie
tucked the ball away. The referee, Mr Aage Poulsen, awarded
the goal and began trotting back to the centre circle only for
the Benfica players to pull him over to the linesman who had
his flag raised. The referee then consulted with his Danish
countryman Mr Hansen and changed his mind, ruling it offside.
I couldn't believe it. Bobby Smith pulled a goal back just before
half-time and Danny Blanchflower scored from the spot two
minutes into the second half. I was convinced that barring
any more ridiculous referring decisions Spurs would go
through. It wasn't to be though, with Dave Mackay's shot
against the bar in the final minute the nearest Spurs came to
salvaging the tie. I wasn't as gutted as you might expect, even
after the Portuguese went on to win the trophy after beating
Real Madrid in the final. Back then I believed Spurs would
play in another European Cup sooner or later. Almost 50 years
on and I'm still waiting!

European Cup Winners' Cup 1962/63

A few weeks after suffering the heartache against Benfica,
Spurs qualified for the European Cup Winners' Cup by beating
Burnley 3–1 in the FA Cup final. When the draw for
Tottenham's second foray into Europe was made, the winners
of the previous season's competition had still to be determined. Fiorentina of Italy and Spain's Atlètico Madrid had
drawn 1–1 at Hampden Park, but the replay had been delayed
as players from both sides were taking part in the World Cup
in Chile. One month before Spurs played Rangers in the first
round, Atlètico Madrid belatedly lifted the trophy. I was
convinced that if we beat Rangers we could go on to become
the first British club to win a European trophy.

    Both teams led their respective domestic leagues when
they met in the first-leg at White Hart Lane. The Scottish
giants included internationals Bobby Shearer, Eric Cadlow,
Willie Henderson, Ralph Brand, David Wilson and the great
Jim Baxter in their ranks. Baxter is regarded today as one of

the greatest Scottish players of all time. He possessed a sweet left foot and I feared he could cause Spurs some damage with it. I needn't have worried, as it was Tottenham's Scots who impressed more that night. Dave Mackay was at his inspirational best and John White scored twice in a 5–2 victory.

Despite the three-goal cushion, I was determined to make the trip north of the border to see them finish the job off. The match was due to take place on a Wednesday night, but I read that Kilmarnock were playing Moscow Torpedo in a friendly under floodlights the night before. I'd never been to Kilmarnock's Rugby Park, so it gave me the opportunity to tick it off my list of grounds that I'd visited. I was booked on the Thames–Clyde Express from St Pancras on the Tuesday morning, but overslept and had to make a mad dash to the station to catch the train. I was in such a rush that I left without having a wash and without my suitcase. I figured that I could buy a change of clothes when I arrived in Glasgow. I only just managed to hop on the last carriage before it pulled away at 6am. On arriving at Glasgow's St Enoch Station, I checked into a hotel and was just about to jump into a bath for a long soak when there was a loud bang at the door.

"Who is it?" I asked.

"It's the hotel manager. There's been a mistake with the room. Could you let me in please." I quickly put my trousers on and just as I unlocked the door two burly policemen came crashing in, pushed me to the floor and handcuffed me.

"What the bloody hell's going on?" I yelled in protest.

"You fit the description of a man wanted for a murder in London."

"What?"

"You were seen running for the London-to-Glasgow train this morning."

"Yes. That was probably me, but I haven't committed any crime. I'm here to see Tottenham play Rangers tomorrow."

"Where's your overnight bag?"

"I haven't got one," I said.

"Why not?"

"I don't need one. I'm going home on Thursday and was going to buy some shirts tomorrow morning."

"It all sounds a bit suspicious to me Sir. You'll have to come with us to the station."

I was taken to the nearest police station, but rather bizarrely released within minutes of arriving. After having the handcuffs removed, one of the police officers asked me to show him my hands. I turned my palms towards him and he declared to his colleague, "It's not him. He's got all his fingers!" He then sat me down and apologised for the rough treatment before explaining that I fitted the description of a man seen running away from a bungled robbery at United Dairies in Cricklewood, West London, in which a milkman had been shot dead. He said that new information about the suspect had come to light that ruled me out as a suspect.

"No hard feelings," said one of the officers.

"We couldn't take any chances as you might have had a gun," added the other.

"I don't suppose you have any spare tickets for the match," said the sergeant, who was looking on. At first I thought he was joking, but he was serious! I couldn't believe his cheek and told him that I didn't.

I still made it to Rugby Park that evening to see Killie beat the Russians 4–3, but the next evening my Scottish adventure went from bad to worse when a dense fog descended over Glasgow and the Rangers versus Spurs game was postponed. I returned home and five days later made my way back to Glasgow for the re-scheduled meeting with the Scottish giants. The game threw up a few extra tickets from my usual sources, and I took a trip back to the police station.

"Is the sarge around?" I asked the bored-looking copper at the desk. He disappeared out the back and moments later returned with the boss. His mouth dropped open when I handed him over two tickets to the re-scheduled match.

"I hope we stuff you!" I cheerfully called over my shoulder as I left.

By the evening of the match, the Scottish press had stirred the Rangers fans into a frenzy by predicting that the Light Blues had the quality to turn the tie around. The 80,000 crowd of baying Scots urged their team on with a deafening roar in the early exchanges. It was nothing compared though to the silence inside Ibrox that greeted Greavsie's opening goal eight minutes into the game. He says today that it was so quiet when the ball hit the back of the net that he could hear Spurs keeper Bill Brown shout "Yes" and clap his hands at the other end of the pitch. I wonder if he heard my cheers too? Rangers pulled a goal back after the interval and the crowd went nuts. I couldn't believe they still thought they were in with a chance, despite trailing 6–3 on aggregate. Three minutes later, Bobby Smith hammered another goal for Spurs to dash any hopes the Scots had of achieving the impossible.

A friend of mine in the rag trade called Freddie Harrison asked to join me on the trip to Czechoslovakia for the quarter-final tie against Slovan Bratislava. "More the merrier," I said. "I'll book the flights."

"Flights? I'm not flying. Can't we go by train?" he asked. I got my map out and plotted the route with my finger.

"Yeah. We can do it. Be prepared for a long haul, but I'm up for the adventure."

Bratislava lies on the banks of the Danube, 40 miles from Vienna. I spent an hour with a travel agent working out a route before setting off from London the day before the game. We caught a train from London to Dover and then boarded a ferry to Calais. From there, we caught a train to Paris and then another that went through West Germany before arriving in Vienna. At some point during our journey, two German border guards boarded the train to check passports. By this time, we'd been travelling for almost the entire day and Freddie was stretched out fast asleep on the seat opposite me. On seeing him snoring, one of the guards gave him a tap on his shoulder to try and wake him from his slumber. Freddie though was well and truly away with the fairies and didn't wake. I laughed out loud, but the guards didn't seem to think it was funny. One then turned towards me and asked, "Do you have coffee?" I wasn't too sure why he was asking, but replied, "No. I don't have coffee." On hearing my voice, Freddie woke up and blurted out, "Yes, please. Two sugars." He then opened his eyes fully and realised that it wasn't the train's refreshment trolley in front of him, but two German guards with guns and they weren't very amused.

"You are smuggling coffee. Yes?" Freddie, who was by now sitting bolt upright in his seat replied, "No. I don't have coffee. I don't even like coffee." The guards weren't convinced and ordered us to empty our bags. After a good rummage through our belongings they checked our passports and swiftly moved on. It was totally bizarre. I can only think that the Germans were cracking down on people who took coffee over the border and into Austria.

When we finally arrived in Vienna, we'd spent 12 hours on a train and still hadn't reached our final destination. We both were in dire need of a good wash and checked into a hotel in the Austrian capital to spruce our selves up before making our way by taxi to the Czechoslovakian border. Once through passport control we phoned for a taxi to take us the few miles to Slovan's Tehelnè Pole stadium. As the game kicked-off, Freddie looked at me and said: "Next time Morris, don't listen to me. We'll fly." Slovan beat Spurs 2–0 on a pitch that resembled the mud baths seen most years at the Glastonbury music festival. I wasn't the best company on the journey home and cursed Freddie during every one of the 800 miles back to London. In the second leg at White Hart Lane, Bobby Smith tore into the Slovan's defence like a rampaging bull after a red rag. It unsettled them and when Dave Mackay scored after half an hour's play the floodgates opened. Spurs were 3–0 up by half-time and had the ball in the net another three times as Slovan were slaughtered 6–0 on the night.

My journey to Yugoslavia for the first leg of the semi-final clash against OFK Belgrade didn't involve any boats or trains, just a return plane ride. Freddie chose to stay at home this time and I travelled with a few of my mates from Fleet Street. The night before the game, I met up with them in a bar for a few drinks. Football writers from the Yugoslav press were also out socialising in the same drinking establishment and good-humoured banter was soon flowing from both corners. Late in the evening and after far too many beers, Ken Jones challenged the Yugoslavs to a game of five-a-side on OFK's training ground the next morning. The Fleet Street mob were a player short and so Ken persuaded me to make up the numbers. I instantly regretted my decision when on turning up with a thumping headache our opponents arrived, but only one of them was a journalist, the other four were over 6ft 3in and ex-Yugoslav internationals! Needless to say we were soundly beaten 5–2, although I did have the honour of scoring what Ken described as "a glorious effort". It involved sliding on the gravel pitch on my backside to tuck away a cross to the far post. It didn't half hurt and took a nice slice of skin off. I believe Peter Lorenzo scored the other goal, although it wasn't nearly as heroic as mine!

A few hours later, Lorenzo was busy writing his match report for the *Daily Herald*. The headline read, 'GREAVES SENT OFF! But Spurs are a goal up'. Greavsie was given his marching orders in the second half for aiming a punch at OFK's centre half Blagomir Krivokuca. It was the first time a Spurs player had been sent off in 35 years, but thankfully it didn't prove costly for the team. Goals by John White and Terry Dyson earned Tottenham a 2–1 win in Belgrade and without the suspended Greavsie in the return leg, Spurs recorded a 5–2 aggregate victory over OFK to become the first British club to reach a European final.

The final pitted Spurs against the trophy holders Atlètico Madrid. It's an occasion that I'll always remember, not only for its glorious outcome, but because it is the only time my father ever came with me to watch a football match. Dad worked seven days a week as a tailor in London's East End and rarely had any spare time to pursue hobbies. I had tried to persuade him many times to put down his scissors and join me for a game, but to no avail.

"I suppose you'll be there," he said on reading the newspaper hype in his daily newspaper one afternoon during a rare lunch break.

"Are you coming?" I asked in jest, rather than hope.

"Where is it?"

"Rotterdam, Holland." I looked at his face, but rather than the usual scrunched-up-nose face pull, swift shake of the head and customary reply of "You're mad", he looked across the table at me and said: "I suppose there's a first time for everything."

I purchased two match tickets and joined the army of 2,500 supporters that travelled to Rotterdam aboard 33 flights organised by Aubrey Morris. It felt strange taking my seat next to Dad in Feyenoord's stadium.

"I hope you're not going to bring us bad luck," I said, on hearing that key player Dave Mackay had failed a fitness test on an injured groin.

"Me too. You'll never forgive me if Spurs lose," Dad replied. I needn't have worried, as if anything, my father brought good luck. Greavsie put Spurs one up after 16 minutes and John White added a second before half-time. The Spaniards pulled one back after the break, but two goals by Terry Dyson and another by Greavsie swept Spurs to an emphatic victory. On the flight home, Dad declared, "He ain't a bad player that Greaves fella."

"I've been telling you that for years," I shouted, trying to make myself heard above the jubilant chorus of singing Spurs fans.

"Is it always this noisy?" asked Dad.

"Nah. Only when you come." My father never did go to another Spurs game. I asked him a few more times, but he always said it was best for him to retire at the top. For that reason, the 1963 Cup Winners' Cup will always be special to me. A couple of years later, Dad became good friends with 'that Greaves fella', when Jimmy opted to stay in Israel for a holiday after a club tour. My father and my stepmother Celia were on holiday and would meet 'James' for lunch on the beach.

UEFA Cup 1971/72

Victory over Aston Villa in the League Cup final of 1971 earned Spurs a place in the inaugural UEFA Cup, the competition that replaced the Inter-Cities Fairs Cup. That win over Villa, then a Third Division side, was scant consolation in a season when local rivals Arsenal became the first club since Tottenham in '61 to do the double. The fact that the Gunners secured the league title with a 1–0 win on our own turf, made it even harder to stomach. It was vital that Spurs won a trophy the next season to restore some pride and redress the balance

in North London. The UEFA Cup was third, behind the FA
Cup and the league championship, on my trophy wish list. I
believed it was also the easiest of the three to win.

Icelandic part-timers Keflavik were Tottenham's opponents in the first round. On paper, they were no better than
a good English amateur side like Enfield or Blyth Spartans.
Their side consisted of a hearty mixture of carpenters, cler-
ical assistants, electricians, mechanics and students. It was
therefore always going to be a one-sided mismatch, but that
didn't prevent me from parting with £36 for a two-day trip
to Iceland with 4S Sports Travel. The price included return
flights with Channel Airways, all coach transfers from the
capital Reykjavik, half-board accommodation at a three-star
hotel, comprehensive insurance, airport tax and a ticket for
the game. Today, you'd be lucky if an outlay of 36 quid covered
the match ticket!

"What's Iceland like in mid-September?" I asked Spurs
and England striker Martin Chivers, the week before the trip.

"It's ICE LAND! It's gonna be freezing! You'd better go
and buy a fur hat," he suggested.

I took Chivers's advice, and that of some of the other
supporters who were making the journey, buying a Russian
fur hat and packing my thermals to keep out the Arctic chill.
I was sweating buckets when I boarded the plane at Stansted,
wearing ski trousers, a thick knitted ski sweater and fur-lined
boots. I also carried a thick sheepskin coat on board in a large
holdall. In my mind, I was happy in the knowledge that I was
fully prepared for the sub-zero temperatures that lay ahead.
As the jet touched down, I looked out of the window and to
my surprise the sun was shining and there wasn't a cloud in
the sky.

"Don't be fooled by the blue sky, it'll be cold when you
get off. You'd better put your coat on," warned the flight attendant. When it was my turn to walk out of the aircraft door,
I braced myself for a blast of freezing air, but instead I was
greeted with a warm glow from the September sun. It was
25 degrees and hotter than London! I turned around and saw
the aircrew in fits of laughter.

"At least you look the part," said one.

"Maybe you can sell your boots to the Eskimos?" said another.

The 30-mile coach drive from the capital to Keflavik took us through some of the most alien geography on Earth. I gazed in wonder at the spectacular lunar-like landscape, where our coach driver said the Apollo 11 astronauts Buzz Aldrin and Neil Armstrong had practised for their moonwalk in 1969. The match the next day wasn't as memorable as the scenery, although a few firsts were duly noted in the record books after Tottenham's 6–1 victory. New signing Ralph Coates notched his first goal for the club and Alan Gilzean scored the UEFA Cup's first hat-trick. Also, youngster Graeme Souness made his one and only competitive first-team appearance for Tottenham. Only 200 Spurs fans were there to witness it, although when Souness replaced Alan Mullery in the 76th minute the 11,000 spectators in the little stadium, which didn't have floodlights, were struggling to pick the debutant out in the fading light.

I was convinced that Souness possessed the attributes necessary to become a top player and was surprised that Bill Nicholson hadn't moved him up the ranks at the same time that Steve Perryman made the leap from youth team to first team. As soon as I heard that Souness was 'homesick' and wanted to leave, I called Stoke manager Tony Waddington and recommended he snap up the precocious youngster, telling him that I didn't believe that Tottenham's reserve team player of the year was the type to be homesick. "He just wants regular first-team action quicker than Nicholson is prepared to give him it." Souness certainly didn't lack confidence and I enjoyed watching the midfielder take charge of youth and reserve team games with some full-bloodied tackles in the middle of the park. Even back then he was an immaculate passer of the ball and had all the makings of being an excellent playmaker. The only flaw that I could see was an occasional petulant streak, which surfaced during the FA Youth Cup final of 1970 when he was sent off for kicking Coventry's Dennis Mortimer. Tony Waddington put the feelers out in December 1972, but when word filtered back to him from sources inside Tottenham saying he should be wary, as the lad could be a troublemaker, he chose to pass on the opportunity. It opened the door for Middlesbrough, whose manager Stan Anderson stepped in and signed him for £30,000, not long after I'd been singing his praises to Boro's trainer Harold Shepherdson. Souness served Boro well during a five-year spell and won the first of 54 Scotland caps as a Middlesbrough player. In 1978, he moved to Liverpool for £350,000 and in seven years at Anfield won five league titles, three European Cups and four League Cup winner's medals. Souness was easily the biggest talent to have slipped through the net during my 66 years as a Spurs fan.

Martin Chivers emulated Gilzean in the second leg against Keflavik, scoring three in a 9–0 victory at the Lane. Goals weren't so easy to come by in the second round against French club Nantes. I sat through a drab goalless draw at the Stade Marcel Saupin and then watched Chivers and Gilzean miss a hatful at home in a match Spurs won 1–0 thanks to a goal by Martin Peters.

The next round saw Bill Nicholson's men take on Rapid Bucharest and that proved to be a far more entertaining encounter. The Romanians were skippered by towering 6ft 5in goalkeeper Rica Raducanu, who belonged in a circus rather than on a football pitch. In the first leg at the Lane, he dropped almost everything that came his way. It got to a point where I was half expecting him to change into a colourful jacket, don floppy shoes, paint his face and put on a big red comedy nose. He stood rooted to his goalline when Chivers launched a long throw into the box from which Peters headed the opening goal. Raducanu feigned injury in the build-up to Tottenham's second goal, throwing himself to the floor before jumping up and waving angrily after Chivers smashed the ball home. I later learned that Rapid's number one was the first Romanian keeper to score in an official match and the first to be caught offside! Chivers scored again before the end and Spurs took a 3–0 first-leg lead to Bucharest.

I was one of only 100 fans who flew to Romania for the return game. On arriving at Bucharest Airport, I changed £50 into the local currency – Romanian lei – and got a taxi to the Intercontinental Hotel, then the tallest building in the city, where the team was also staying. When I arrived Pat

Jennings and Phil Beal sought me out and asked if I wanted to buy their Romanian lei off them. "The club has given us an allowance of five quid's worth per day and we don't know what to do with it," said Jennings. As I planned to go on a shopping trip, I agreed to take it off their hands. Word spread throughout the team and soon most had exchanged their Romanian lei allowance with me for sterling. I ended up with about 200 pounds worth, but was unhappy to find that almost all of the shops that I went into only accepted US dollars or sterling!

The next day, Spurs won the match 2–0. Substitute Jimmy Pearce was only on the pitch for 12 minutes before getting sent-off for retaliation in what was an ugly encounter. He did though score the first goal and have another disallowed. Rapid's goalkeeper provided another entertaining moment, throwing the ball at the referee after Pearce had scored. Raducanu wasn't even booked, although the Romanian FA later took action suspending him for three games. It was comical, but I wasn't laughing the next day when I feared the authorities might put me in prison after being accused of buying Romanian currency on the black market!

I had tried to pay my hotel bill using Romanian lei, but the American hotel wouldn't accept it. "We only accept American dollars or pounds sterling," said the hotel manager.

"I haven't got any. I've only got Romanian money," I lied. I had a wad of lei and was by now desperate to get rid of it.

"Can't you borrow some from your travelling companions?

"No. I can't. You're a hotel in Bucharest. Why can't you accept my Romanian money?"

"We'll make an exception and accept your Romanian lei, but only if you prove to us how much you bought on entering the country. Have you got the receipt?

"I've lost it," I replied, knowing full well that I only had a white slip showing that I had changed up fifty pounds worth of lei and my hotel bill came to more than that.

"Sorry Sir, without the slip we can't help you." For 20 minutes I argued with them. The manager warned me that without a receipt the authorities would accuse me of changing money on the black market and probably throw me in jail. On hearing that I was ready to cave in and was just about to miraculously produce some sterling out of my wallet, when the manager took pity and grabbed enough Romanian lei out of the pile I'd placed in front of him to cover the bill. At the airport, I produced my white slip and got £50 back and took the remainder of the Romanian lei home with me. I was unaware at the time, but I was actually breaking the law, as you weren't allowed to take the currency out of the country! I was glad to see the back of Romania, so you can imagine how exasperated I was when Spurs were drawn to play Unizale Textile Arad, another Romanian club in the quarter-finals. On the second trip, I made sure that I had plenty of sterling and even stuffed some dollars into my wallet just to be safe.

UT Arad's players were traditionally drawn from the workers of a textile plant in the town of Arad, located in Dracula's territory of Transylvania. The previous season they had knocked the holders Feyenoord out of the European Cup and I expected them to be a tougher nut to crack than Rapid. In Romania, Spurs ruled supreme, winning 2–0, but two weeks later in the home tie, they were given a fright. Alan Gilzean salvaged a 1–1 draw with a late headed goal to book a semi-final date with Italian giants AC Milan. My mate Philip Isaacs was due to fly home with me the next day, but as he had an important meeting to attend early the following morning asked club chairman Sidney Wale if he could fly back on the team's plane that evening. Philip offered to pay his way, but Wale refused to allow him, saying: "Only players and club officials can board our plane. Lord Ted Willis just asked the same question and I told him the same." It proved that social standing meant nothing to Wale. He preferred to have empty seats than offer them to outsiders. Philip flew back to London with me the next morning. He only just made his meeting on time following an uncomfortable dash through busy London traffic. He cursed Wale for most of the journey home.

Two days before Tottenham's home clash against AC Milan, midfielder John Pratt broke his nose against Ipswich. Bill Nicholson acted decisively, recalling Alan Mullery from Fulham, where the club captain had been on loan after failing to convince Nicholson that he was over a pelvic injury. In three days, Mullery went from playing in front of a few thousand against Orient at Brisbane Road in the Second Division to leading Spurs out in a European semi-final. A crowd of 42,000 packed into White Hart Lane and welcomed him back from the wilderness like a returning hero. The joy though soon turned to despair when Romeo Benetti gave Milan the lead in the 25th minute. Steve Perryman saved the day with two glorious volleys to give Spurs a slender lead to take to Milan. I was convinced that it wouldn't be enough, with the Italians boasting Gianni Rivera, one of the outstanding strikers in world football, in their side. I took my seat up in the gods of the San Siro and danced a jig when Mullery silenced 68,000 Italians after just seven minutes with a 20-yarder that curved into the top corner. Rivera later equalised from the spot, but Spurs hung on to book a place in the final against Wolves, who beat Ferencvaros of Hungary on the same night.

The first ever UEFA Cup final was played over two legs, with the first leg at Molineux. I had to stand up for the entire match at Wolves, as when I went to take my seat in the back row of the stand, I found it had been removed! Martin Chivers gave Spurs the lead in the 57th minute with a pinpoint header but Wolves skipper Jim McCalliog levelled the scores following a quick free kick midway through the second-half, but Chivers scored the winner three minutes from time with a thunderous drive from 25 yards. Spurs warmed up for the second leg with a 2–0 victory over Arsenal at Highbury. Six days later, over 54,000 crammed into White Hart Lane for the decider. Mullery headed Spurs into a 3–1 aggregate lead after 29 minutes. Before the interval, Wolves winger David Wagstaffe reduced the deficit with a 25-yard strike, but Jennings ensured Spurs became the first British club to win two different European trophies with some superb saves in the second half to keep Wolves at bay. Mullery received the trophy from a rickety old table and I watched with pride when he lifted it high into the air. The crowd then streamed on to the pitch and carried him shoulder-high around it. It proved to be his final match in the club's colours and capped a memorable season in Europe for me.

The Riot in '74 and the Glory of '84

I continued to follow Spurs in Europe during their UEFA Cup campaigns of 1972/73 and 1973/74. Problems with my gall bladder in September '72 forced me to pull out of a trip to Norway where Tottenham's first-round opponents were part-timers Lyn Oslo. It was only the second European tie that I'd missed in 11 years! I gave my ticket to my good friend Derek Ufton, the former Charlton and England footballer and Kent cricketer. He witnessed an entertaining 6–3 victory for the Lilywhites in a match when three goals were scored in less than two minutes. Alan Gilzean scored two of them and Lyn's full-time student Trygve Christophersen got the other. Liverpool ended Tottenham's grip on the trophy, winning a hard-fought semi-final on the away goals rule.

Spurs qualified for a third successive year of UEFA Cup football after beating Norwich in the 1973 League Cup final, courtesy of a Ralph Coates shot from outside the 18-yard box. Tottenham reached the final of the UEFA Cup of '74 without losing a match home or away. I travelled to Zurich and saw them thrash Grasshoppers 5–1 in the first round and then to Cologne in the fourth round, where they played magnificently and beat the West Germans 2–1. Coates scored a vital goal in East Germany that helped Nicholson's men to a 4–1 aggregate win over Lokomotiv Leipzig in the semi-final. Tottenham faced Feyenoord in the final, but a 2–2 draw in the first leg at White Hart Lane meant the Dutch were firm favourites to lift the trophy in Rotterdam.

The odds may have been against skipper Martin Peters lifting the trophy, but I arranged a three-day trip with Terry Venables and Philip Isaacs nevertheless. When our wives discovered that Rotterdam was just 35 miles from the Hague with its rather nice beach resort of Scheveningen, they decided they were coming along too. It certainly made sense to base ourselves away from hordes of invading Spurs fans to give us more chance of having a relaxing break. My children Shelley and Allan had both developed into keen Spurs fans by then and although they were aged just 17 and 15 respectively, I gave them permission to travel to Holland to see the game accompanied by their older cousin Lawrence. They flew out on a chartered flight on the morning of the match and I met them outside the stadium before kick-off. We'd heard that there'd been some disturbances in the town centre involving drunken Spurs fans and told the kids that if there was any hint of trouble inside the De Kuip stadium they should leave and meet us at the same spot outside.

Sadly, the hooligan minority amongst Tottenham's huge travelling support turned on the home fans when right back Wim Rijsbergen scored just before half-time. Bottles, banners and broken chairs rained on Feyenoord's supporters and a full-scale riot got underway. It was frightening and heartbreaking at the same time. Bill Nicholson made an appeal over the stadium Tannoy for Spurs fans to behave themselves, but the majority of hooligans took no notice and continued their battles on the terraces. I looked at the scene going on in the Tottenham end of the ground and my blood ran cold. I feared that my kids were caught up in it and immediately left my seat, as did Terry, Philip and our wives and hurried to the pre-arranged meeting point. On our way there, I ran into a friend of mine called Clive Bednash. He too was leaving the ground at the same time after being sickened at the sight of our fans wrecking the stadium.

"I'm praying my kids and nephew are OK. They're in the area of the ground where the trouble has started," I said to Clive, as we hurried out of the exit.

"I've seen enough," he said. "I drove here in my Roller and I'm leaving before they smash that up too."

"Could you give my kids a lift to the airport?" I asked. Clive was only too pleased to help out. Thankfully, Shelley, Allan and Lawrence were waiting as instructed at the meeting place. They were shook up, but happily weren't amongst the 200 people injured in the rioting. Clive got them to Rotterdam Airport 20 minutes before the game had even ended. We were also long gone and on our way to The Hague by the time the Feyenoord captain Rinus Israel was holding the trophy aloft after their 2–0 victory. It was the first major final that Spurs had ever lost, but I couldn't have cared less about the result. Hooligans had tarnished the great name of Tottenham Hotspur and for the first time in my life I felt ashamed to be a fan of the club. Bill Nicholson's daughter Jean had also been caught up in the trouble. A brick was thrown through a window of the coach in which she was travelling. Nicholson later cited the riots in Rotterdam as one of the contributing factors in his decision to resign four games into the next season. The club were banned from playing their next two European home games at White Hart Lane, although this was largely academic as Spurs failed to qualify again for Europe before UEFA's 25th anniversary amnesty annulled the ban in 1980.

The riot in Rotterdam seemed to spark a wave of hooliganism involving British clubs. Twelve months later, I was caught up in trouble at the European Cup final between Bayern Munich and Leeds in Paris. Some rather questionable decisions by the French referee Michel Kitabdjian, including denying Leeds a penalty when Franz Beckenbauer tripped Allan Clarke and disallowing a perfectly good goal by Peter Lorimer led to some ugly scenes after the West Germans won 2–0. I watched missiles rain down on to the pitch and saw Leeds fans destroying cars and smashing windows outside the stadium afterwards. They were banned from Europe for four years, reduced to two on appeal, after those riots.

By the time Spurs were next in Europe, my daughter Shelley had married the club's central defender Paul Miller. I went to all the team's matches in the European Cup Winners' Cup campaign of 1981–82, including the fateful night in Barcelona when the lights went out in the Nou Camp and on Tottenham's hopes of a place in the final. The first leg at the Lane had been an X-certificate encounter with Barcelona defender Juan Estella sent off for a horrendous tackle on Tony Galvin. Seconds later, Ray Clemence let a speculative 40-yard shot slip out of his grasp and into the net. Graham Roberts equalised five minutes from the end to give Keith Burkinshaw's men a lifeline. Paul told me that before the match in Barcelona, the referee went into both dressing rooms and warned the teams about their conduct. The only trouble was our lads heeded the warning, whereas the Spaniards took no notice and the lenient referee allowed Barcelona to hack and kick their way to a 1–0 victory.

In an earlier round of the competition that year, I travelled with my friends from Fleet Street to Dundalk, a small town in County Louth, situated 13 miles from the border with Northern Ireland. This was during the time of the Troubles and Dundalk was known to be a safe haven for the IRA. It was a particularly sensitive time due to the deaths of ten Irish republicans following hunger strikes at the Maze Prison. The strikes had ended just a couple of weeks before the match. As a result, although unknown to me at the time, the security forces had insisted that they ride with us to the game on the two buses hired by the club. The Press travelled on the first bus and the players and club officials followed on the other bus behind. Paul tried to make light of the situation by joking, "if there is a bomb at least the press will get blown up first". In truth, everyone was a bit on edge during the journey to Dundalk's Oriel Park stadium. I spent most of the journey looking out of the window, scared what might happen as we passed through an area of countryside known as 'Bandit Country'. It wasn't until I got back to London after the 1–1 draw that Paul asked me if we'd also had guys on our bus wearing tracksuits that read 'Irish Judo Association'. I remembered that I had seen a few guys in tracksuits. He said: "I bet they were the SAS in disguise!" Who knows? Maybe they were!

Bayern Munich ended Tottenham's hopes in the Cup Winners' Cup at the second-round stage the next season. I didn't go to the 4–1 defeat in Munich, although Paul told me on his return that the match turned into a farce when fog descended onto the pitch soon after kick-off. He said at least two of their goals were down to the weather and claimed he couldn't even see Bayern's forwards until they were bearing down on goal.

Spurs made light work of some really good sides in the UEFA Cup of 1983/84. Dutch master Johan Cruyff tried to man-mark Glenn Hoddle in the second-round tie against Feyenoord, but the move backfired. Hoddle created four first-half goals, two each for Steve Archibald and Tony Galvin, in the first leg in what was one of his best performances in a Spurs shirt. Tottenham won 4–2 on the night and 2–0 in Holland two weeks later. Archibald got his name on the scoresheet again, when the team avenged the defeat over Bayern Munich the previous season by beating them 2–1 on aggregate to progress to the quarter-finals. I enjoyed watching Archibald play and liked the fact that he created goals as well as scoring them with his deft touches in and around the box. I especially liked seeing him in tandem with Garth Crooks in attack, whom I also rated highly. Tony Waddington at Stoke City had told me about 'Crooksie' a few years before Keith Burkinshaw signed him for Spurs. Tony reckoned one of the 'big four' clubs would snap him up sooner or later and he was right. (Spurs were one of the big four back then) I remember Tony asked if I could get Garth a ticket for Wimbledon – not the football team, but the tennis tournament. I couldn't get a ticket in the stands, but I got Garth closer to the action that he probably dreamed possible. My mate Monte Fresco was at Wimbledon taking photographs for the *Daily Mirror* and he agreed to take him as his 'runner'. Back in those days before computers and Internet connections made it easy to upload pictures to newspaper offices, Monte needed someone to run the film he took to dispatch riders, who would rush through busy traffic to deliver their film. That's what Garth did and he loved it. Monte says today, "Crooksie was definitely the fastest runner I ever had!"

A comfortable 4–2 aggregate win over Austria Vienna followed by victory over Hajduk Split on the away goals rule in the semi-final gave Tottenham a place in the final against Anderlecht. For the first leg in Brussels, I arranged for a small 11-seater private plane to fly me and a few of my friends to the game. The cost of hiring the plane worked out at about £1,100, which actually wasn't much more than buying a ticket each from an airline. Bobby Robson, then manager of England, was one of my guests, as was Paul's father, Dick, and Allan Harris, who at the time was Terry Venables's assistant at QPR. For some reason, Terry didn't come with us to Brussels, although I remember that when I told him Bobby Robson was flying with me to the game, he said: "You'll do anything to get your son-in-law an England cap!" The late Sir Bobby was a very good friend of mine. I used to pick him up from Liverpool Street station when he travelled down from Ipswich to watch

Spurs games. I was truly honoured when he accepted my invitation for the UEFA Cup final. As the England manager, he could easily have chosen to sit with the dignitaries, but instead he joined me in the stands with the rest of the Spurs fans. He even stood up, cheered and punched the air when Paul opened the scoring for Tottenham. He was truly passionate about the English game and always wanted to see our clubs do well in Europe. He showed the same loyalty to his friends and always went the extra mile if they asked for his help. Like the time I called him up in 1979, on the day Ipswich were playing Barcelona in the European Cup Winners' Cup.

"Any chance of two tickets, Bobby?"

"Blimey Morris, you're leaving it a bit late. I'm not sure I'll be able to get any, it's a sell-out." He phoned me back half an hour later and said: "I've had to move mountains to get these, but I'm sorry they aren't in the directors' box."

'Maxie' Miller did himself justice that night in Brussels, not just scoring in the 1–1 draw, but playing brilliantly at the back with Graham Roberts. He tells a good story about how BBC commentator Barry Davies had interviewed him before the game and reminded him that he usually scored at least one goal a season. He told Davies that there would be no better time to score than in the final. Apparently, Davies likes to take some credit for Paul's bullet-headed goal from Mickey Hazard's corner. We left three minutes from the end of that match, just as Spurs goalkeeper Tony Parks fumbled a shot by Frank Arnesen and sweeper Morten Olsen toe-poked an equaliser. We got a taxi to the airport and were back in London in time to watch the highlights of the game on TV.

"I can't believe we were there an hour ago watching the game," said Bobby, as we sipped our drinks in the Rendezvous Casino at the Hilton Hotel. Tony Parks more than made up for his mistake in the second leg at White Hart Lane, saving two penalties in a shootout following a 1–1 draw as Spurs secured the UEFA Cup for a second time in their history. Bobby never did award Paul an England cap, despite my endeavours!

In May 2009, 25 years after that famous victory, the players and management team from that triumphant side were honoured in an anniversary dinner at the Dorchester Hotel in

London. All of the players were present, with the exception of Glenn Hoddle, Steve Archibald and Alan Brazil. Glenn had an important game to watch at his academy in Spain, while Steve and Alan had committed to media work in the build-up to the Champions League final between Barcelona and Manchester United. The event was organised by Paul, who was the players' social secretary during his time at the club, and Spurs fanatic Mark Jacob. Matt Lorenzo was the evening's master of ceremonies and celebrity Spurs fan Bobby Davro provided the cabaret. Sky Sports presenter Clare Tomlinson, herself a Spurs fan who boasts a home-and-away season ticket, also took part by conducting an auction for prizes that included tickets to see Michael Jackson at the O2 Arena. (I believe the winners got to see another top act after Jackson died during rehearsals for the O2 concerts.) I won a signed football in the raffle and gave it to Clare for the auction: what do I need with a football at my age? It fetched £1,300 for the Noah's Ark Children's Hospice, which was a brilliant gesture by the Spurs fans who bid for it on the night.

A few weeks before the event, I sat down with Tomlinson and journalist Richard Littlejohn, another Spurs nut, at Les Ambassadeurs in Mayfair to muse over a dream-team selection of players that had played in any of the club's three European trophy wins of 1963, 1972 and 1984. Our discussion went on for quite some time and was documented over eight pages in the souvenir brochure for those 25th anniversary celebrations at the Dorchester. The team we selected was: Pat Jennings, Steve Perryman, Cyril Knowles, Mike England, Dave Mackay, Glenn Hoddle, Danny Blanchflower, Ossie Ardiles, Cliff Jones, Jimmy Greaves and Martin Chivers. The three substitutes were Bobby Smith, Graham Roberts and Tony Galvin, with Littlejohn and Tomlinson picking Bill Nicholson as the team's manager, although I caused a bit of controversy by disagreeing with their selection, opting for Keith Burkinshaw instead. I told them that the players always said Nicholson was too negative in his pre-match team talks, building the opposition up and putting doubts in players' minds. I believe the captain Danny Blanchflower deserved as much credit as Nicholson for the club's success during the golden period in the early sixties. Littlejohn disagreed, saying, "I think there should be a special place at this dinner where Morris stands up and explains why Bill Nicholson was useless." Thankfully, nobody asked me to do that and at least it caused a talking point amongst people who read my comments. There may be a debate over some of our choices, but I reckon the first supporter allowed through the turnstiles to watch Tottenham's European dream team deserved to be me!

6 GEOFF HURST, PAT JENNINGS AND STOKE CITY

"Morris is a lifelong friend and a true supporter of football."
Sir Geoff Hurst (West Ham and England, World Cup winner 1966)

"Back in the seventies, Tottenham's directors mistakenly regarded Morris as a hanger-on when nothing could have been further from the truth. The players never understood their attitude."
Pat Jennings OBE (Spurs and Northern Ireland, 119 caps)

B obby Moore introduced me to Geoff Hurst in 1964, two years before his West Ham teammate scored that infamous hat-trick for England against West Germany in the World Cup final. A little while before we first met, I watched the Hammers beat Second Division Preston in the 1964 FA Cup final, when Geoff, playing as an inside left, headed West Ham's second equaliser in their 3–2 victory. His performance that day convinced me that he had the potential to become an England international, although I believed that his strength in the air made him better suited to a centre forward position, rather than the midfield one that he occupied for the Hammers. In fact, West Ham boss Ron Greenwood converted him to that very role soon after the '64 Cup final. Indeed, England coach Alf Ramsey awarded Geoff his first cap as a centre-forward in February 1966, just five months before the World Cup finals. I like to think that I was ahead of the time when it came to realising Geoff's best position.

I took a keen interest in West Ham's fortunes the next season, in particular their run in the European Cup Winners'

Cup competition. I had followed Spurs all over Europe two years earlier, when Bill Nicholson's team became the first British side to win a European title. My mate Jimmy Greaves scored twice in the 5–1 victory over Atlètico Madrid in the final. At the start of the 1964/65 season, Greavsie, Bobby and myself had discussed how West Ham might fare against some of the best sides in Europe. Bobby was sure they had a good chance of emulating Tottenham's achievement, but I wasn't so sure. Geoff Hurst soon entered the debate when Bobby introduced me to him on 12th September 1964. Bobby had provided me with complimentary tickets for the clash between Spurs and West Ham at Upton Park. The game that Saturday afternoon was a real ding-dong affair, with Greavsie scoring twice and Johnny Byrne bagging a hat-trick for the Hammers, who fought back from 2–1 down to win 3–2 thanks to Byrne's late goal. I joined Bobby and Greavsie in Upton Park's hospitality rooms after the game. As you can imagine, the West Ham lads were in full swing and rather enjoying the banter after beating their London rivals. One by one, in his own quiet way, Bobby introduced me to his West Ham teammates.

"Geoff, meet Morris, Tottenham's number-one fan, although I don't think he'll admit to that today." Geoff roared with laughter. After a few minutes of mickey-taking, I sat down with 'the West Ham Academy' at the bar. Amongst its members that night were John Bond, John Sissons, Ken Brown, Ronnie Boyce and a young reserve by the name of Harry Redknapp, who took great delight in winding me up after Tottenham's defeat, telling me, "Spurs could get relegated without Dave Mackay." The Spurs star was out at the time after breaking his leg against Manchester United the previous season.

West Ham were due to make their first trip into Europe the following week and they were expecting European football to be an easy ride. Ron Greenwood's men were off to Belgium to play La Gantoise in the preliminary round of the Cup Winners' Cup, but I warned Geoff and young Redknapp: "Don't count your chickens. It's not an easy cup to win". Their over confidence reminded me of what had happened to Man United the previous season, when they had been stuffed 5–0 by Sporting Lisbon in Portugal, following a 4–1 first-leg victory at Old Trafford.

"If you are drawn against the Portuguese and are complacent, you'll suffer a similar fate."

As it turned out, West Ham progressed to the quarter-finals, albeit unconvincingly, beating La Gantoise 2–1 on aggregate and then dumping out Czechoslovakian side Sparta Prague. Sporting Lisbon on the other hand suffered a shock exit to Cardiff City, with the Welshmen securing a famous 2–1 victory in Lisbon. The Hammers then faced Lausanne in the quarter-finals, and with Spurs not competing in Europe that season, Bobby invited me to join the team on their trip to Switzerland. A few friends of mine also came along and I arranged through Bobby for our party to stay in the same hotel as the team, a move that Ron Greenwood was happy to sanction. On the evening before the game, we joined the players on a fantastic boat trip across Lake Geneva, stopping for a few beers at a bar which commanded a glorious panoramic view of the Alps. With an ice-cold beer in our hands, we watched a glorious sunset over the mountains.

Geoff recently reminded me of an incident that occurred on the morning of the game against Lausanne. A few of us were sitting around the hotel swimming pool, when the team's striker, Brian Dear, known as 'Stag' to the lads, got out of his depth when wading into the pool. As a non-swimmer, Brian wasn't prepared for the steep descent into the deep end and Geoff, the only other person in the pool at the time, had to pull him out when he got into trouble. Despite that scare, Brian, just 21 at the time, recovered well from the fright and scored one of the goals in West Ham's 2–1 victory that evening. The favourable result helped round off a great trip and some lasting friendships were made with many of the West Ham players, Geoff in particular, who soon joined Bobby and Tina Moore as one of my regular dinner guests, along with his wife, Judith. I went on to organise his testimonial match against a European select XI side at Upton Park in 1971.

Brian Dear's great goalscoring form continued in Europe that season, scoring twice in a thrilling 4–3 victory over the Swiss in the second leg at Upton Park. He also scored in a

3–2 aggregate win over Spanish side Real Zaragoza, which booked West Ham a place in the final. By chance, the final that season was at Wembley, and I was one of the 97,974 sitting beneath the Twin Towers who witnessed West Ham become the second English winners of a European trophy. Right winger Alan Sealey scored both West Ham's goals in a 2–0 victory over 1860 Munich. I must admit the Hammers played some magnificent football that night and I was more than happy to see them beat the Germans.

The European Cup Winners' Cup of 1965 was to be the last piece of silverware that Bobby and Geoff won in West Ham's colours, although they got close a couple of times before leaving Upton Park in the early seventies. In 1966, the Hammers lost a two-legged League Cup final against West Brom, and in the same season, Borussia Dortmund ended the East Enders hopes of retaining the European Cup Winners' Cup at the semi-final stage, winning 5–2 on aggregate. The Germans beat Liverpool 2–1 in the final at Hampden Park, which was inconveniently played the night after England's last match at Wembley before the 1966 World Cup finals. I had hoped to travel up to Scotland to cheer on Liverpool, having watched the Reds overturn Celtic at Anfield in their semi-final encounter. However, I couldn't guarantee getting a train north of the border in time for the kick-off, and instead watched Greavsie and Geoff lead the England attack against Yugoslavia at Wembley. Greavsie scored England's first goal in a 2–0 victory that night. He then cemented his place in Alf Ramsey's World Cup line-up when he scored four in a 6–1 victory over Norway in Oslo, 12 days before the tournament kicked off. I was over the moon for my old mate Jimmy, but disappointed that it was Liverpool's Roger Hunt, and not Geoff, who had won the race to partner him in attack.

In fact, of course, the tournament was one of joy for Geoff and despair for Jimmy, following England's World Cup triumph, Geoff established himself as his country's number one striker, winning a total of 49 caps and scoring 24 goals in an international career that lasted five more years. On the other hand, despite managing to regain his place nine months after losing it, Jimmy only earned three more caps. His last came against

Austria in Vienna in May 1967, a match I attended with the England Supporters' Club. Greavsie called time on his international career the following year, after failing to make any of Alf Ramsey's starting line-ups during the 1967/68 season.

Three months after Greavsie's final cap, I made another new friend in football, one who by chance was to become an influential figure in Geoff's career. On 28th August 1967, I travelled by train to Liverpool for Tottenham's league match against Everton, due to be played the following day. At this time, whenever I travelled to Merseyside to see Spurs matches, I always travelled up the night before. It gave me time to meet up with the friends that I'd made in the area and enjoy a night out with them before the game. On this occasion, I booked myself into the Adelphi Hotel in Liverpool and arranged to meet my friends at a regular haunt close by called the Cabaret Club. Over the years, I had got to know the club's manager quite well and he always saved me a good table if I let him know beforehand that I was coming up for a game. The club always had its fair share of celebrity faces at the weekend, but this was a Monday night and it was quieter than usual. However, there was one familiar face sitting just a few tables away from mine.

"Morris. You're a football man," said the club's manager. "Do you recognise that guy sitting over there?" I did.

"It's Tony Waddington, the Stoke City manager," I replied.

"Come with me, I'll introduce you to him," he said.

I followed him over to the table, excited at the prospect of meeting one of the top managers in English football.

"Mr Waddington. Please allow me to introduce you to Morris Keston of Tottenham Hotspur."

"Hello Morris. Pleased to meet you," said Tony before asking me: "Are you a club official?"

"No, I'm just a fanatical supporter who goes to all of the matches," I replied.

"So you're here for the Everton game," he smiled.

"That's right," I said, before telling him. "Nice win for your boys over Man City the other day.

"Yes, but the 3–0 score line flattered us a bit."

I sat at Tony's table for the entire evening and listened to his opinion about the Spurs players of the day, whilst also discussing the merits of his own team. I remember that Waddington had only just signed England goalkeeper Gordon Banks from Leicester and was very pleased to have got him. "He'll save us 20 goals a season," he predicted. It was certainly a thrill to hear the views of one of the most respected managers in the game. However, the biggest thrill that night came soon after the barman called last orders. Just as I was getting my coat from the cloakroom, Tony walked over and said to me, "We're due to play your mob at the Victoria Ground later this year. Do you think you'll go to the match?"

"Yes, I'll be there, cheering Spurs to victory," I laughed.

"Good joke Morris," he said. "But I think you'll find that it will be me laughing after we've beaten Nicholson's boys. I tell you what, you can be my guest at the Spurs match. I'll save you two seats in the directors' box. All you need to do is collect them from our ticket office on the day of the game. After we've beaten you, I'll meet you in the boardroom for a celebratory drink."

I thanked him for the offer, although to be honest, we'd both had a few drinks that night and I didn't expect him to even remember me or his generous offer come the day of the game. However, when I made my way to the ticket office at the Victoria Ground on the day of the match, unbelievably, two directors' box tickets were in an envelope awaiting my collection, courtesy of Tony Waddington. I was absolutely gobsmacked. That afternoon, I cheered as my mate Terry Venables gave Spurs an early lead and groaned as Stoke winger Harry Burrows scored twice to give them victory. True to his word, Tony Waddington greeted me with a huge smile in the boardroom after the game.

"Good to see you Morris," he said. "I told you Spurs would come a cropper against the mighty Stoke City." Tony roared with laughter and introduced me to Stoke's club officials. From that day onwards, every time Spurs made the trip to Staffordshire, Tony and the directors would invite me to watch the game with them. Likewise, whenever Stoke visited London, I would meet up with Tony and the club's officials, who at the time included chairman Albert Henshaw and directors Alex Humphreys and Gordon Crowe. We would have a meal together before the game

Army days in Egypt - It's a forced smile as I'm missing Spurs' championship-winning season of 1950/51.

SEASON 1952-3

TEAMS			LEAGUE	RESULT
	DERBY COUNTY		TRIAL MATCH	2-1
	SPURS V WBA		1ST DIV	3-4
	WORKSOP V DONCASTER RES		MIDLAND LEAGUE	0-2
	DONCASTER V SWANSEA		2ND DIV	2-3
	LEEDS V PLYMOUTH A		2ND DIV	1-1
	YORK V CHESTER		3RD DIV NORTH	0-0
	BRENTFORD V HUDDERSFIELD		2ND DIV	1-3
	SPURS V CARDIFF		1ST DIV	2-1
	BRISTOL ROV RES V ALDERSHOT RES / BOURNEMOUTH RES		F. COMB 2ND DIV	1-1
ITORE PARK	PLYMOUTH V ROTHERHAM		2ND DIV	4-3
"16TH" ASHTON GATE	BRISTOL CITY RES V BOURNEMOUTH RES		F. COMB 2ND DIV	1-1
-18TH DEAN COURT	BOURNEMOUTH V NEWPORT		3RD DIV SOUTH	1-2
-23RD WORKSOP	WORKSOP V FRICKLEY COLLIERY		MIDLAND LEAGUE	2-0
ELLAND RD	LEEDS V SOUTHAMPTON		2ND DIV	1-1
WHITE HART LANE	SPURS V BURNLEY		1ST DIV	2-1
MAINE RD	MAN. CITY V CARDIFF		1ST DIV	2-2
WHITE HART LANE SPURS	SPURS RES V CHARLTON RES		F. COMB 1ST DIV	3-0
	ARSENAL RES V WALTHAMSTOW. AVE		L.F.A.C.C. (FLOODLIGHT)	8-3
	ARSENAL RES V FULHAM RES		F.C.S.F. (FLOODLIGHT)	0-1
T LANE.	SPURS V BLACKPOOL		1ST DIV	4-0
ARK	W.HAM RES V SPURS RES		L.C.C. 2ND RND	2-1

OCTOBER 1959

THE *Lilywhite*
OFFICIAL ORGAN OF THE SPURS SUPPORTERS CLUB

VOL. 10 No.

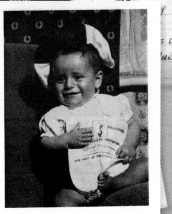

A GOOD START

MR. M. KESTON of London, N.W.9 is a staunch member of the Spurs Supporters Club, and enrolled his son Alan as a member when he was two days old! Here is lovely photo of young Alan at five months. Doesn't he look cute.

"A good start" for my son Allan in 'The Lilywhite'.

My daughter Shelley aged 12 with her "uncle" Terry Venables.

Walking off the pitch and straight to the bar after a charity game with referee Mr. Venables and another ex-Spur Micky Dulin.

Taking a stroll with Bobby Moore and some autograph hunters in Basle, Switzerland in October 1971.

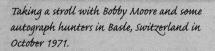

Dancing with my beautiful wife Sylvia at the Goaldiggers Ball, a charity function organised by Jimmy Hill.

Bobby Moore gives a speech at one of the testimonial dinners that I organised for him in 1970. In the background, Jimmy Hill lights up a cigar.

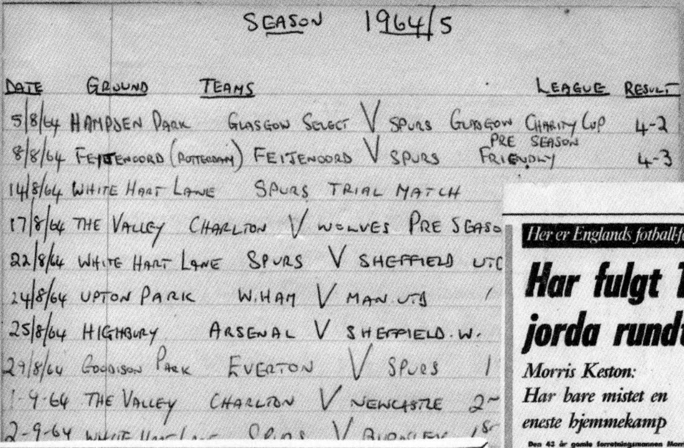

Handwritten ledger:

SEASON 1964/5

DATE	GROUND	TEAMS	LEAGUE	RESULT
5/8/64	HAMPDEN PARK	GLASGOW SELECT V SPURS GLASGOW CHARITY CUP		4-2
8/8/64	FEIJENOORD (ROTTERDAM)	FEIJENOORD V SPURS PRE SEASON FRIENDLY		4-3
14/8/64	WHITE HART LANE	SPURS TRIAL MATCH		
17/8/64	THE VALLEY	CHARLTON V WOLVES PRE SEASON		
22/8/64	WHITE HART LANE	SPURS V SHEFFIELD UTD		
24/8/64	UPTON PARK	W.HAM V MAN UTD		
25/8/64	HIGHBURY	ARSENAL V SHEFFIELD W.		
27/8/64	GOODISON PARK	EVERTON V SPURS		1
1.9.64	THE VALLEY	CHARLTON V NEWCASTLE		2-
2-9-64	WHITE HART LANE	SPURS V BURNLEY		18

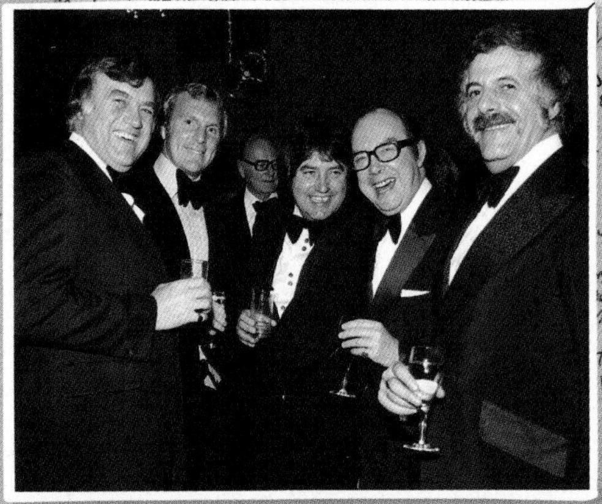

Big smiles and big bow ties all round with Derby chairman George Hardy, Bobby Moore and comedians Jimmy Tarbuck and Eric Morecambe.

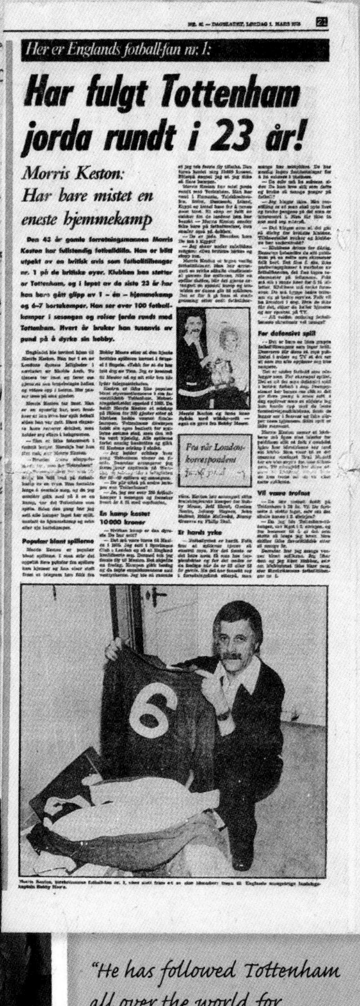

Newspaper clipping (Norwegian):

Her er Englands fotball-fan nr. 1:

Har fulgt Tottenham jorda rundt i 23 år!

Morris Keston:

Har bare mistet en eneste hjemmekamp

"He has followed Tottenham all over the world for 23 years!" (Interview in Norwegian newspaper 'Dagbladet', March 1975) Holding the shirt that Bobby Moore gave me. Was it the 1966 jersey? Did I throw away £250,000?

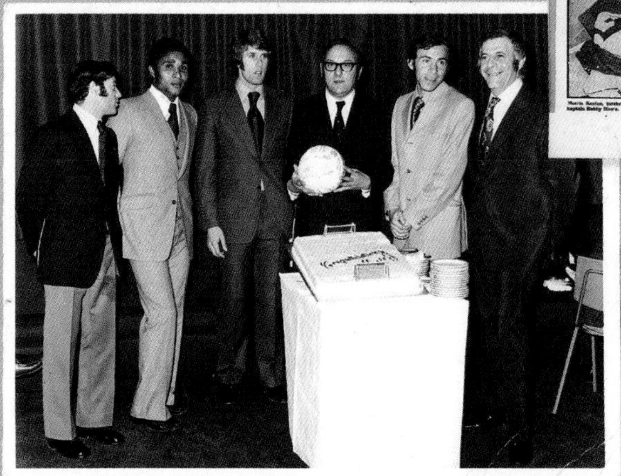

"Hurry up and cut the cake!" - Awaiting a slice after Geoff Hurst's testimonial in November 1971 are Uwe Seeler, Eusébio, Geoff, Philip Isaacs, Mordechai Spiegler and me.

"How are your Spurs doing Morris?" - Frank Sinatra stops for a chat after seeking out Sylvia at the Ritz. Also standing around the table are Sinatra's lawyer Mickey Rudin (red bow tie) and American casino developer Steve Wynn (grey tie).

To Sylvia —
I saw morris here —
Where were you!
All the Best,
Frank Sinatra
mar '78

"One legend to another" - Bobby Moore sizes up boxer Sugar Ray Robinson for one of the suede coats that we sold in partnership with Freddie Harrison.

Suited and booted at the Hilton for the Anglo-American Sporting Club dinner. That's me sitting opposite Bobby Moore with Terry Venables on my right and Bobby Butlin on my left. Footballers Phil Beal and Johnny Byrne are sat behind Terry. On the left side with Bobby are Hendon F.C. official Charles Geary, boxing promoter Mickey Duff and entertainer Kenny Lynch.

"Who's a Sissy?" - Connecting with The Champ's chin in 1975 at a function in his honour at The Sportsman in London.

1973/74

DATE	GROUND	TEAMS	LEAGUE	RES
8/8/73	OLYMPIC STADIUM	AJAX (AMSTERDAM) V SPURS	SJAAK SWART TESTIMONIAL	4-1
11/8/73	NINIAN PARK	CARDIFF C. V SPURS	PRE SEASON FRIENDLY	1-3
14/8/73	CRAVEN COTTAGE	FULHAM V NORWICH	PRE SEASON FRIENDLY	3-1
15/8/73	VICTORIA GROUND	STOKE		
18/8/73	"	STOKE V		
25/8/73	HIGHFIELD RD	COVENT		
27/8/73	UPTON PARK	W. HA		
28/8/73	HIGHBURY	ARSENAL		
1/9/73	WHITE HART LANE	SPURS		
4/9/73	LOFTUS RD	Q.P.R.		
5/9/73	WHITE HART LANE			
8/9/73	UPTON PARK	W. HAM		
10/9/73	"	W. HAM		
11/9/73	TURF MOOR	BURNLEY		
15/9/73	WHITE HART LANE	SP		

LIFE'S A BALL FOR SOCCER'S SUPER FAN!

For football's 'big spender' spends more than a little time following the team he loves . . . he Spurs them on with lavish parties at the Hilton Hotel!

for fulgt Tottenham arts rundt i 23 år!

FASHION tycoon Morris Keston has reached his "goal" in life! Now he can combine business with pleasure. Business . . . as boss of one of the East End's biggest clothing empires. Pleasure . . . in following his favourite team, Spurs. In 24 years faithful devotion to the team, he hasn't missed one home league match! And it doesn't end there! Globe-trotting Morris will go anywhere to follow the sport he loves—including a £750 whirlwind trip to see England play West Germany in the World Cup. Here, the editor, Bob Hutchins, looks at the life of this remarkable man, who "doesn't count the cost" when it comes to throwing lavish parties at the Hilton Hotel to celebrate his team's successes!

HE HASN'T MISSED A SPUR'S HOME-TIE IN 24 YEARS

"The King of Vegas" - At Caesars Palace with Bobby and Tina Moore and Philip and Ruth Isaacs.

The terrifying flash floods - Las Vegas, July 1975.

"The one that got away" - Graeme Souness - Only one game for Spurs, but a friend for life.

*"Spurs in the family"
- Paul Miller and
granddaughter
Charlotte in 1987.*

*Sylvia and Glenn Hoddle
with the FA Cup in 1981.*

1980/81

	ROUND	TEAMS	LEAGUE	RESULT
		SAN DIEGO SOCKERS V ATLANTA CHIEFS	N.A.S.L.	4-0
		" " V TAMPA BAY ROWDIES	NA.S.L.	3-0
	HALL	SOUTHEND V SPURS	PRE-SEASON FRIENDLY	1-1
	LANE WIMBLEDON	V BRENTFORD	"	2-1
H 8/80	CRAVEN COTTAGE	FULHAM V NOTTS.C.	ANGLO SCOTTISH CUP	0-1
5 8/80	PLOUGH LANE WIMBLEDON	V C. PALACE	PRE-SEASON FRIENDLY	0-3
6 8/80	GRIFFIN PARK	BRENTFORD V CHELSEA	" "	3-0
9 8/80	WEMBLEY	LIVERPOOL V W.HAM	CHARITY SHIELD	1-0
12 8/80	CRAVEN COTTAGE	FULHAM V PETERBOROUGH	F. LEAGUE CUP 1ST RND 2ND LEG A.E.T.	1-1
				2-0
				1-0
				3-4
				3-0
				6-0
				2-2
			L	0-2
			EF	0-0
				0-1
				1-0
				2-0
				3-1
				0-0
			GAME	3-0
			ND	1-2

*"Smudger" Monte Fresco's retirement party - (front step - Bob Thomas, George
Cohen, me, Monte, George Graham, John Hollins - and on the steps above -
David O'Leary, Gary Lineker, Dave Mackay, Lawrie McMenemy, Sir Trevor
Brooking, Frank McLintock and Sir Henry Cooper).*

Sylvia organised a garden party for my 70th birthday. I spent a lovely day with family and friends, including Phil Beal, Martin Chivers and Sir Geoff Hurst.

"The next two generations of Spurs fans!" – The beautiful treble – My granddaughters Amy and Charlotte and great-granddaughter Grace.

Getting my hands on some silverware in 2008.

and I always thoroughly enjoyed their company. I remember once sitting in the Potters Club restaurant having lunch before a game, when I asked Henshall why it was that Stoke and Port Vale always kicked off at 3.15pm on a Saturday afternoon, when everyone else kicked off at 3pm. Albert looked over at Bill Williams, the club's secretary and asked him.

"That's because of the Wedgwood factory. We kick off later to give the half-day Saturday workers enough time to make it to our matches."

"But the factory workers don't work on Saturday mornings any more," exclaimed Albert.

"I suppose we'd better see about changing that to 3pm, so we are in line with the rest of the country," smiled Bill.

"That would be nice," I laughed. "It would also mean that I wouldn't have to rush off a few minutes before the end of the match to catch my bloody train each time I come here". Bill Williams made a note of my request and the following season, Stoke kicked off at 3pm just like the rest of the country and I believe Port Vale followed in Stoke's footsteps a little later.

Around about the same time, Albert Henshall actually got the kick-off delayed for one of Stoke's games so that we could watch my horse running in a three o'clock race. It's true! The match was played on 26th May, 1971, an Anglo-Italian Cup game against AS Roma.

"Don't worry Morris, you won't miss the race. I'll ask the referee to delay the kick-off by five minutes so that we can watch it on the TV." And that's exactly what he did. My horse Sylvange, racing in Spurs colours and named after my wife Sylvia and my friend Freddie Harrison's wife Angela, finished out of the places.

I suppose you could say I was well in with the great people at Stoke. In fact, they even offered me a directorship at the club. I must admit, I thought long and hard about accepting their offer, but Tottenham were my club and in the end I decided to turn it down as I couldn't bear to miss any Spurs games. However, the Potters became my second club and I still have a soft spot for them today.

Looking back over my friendship with Tony Waddington, I guess our personalities just clicked. From that very first meeting in 1967 our friendship grew and we were often swapping opinions on the players and teams of the moment.

During the 1971/72 season, I probably watched Stoke more than at any other time during Tony's 17-year spell as their manager. The reason was the amazing number of replayed Cup matches that Stoke needed to progress in the Cup competitions. The League Cup semi-finals that year pitted Spurs against Chelsea and West Ham against Stoke. Spurs were the Cup holders at the time, having beaten Aston Villa at Wembley the previous year with two goals from Martin Chivers. As you can imagine, there was a fair bit of banter between Tony and myself in the days leading up to the semi-finals. He was convinced that their name was on the Cup, having knocked out Manchester United in the fourth round following a second replay at the Victoria Ground. I, however, quite fancied our chances of retaining the trophy during a season when Bill Nicholson's side were playing some good football. As it turned out, it was Chelsea who were first to book their place in the final, beating Tottenham 5–4 on aggregate. Alan Hudson scored the Blues' winner in the last minute of the tie at White Hart Lane with a freak free kick taken near the corner flag. On the same night, Stoke, having drawn 2–2 on aggregate against West Ham, drew 0–0 in a replay played at Hillsborough. The next day, Tony called me up at home to commiserate.

"Unlucky Morris, but what the hell was Cyril Knowles doing? It looked like he completely miskicked the ball on the goal line."

"He did," I said. "And that's how Hudson's free-kick ended up in the net."

"What a disaster. Anyway, do you fancy coming along to our second replay against the Hammers?"

"Yes. I'd love to." The conversation was a pretty run-of-the-mill one. Tony and I often dissected big matches over the phone and having discussed Spurs' disaster, we turned our attention to Stoke's performance against the Hammers.

"I'll tell you something for certain Morris, that Geoff Hurst may be 30 years old, but he has played superbly against us and been a constant menace for our back four. He's the one I've told our boys to watch."

"I couldn't agree more. I'm actually a good mate of Geoff's. I organised a fund-raising testimonial dinner for him last week, and he told me that Ron Greenwood hasn't yet offered him a new contract."

"When does his West Ham contract expire?"

"At the end of the season."

"Really? That's a surprise. Are West Ham mad? Do me a favour Morris. If you hear that West Ham haven't offered Geoff a new contract by May, then please let me know,"

"Will do."

Three weeks later, I joined the Stoke officials in the directors' box at Old Trafford, and along with almost 50,000 fans witnessed another great tussle between the two sides that ended in a 3–2 victory for Stoke. After the match, Tony Waddington, as you'd expect, was overjoyed at having got his team to Wembley for the first time in the club's 108-year history. He and the directors wanted me to join him for the final, saying I was a 'lucky omen', but with the match against Chelsea clashing with Tottenham's home league fixture against Manchester United, I declined the invitation. At the time, I hadn't missed a Spurs home game for 21 years and wasn't about to start then, even for my mates at Stoke. Tottenham beat United 2–0 that day, in front of their biggest crowd of the season, 54,814. At Wembley, Stoke carried off the famous three-handled trophy, courtesy of striker George Eastham's late winner in a 2–1 victory over Dave Sexton's Kings of the King's Road. I hurriedly made my way to Stoke's celebration party that night. It was a cracking evening with entertainment provided by musical duo Jackie Trent and Tony Hatch. Singer Trent, whose real name was Yvonne Ann Burgess, changed her stage name from Jackie Tremayne to Jackie Trent in honour of her Stoke origins. She certainly went down a storm that night with her then-husband Hatch, singing their hits from 1965, *Where Are You Now (My Love)* and *On the Other Side of the Tracks.*

Despite being the second-oldest professional club after Notts County, Stoke had never won a major trophy in its history. Now, finally with some silverware in their trophy cabinet, Tony had the task of strengthening his squad for the club's first season in Europe, having qualified for the 1972/73 UEFA Cup competition. With Wembley match-winner George Eastham fast approaching his 36th birthday, Tony called me up at home to find out the latest news on the Geoff Hurst situation. Here now, for the first time, is the full account of how Geoff came to sign for Stoke City in August 1972.

After exchanging pleasantries, Tony asked me, "Morris, what's happening with Geoff at West Ham?"

"Not sure. Shall I give him a call to find out?"

"Yes. That would be great. I've just signed the old Spurs winger Jimmy Robertson from Ipswich and I'd love to sign Geoff to head home Jimmy's crosses."

"OK. I'll call you back as soon I've spoken to him."

I got straight on the phone to Geoff.

"Have West Ham offered you a new contract yet?" I asked.

"No. It looks like the club are going to release me. I was expecting Ron to come up with a new deal, but nothing has materialised. I must admit, I'm a bit gutted about that. You know me Morris. I love West Ham and the fans, and don't really want to leave."

"I can't understand Ron Greenwood's thinking. You're only 30 and an England player. Is he mad? Have any clubs shown an interest in signing you?"

"Well, I don't know if it's common knowledge that I'm available, although Ron did tell me that Bournemouth want to sign me."

"Bournemouth? Are you kidding me? They're in the Third Division!"

"I know Morris. I don't think I'm quite ready to retire to Bournemouth just yet. But according to Ron, they are keen to sign me after only just missing out on promotion last season."

"Well, you know why Ron wants you to go to Bournemouth. If you go there and score a hatful everyone will say, 'It's only Bournemouth.' If you sign for another First Division club and score a hatful, everyone will be pointing the finger at Ron and asking him, 'Why did you let Geoff Hurst leave?'"

"I make you right Morris."

"How about Stoke City?"

"Funny you should say that. Banksy is always banging on about how good Stoke are and that I should join him there."

"Well. I can tell you that I've just got off the phone to Tony Waddington, and he wants to sign you."

"Really?"

"Yeah. I tell you what, why don't you come over tomorrow afternoon. I'll arrange for Waddo to meet you here and you can have a chat with him."

"Sounds good to me Morris."

The next day, Geoff and Tony met at my flat in London's West End for their 'secret meeting'. Tony arrived a few minutes before Geoff and greeted the World Cup winner with a warm handshake. I left them alone and Tony went about selling his club to Geoff, a loyal professional who had up until then only ever known the Claret and Blue of West Ham. Stoke had been graced with some brilliant strikers over the years, like Freddie Steele, who scored a hat-trick for England against Sweden in May 1937 and Dennis Wilshaw, who I watched score four times for England in a 7–2 win over Scotland at Wembley in 1955. I wondered, as I stood in my kitchen searching for some champagne flutes, whether Geoff Hurst was about to join Stoke's list of great England hat-trick heroes by agreeing a transfer sat around my living-room table.

After a conversation that lasted no longer than 20 minutes, Tony piped up: "Morris. I think some bubbly is in order. Geoff has just agreed to sign for Stoke City."

"Great. I had put some champers on ice, just in case."

Tony Waddington phoned Hammers boss Ron Greenwood the next day to register his interest in Geoff, only to be told that Geoff was signing for Bournemouth. However, after Stoke agreed to pay £80,000, the deal was agreed "subject to Geoff agreeing personal terms with Stoke". Terms that were already agreed in my flat the day before!

Suffice to say that Ron Greenwood wasn't too pleased to see Geoff move to another top-flight club, especially when a quiet exit to sleepy Bournemouth looked on the cards. I suspect he also wasn't too happy when Geoff scored on his first return to Upton Park in Stoke's colours in December 1972. A terrific match that West Ham won 3–2. Even so, I reckon that if Ron had known that I'd been instrumental in Geoff's move to Stoke, I wouldn't have received a Christmas card from him that year.

Geoff and Judith settled well in the West Midlands, moving into a lovely detached bungalow set in five acres complete with stables in the small village of Madeley. Geoff's Stoke and England teammate Gordon Banks lived close by in the same village with his wife Ursula and their three children. Sylvia and I met up with them all during my trips to the Potteries to see Stoke in action.

With a world-class striker now in the side, Tony had high hopes of challenging the likes of Arsenal, Leeds and Liverpool for the Championship in 1972/73. However, the team got off to a bad start, especially on their travels, picking up just three league points on the road before Christmas. They were also knocked out of the UEFA Cup at the first-round stage in late September. I sat with Tony in the directors' box when Stoke beat Kaiserslautern 3–1 in the first leg at home and fully expected them to progress quite comfortably. However, their deficiencies away from home were cruelly exposed in the second leg, and the then unknown West Germans won 4–0.

Worse was to come for Stoke when Gordon Banks was involved in a car accident, from which the England 'keeper tragically lost the sight in his right eye. It was a devastating blow. Banksy tried to make a comeback, but after six months' training decided that it was impossible for him to play again at the top level. When Tony called me to tell me of Gordon's decision, I was gutted. Aged 34, Gordon was at his peak and had been named the Football Writers' Association Footballer of the Year only a few months before his accident. Not long after his decision to retire, I helped organise a testimonial match and dinner for him. It was the least I could do for a great goalkeeper and a great man.

Despite the loss of Gordon Banks, Stoke still managed to finish 15th that season, with Geoff scoring 13 goals in 43 competitive appearances. It was a decent return considering it was his first season at a new club, and had gone down with pneumonia after playing with a heavy cold over the Christmas period.

For the campaign of 1973/74, The Football League opted

to change the number of teams to be promoted and relegated, from two to three. It was clear that Tony Waddington would have to strengthen his squad if Stoke were to avoid another relegation battle. By Christmas, the Potters occupied a place in the bottom five, just three points ahead of rock-bottom West Ham, who were obviously missing Geoff Hurst's contribution in the 'goals for' column of their stats. In January, Tony telephoned me to ask for an opinion on 22-year-old Chelsea midfielder Alan Hudson. 'Huddy' and teammate Peter Osgood had been placed on the transfer list by Dave Sexton after refusing to train, having been dropped by the Chelsea boss.

"What do you reckon on Alan Hudson, Morris?"

"Smashing player. If Alf Ramsey manages to keep his job after that debacle against Poland, then he should think about building the England team around him. I rate him that highly."

"We're on the same wavelength Morris. I can't understand why he hasn't won an England cap yet. I'd need to get him to concentrate on his football though. Away from London's bright lights, I reckon there's a good chance of that."

"I've heard he likes a beer. He and Peter Osgood are great pals and the pair of them certainly know how to enjoy themselves."

"I must admit, I wouldn't mind having Ossie at Stoke too."

"Well, they're both great players and I bet they wouldn't come cheap. Of the two, I'd say Hudson would make the greater impact. You could really do with a creative, attacking midfielder of his calibre. You already have Geoff Hurst doing the business up front, so I can't see that you need Ossie, to be truthful. Finding someone to keep Huddy on the straight and narrow is the key to him being successful at Stoke."

"I agree Morris. I'm going to sleep on it. As always, thanks for your opinion."

One week later, Tony Waddington snapped up Hudson for a then staggering £240,000, which more than doubled the club record fee paid by Stoke. Soon afterwards, Judith Hurst revealed to my wife that Alan Hudson had moved into their home in Madeley. The Hursts had a lodger and I thought to myself, "Waddo's pulled a masterstroke there". With Geoff and Judith keeping an eye on the youngster, Stoke got the best out of their new signing. I travelled up to Staffordshire on a Sunday, to watch Alan Hudson's second home game for his new club. The match, against his old club Chelsea, was the first-ever top-flight game to be played on a Sunday. It was memorable one, with Alan putting in a superb performance and winning an 81st-minute penalty, from which Geoff converted to give Stoke a 1–0 victory.

With Hudson pulling the strings in midfield, Stoke rapidly climbed the table in the second half of the 73/74 season, ending the campaign in fifth place. It was the highest league finish that Geoff Hurst had ever experienced, having only managed eighth spot during his 13 seasons in West Ham's first team. It also earned Stoke a place in the UEFA Cup the next season. I watched them draw 1–1 at home against Ajax, before being invited by Stoke's directors to travel with them to Amsterdam for the second leg. The match ended goalless and the Potters went out on the away-goals rule. It was another missed opportunity for Stoke in Europe, but at home they were genuine title contenders. Tony Waddington signed England goalkeeper Peter Shilton from Leicester in November 1974. The signing tightened them up at the back and as a result they topped the table in late February 1975. With three matches of the 1974/75 season to go, the bookies made Stoke favourites to win the title, but a damaging defeat against Sheffield United followed by draws against Newcastle and Burnley saw them finish fifth, just four points behind champions Derby County and two behind the runners-up Liverpool. They also missed out on a UEFA Cup place by one point. I rang Tony to commiserate.

"Hats off to Derby, they stayed cool and got the results whilst everyone around them buckled under the pressure," reasoned Tony, doing his best not to sound too downhearted.

"It's tough at the top, but at least you're at the right end of the table," I said.

"Yeah I know. You must be relieved that Spurs stayed up."

"You're not wrong there. I was convinced that when Alfie Conn sat on the ball, Leeds would take umbrage and send us down. In truth, if it hadn't have been for Jennings we'd have been down by Christmas."

"Funny you should mention Jennings, I could do with borrowing him for a week."

"Really? How come?"

"We're off on tour to Indonesia and Shilton can't make it. He made other commitments before the tour was arranged. The thing is we've promised our tour sponsors that we'll be bringing along our star players. They're parting with big bucks to get us over there and we need to take some internationals."

"Shall I have a word with Pat?"

"If you don't mind. Tell him we'll make it worth his while."

I called Big Pat and put the question to him. He was apprehensive, as he didn't want the Spurs supporters to think he was being disloyal. I told him that I doubted the press would even hear about it, as Fleet Street's finest didn't often travel overseas to report on friendly tour matches in those days.

"I'll do my best to keep it a secret," I said and then revealed to Pat what Stoke were willing to pay him for his services out of season.

"It's too good to turn down. Count me in," he said. The wheels were set in motion. Tony got the OK from Spurs boss Terry Neill, who was only too pleased to make Pat available. I'm sure Bill Nicholson wouldn't have entertained the idea if he'd still been in charge.

On his arrival home after the tour, Pat called me at home.

"Thanks Morris. I don't think I've ever been on such a happy tour." He explained that his enjoyment was all down to the relationship Stoke's directors had with the players.

"At Stoke, there's no them-and-us divide like at Spurs. The directors treated the players on equal terms and the chairman is always the first at the bar. When you compare it to the trip I made with Spurs last year, it was worlds apart."

Pat had told me that when Spurs toured Mauritius in 1974, there was a great deal of resentment towards the directors after the players had been left with a bill of £400 for drinks they'd had with their meals. Alan Gilzean, who was on his last tour with the club, having decided to hang up his boots, was so incensed at the directors' mean attitude that he offered to sign a cheque there and then. The team refused to allow this and instead placed a £40 bet at a local bookmakers that they'd win the final tour match 6–0. The odds were 10–1, so if they managed it they'd have had the money to pay the drinks bill. Pat said that he'd never felt under more pressure to keep a clean sheet, but with the score at 5–0 the home keeper began to pull off some remarkable saves. It wasn't until the 89th minute that the sixth was duly converted and the players celebrated like they'd just beaten the Arsenal 6–0. Gilzean scored three of the six goals in his final game for the club and was carried off the pitch by his jubilant teammates.

It was interesting listening to Pat's reasons for why the trip with Stoke had been so enjoyable. I agreed with his sentiments and told him that was why I got on so well with Tony Waddington and the directors at Stoke.

"They're down-to-earth people, not standoffish like our lot." I warned him though, "Don't go getting any ideas about jumping ship and joining Stoke. We need you at Spurs." As far as I know, news of Jennings's loan to Stoke never made the national newspapers. Two years later, and after making almost 600 competitive appearances for Tottenham, Terry Neill's successor Keith Burkinshaw sold Jennings to arch-rivals Arsenal. It was a deal that rocked the very foundations of North London and it broke my heart to see Pat leave. I remember looking at the cover of the first match programme of the 1977/78 season, and seeing 32-year-old Pat standing in line with the rest of the players modelling the club's new Admiral kit. I was dumbfounded that Burkinshaw had sold him, only a year after Pat had been named the PFA's Players' Player of the Year. It took a while before I got used to the fact that he'd gone. At the time, I think Pat would have preferred to have joined Ipswich. Bobby Robson was keen to sign him on a two-year deal, but Ipswich striker Trevor Whymark broke his leg during a pre-season game in Holland and Robson's priorities changed.

Three years after Keith Burkinshaw allowed Pat to leave, I got my chance to quiz him about his decision. Spurs were playing Nottingham Forest on the opening day of the 1980/81 season and ITV's *Big Match* were there to cover it for their Sunday broadcast. These were the days before Sky Sports and before league football was transmitted live. Jimmy Hill, who worked as an analyst on the programme, called me up and told me that he'd introduced a new five-minute feature called 'Fan Interviews the Manager' and asked me if I'd interview Keith. I agreed and knew exactly what would be my first question to the Tottenham boss. However, before they began filming me walking across the pitch with Keith, he made it abundantly clear that I wasn't to ask him any leading questions. I nodded, and off we strolled across the turf with the cameras rolling. As we walked, I expressed my disappointment and surprise at Brian Clough's defensive tactics, but pleasure at seeing Spurs win 2–0. As we hit the centre circle, I turned and said, "By the way Keith, every Spurs fan would like to know why you sold Pat Jennings."

Keith reacted brilliantly. He kept cool and stayed professional and explained that with Barry Daines and Mark Kendall coming through the ranks, he thought it was the right time to let Pat go. After Keith's reply, I added, "But why to the Arsenal? We hate them you know!" He smiled and the cameras stopped rolling. When the interview was broadcast on the Sunday, it was cut to just two minutes from the allotted five-minute slot, as the programme needed three minutes to report on a fire overnight at Bristol Rovers' Eastville Stadium. However, they kept in my question about Pat's sale to Arsenal. In the end, I wished they hadn't. For the next few days I received an endless stream of abusive phone calls from Arsenal fans at all times of the day and night. It got so bad that I had to think of something to stop them. One night when the phone rang, I allowed the person to finish the tirade of abuse and then shouted, "Operator, connect". I think it made the caller believe I was asking the operator to trace the call for the police. Thankfully, the abusive calls ended after that.

Pat's transfer to Arsenal ended up being a good move for him. He played on for another eight years, helping the Gunners to reach three successive FA Cup finals in 1978, 1979 and 1980, winning the second one. He returned to Tottenham during the 1985/86 season to act as first-team cover for Ray Clemence, and to hone his fitness before representing Northern Ireland at the World Cup in Mexico. He played just one more first-team game for Spurs, against Liverpool in the

Screen Sport Super Cup, the competition contested by clubs who would have qualified for Europe, but for the ban following the Heysel Stadium Disaster. Needless to say, I was one of only 10,078 people who paid to see Pat don a Spurs shirt for a final time. Today, Pat works as a goalkeeping consultant at Tottenham and on match days in the hospitality suite at White Hart Lane. He is Tottenham through and through. I try to forget that he ever played for Arsenal; maybe he does too?

Sadly for Stoke, it went all downhill after that tour to Indonesia. Geoff Hurst left for Second Division West Brom that summer. The roof then blew off the Butler Stand at the Victoria Ground during a violent storm in January 1976 and with a repair bill of almost £250,000 the club hit financial trouble. Alan Hudson was sold to Arsenal for £200,000 in December 1976, where he replaced Alan Ball in the Gunners' midfield. Three months later, on 22nd March, 1977, Tony Waddington, then the First Division's longest serving manager, resigned with Stoke struggling in the bottom half of the table. George Eastham took over as caretaker manager, but he couldn't halt the club's slide in 1976/77, the season I refer to as my 'Annus horribilis'. Like Stoke, my beloved Spurs were also relegated to the Second Division the same year.

My friendship with both Tony and Geoff outlived their Stoke careers. Tony continued to seek out my advice when he managed Crewe between 1979/1981, signing former Spurs defender Phil Beal on my recommendation. We remained friends until his death in 1994 and I miss him greatly. Geoff and me are still good mates today, and I was honoured when he invited Sylvia and I to join his celebratory dinner when he was awarded a knighthood in 1998. I feel privileged to have played a small part in his career through that secret meeting in my flat in 1972 during the glorious Waddington years at Stoke City.

FRIENDLY TRIPS

"Morris is certainly the biggest football supporter I've ever come across. We've travelled all over the globe together with Spurs and England. We've enjoyed many laughs and even shed a few tears along the way."
Alan Mullery MBE (Spurs and England, UEFA Cup winner 1972)

"Although Morris is and was consumed with football, and was well known by many other boards and directors, his love of Tottenham Hotspur was all-consuming. A very generous man and friend to all of us."
Phil Beal (Spurs, League Cup winner 1971 and 1973)

I would never think twice before leaving my wife, kids and business to look after themselves and jetting off to some foreign land to watch my beloved Spurs play a meaningless friendly match against a team I'd probably never even heard of. The highlights of these trips were seldom the matches themselves, but more the chances to mix with the players, as they took the chance to enjoy themselves without the pressure of a high-stake match to grapple with.

Losing My Religion

In November 1962, Spurs boss Bill Nicholson arranged a trip to Egypt with the aim of keeping the team's spirits high and boosting morale ahead of an important European Cup Winners' Cup game against Scottish giants Rangers. I was desperate to join them on their four-day trip, as I'd been stationed in Egypt during my Army days and wanted to show them around my old stomping ground. The only thing stopping me was my religion, as being Jewish I was banned from entering Egypt during what was a very sensitive time in the Middle East. Undeterred, I applied for an entry visa and when filling out the form wrote 'Church of England' in the box marked religion. My application was accepted and I joined Nicholson and the players on the 2,200-mile flight to Cairo.

When we arrived, I booked myself into the the Nile Hilton, the same hotel as the team, and at breakfast the first morning told my mates Greavsie and Bobby Smith about my little white lie. They found it highly amusing and the next day, when I came down for breakfast, they greeted my arrival by calling out "Shalom," which of course means "Hello" in Hebrew. When Bill Nicholson got wind of their little joke, he started to worry and asked them to be careful not to upset their Egyptian hosts. His consternation only encouraged them more, and by the third day, the entire squad were in on it; I was greeted with an ever-louder chorus of "Shalom" each morning, as the players pushed Bill to the brink. By the end of the trip, I think he was convinced the players had caused a diplomatic incident and we'd need to contact the British Embassy to get a safe passage home.

The day before the team's friendly against the then Egyptian Cup holders, Zamalek, the club organised a day trip to the pyramids. Bobby Smith had told me to jump on the team bus and hitch a lift with them, but I always preferred to keep my distance from the club's officials, as I was after all only a supporter.

"It's OK Bob. The directors are with you and they won't like me intruding."

"Don't be bloody stupid. Get on."

"Nah. I'll see you there."

"If you won't come with us, then we're coming with you!" he said, before hurtling towards the front of the bus and jumping off, just as it started to pull away. Following closely behind were Ron Henry and Terry Medwin. The trio ran towards the taxi I'd just hailed and all three then jumped into the back of the Mercedes-Benz 180 Ponton.

"To the pyramids and step on it. Quick, quick, fast, fast,

we must beat that bus," said Smithy pointing at the team bus, which was by now pulling away into the distance. That 40-minute journey was the most terrifying of my life. The driver sped off at 80mph and proceeded to weave in and out of the busy traffic like Stirling Moss at the Monte Carlo Rally. I lost count of the number of times we almost went into the back of the car in front. Even when we overtook the team bus, waving at an unimpressed Bill Nicholson as we did so, the driver continued to travel at breakneck speed.

"You can slow down now," said a worried-looking Terry. But the taxi driver didn't take any notice, and just kept his foot to the floor.

"You're bloody mad," said Smithy, when we arrived at Giza with our hearts still in our mouths and each close to requiring a new pair of underpants.

"You could have killed us," screeched Ron. Needless to say, we arrived at the Great Sphinx long before the rest of the party. When they caught us up, I organised camel rides for the players and some of the touring party had their picture taken riding them in front of the Pyramid of Khafre. It appeared in the home match programme a few weeks later. It wasn't the only picture from that trip to make a Spurs publication. A photo was also published in Dennis Signy's Tottenham Hotspur Football Book of myself, team captain Danny Blanchflower, goalkeeper Bill Brown, winger Terry Medwin and renowned *Daily Express* sports reporter Desmond Hackett sitting around a table with the staff at the Nile Hilton. Desmond wasn't the only journalist reporting on Tottenham's trip to Cairo: Peter Lorenzo of the *Daily Herald* was another, who like Desmond stopped off on their way to the Commonwealth Games in Perth, Australia. I remember one of their stories ran with the headline, 'EGYPT – YOU'VE GOT THE PYRAMIDS, BUT WE'VE GOT SPURS'.

At the Zamelek match the next day, I was one of only a handful of Tottenham fans in the 60,000 crowd. It was an entertaining 7–3 victory for the tourists, with substitute Terry Dyson replacing Cliff Jones and scoring twice. As I stood up and cheered Dyson's second goal, a local sitting in front of me turned round and said in English: "What kind of manager puts their best player on the bench!" I think Terry was quite pleased when I told him about that, but I didn't dare tell Bill! That night, I took a few of the lads to the Sahara City nightclub to celebrate the end of the winning trip. I've still got a picture of Greavsie and me standing outside the club smiling for the camera. Of course, in truth, I never should have been there, but I've always been against politics or religion interfering with sport. On my arrival home, a newspaper published the story about my trip under the headline 'JEW DEFIES NASSER TO SEE SPURS', Nasser being the Egyptian president at the time. It's probably the story that's been told the most about me by the old pros in their autobiographies.

When the Players Got Arrested

My mate Greavsie had just notched up his 100th league goal for Spurs, when Bill Nicholson decided to take the team to Denmark to play a friendly ahead of a tough fixture at Old Trafford that weekend. The side had struggled away from home at the start of that 1964/65 season, losing three out of four games, and my spies (the players) told me that Nicholson believed a midweek game would be good preparation before facing the likes of Charlton, Best and Law. He also felt it might lift the players' spirits, after captain Dave Mackay had broken his leg for a second time in his comeback game against Shrewsbury Town's reserves. Little did Nicholson know, that the trip was to put him dangerously close to having to field the reserves against Manchester United, after four players were arrested by Danish police following an incident involving my hot-headed mate Mick O'Shea.

Mick didn't like football much. In fact, I think the only sport he liked was boxing. He was a very good boxer, a real tough guy. No one messed with Mick O'Shea. Now and again, he'd join me on my jaunts to see Spurs, but only rarely would he go to the game. He'd prefer to sit in a pub during the match and meet me for a few beers afterwards. That's what happened on this trip. While I watched Nicholson's big match preparations end in a disappointing 2–1 defeat against a Copenhagen select side, Mick was making himself at home in a bar opposite the City Hall. After the match, I returned to my hotel, where the team were also staying. I spruced myself up and told Jimmy Greaves where I was going to meet Mick and asked him to join me if he fancied a social drink.

"We're under orders from Bill not to get back too late as the flight leaves early tomorrow morning, but I dare say a few of the lads will come along," said Greavsie. As it turned out, the entire team showed up at the bar, where many of the Danish footballers that had played in the match were also drinking. At about 11pm, one of them suggested that the Spurs contingent join them at a nightclub across the road. After an impromptu team meeting conducted by Alan Mullery, half of the lads decided to call it a night and returned to the hotel and the rest followed Mick and myself over to the nightclub. By this time, Mick had downed quite a few pints, but he could always take his drink so I wasn't too worried about him. At the nightclub, the time soon raced away, as we happily mixed with the locals and chatted to some gorgeous looking blondes. At about 1am, Cliff Jones suggested that we start making our way back.

"I'd like to get a few hours kip before breakfast and that 10am flight home. Who's coming with me?"

"I'm getting some moves going here!" yelled Greavsie from the dancefloor, but Cliff managed to coax him away and like dominoes, once one made the move the rest soon followed, except my mate Mick O'Shea.

"You're not going already are you boys?" he asked.

"Yeah. I've had enough for one night," said Ron Henry.

"Me too. And it will take more than one man to carry you home," I said to Mick, grabbing his arm and helping him down the stairs.

"I'm alright. I'll run over the road and get us a couple of taxis," said Mick, before making a dash for the nearest taxi rank in a drunken zig-zag. We watched him cross the road and laughed at the spectacle.

"He'll get run over if he doesn't watch himself. I'll catch him up," said a concerned Cliff Jones. He did indeed catch him up and we watched in horror as Cliff just managed to pull

Mick out of the way of an oncoming taxi. As the vehicle came to a sudden stop, Mick leaned through the window and asked the driver to take them to the hotel.

"Sorry Sir. I'm busy," he replied. For some drunken reason, Mick took offence, and gave an almighty kick to the driver's side door, putting a huge dent in it. The cabbie, as you'd expect, was livid, and let rip with a stream of furious, rude-sounding Danish words.

"You can get stuffed," slurred Mick to the irate driver, before threatening to kick another nice dent in what looked like a brand new car.

"Come on Mick, let's go," I said, leading him by the arm away from the confrontation. The rest of the lads, who included the club's new signing Cyril Knowles, helped me drag him away. We continued on our way through City Hall Square and headed towards another taxi rank. As we walked, the sound of car horns began coming from all directions. The noise became louder and louder and we soon realised that the noise was coming from a fleet of about 20 taxis, all of which seemed to be circling the paved square. As we continued our march towards the road, we watched as one by one they screeched to a halt and blocked our exit. We were hemmed in like sheep in a pen. Before long, a black police van appeared with its blue lights flashing and six policemen piled out of it.

"Stop where you are!" said one of them in English.

"Which one of you kicked the taxi back there?" He was greeted with a wall of silence.

"If we don't get an answer, you'll all be spending the night in the cells. Who was it?" Everyone stood together and like teammates on the field of play, not one was willing to buckle under the pressure and grass on our stupid mate. It was up to Mick to come clean, but he just looked at the floor and said nothing, probably because he could barely string a sentence together by then.

"OK. You're all arrested," the policeman said resignedly, and with that each copper grabbed hold of the nearest suspect and forced them into the back of the police van.

"Bloody hell Mick. We've got a plane to catch in eight

hours. If this lot aren't on it, Bill Nicholson's going to hit the roof and dock them a week's wages."

"Sorry lads. I didn't think they'd throw us in the van that quick!" said Mick, who had suddenly sobered up at the prospect of a night in a foreign police cell. "I'll come clean when we get to the cop shop and hopefully they'll let you go straight away."

When we arrived, Mick immediately confessed to the police chief.

"I kicked the dent in the car because he tried to run me over," pointing at the taxi driver who had followed us to the police station to pick the culprit out of a line-up that included Jimmy Greaves, Cliff Jones, Cyril Knowles and Ron Henry – four of Tottenham's greatest players!

The police chief certainly didn't believe drunken Mick's accusation and after some sobering compensation talks, Mick handed over a wad of cash to the taxi driver, much of it borrowed from his supposed partners in crime. Greavsie cheekily asked the 'victim' if he'd give us a lift back to our hotel, but his reply was riddled with English expletives.

It was almost 6am when our heads finally hit the pillow back at the hotel. Fearful of Bill's Nicholson's wrath, the players still managed to drag themselves out of bed to make the manager's 7am breakfast roll call. For once, though, Nicholson hadn't got wind of what the players had got up to on their night out. Everyone was certainly relieved about that, as it wouldn't have made good reading back home if the press had got hold of the story about the players' trip in the Black Maria, or "Irish Mick's Paddywagon" as Greavsie called it. Today, it's the sort of story that would make the front page of the tabloids! There were definitely some weary and relieved footballers on that flight back home.

The Trip to the Bar Mitzvah

Three weeks after beating Burnley in the 1962 FA Cup final, Spurs made their first ever trip to Israel. When I found out that my good mate Jimmy Greaves wouldn't be going, I decided not to accompany them. Greavsie was in Chile preparing for the World Cup finals with England. Cliff Jones and Mel Hopkins were other notable absentees on the flight to Tel Aviv that year, as they were representing Wales on tour in South America. Tottenham's Scottish contingent of Bill Brown, Dave Mackay and John White went along, following Scotland's failure to beat Czechoslovakia in a World Cup play-off in neutral Belgium. Sadly, by the time Spurs made their second trip to Israel in 1965, John White was dead, having been struck by lightning when out playing golf.

John was very much in everyone's thoughts when I joined the touring party on the second visit. A memorial match had been played between Spurs and a Scotland XI during that season and our Israeli hosts were keen to remember the man who had been in the Spurs side that had thrilled the crowds three years earlier. With the help of the Israeli FA, two games were organised for the touring Spurs team, the first against the newly crowned Israeli league champions Hakoah and the second against Maccabi Tel Aviv, for which a cup named in John's honour would be contested.

The Israeli national team manager Joe Mirmovich acted as our guide and fixer during the stay. Nothing was ever too much trouble for Joe. A few years later, I took him to an Ipswich match and introduced him to Bobby Robson. They became good pals after that and Bobby told me a good story about the time he took the England team to Israel to play a friendly in Tel Aviv. It was in 1988 and Mirmovich had just finished a third spell in charge of the national side, but was helping out new Israeli manager Miljenko Mihic. Joe decided to go and watch England train before the game, although Bobby wasn't too impressed when he caught him making notes on England's set-play tactics. Bobby told Joe and an assistant, who was holding an umbrella to shelter him from the rain, to clear off. Bobby had to laugh though when Joe turned up a few hours before the match asking Bobby to go over his tactics again as his jotter got wet and he could no longer read the notes he'd made!

In the first of Spurs' two Israel matches, two goals from Greavsie and one by Cliff Jones earned the tourists a 3–1 victory over Hakoah in front of a sell-out 15,000 crowd. After the match, a distant relative of mine contacted me at the team hotel and told me that his friend's son was having a coming-of-age party the next day and invited me along. I accepted his invitation and then the real reason for his hospitality became clear.

"Of course, any of your Spurs friends would be welcome to join us". I was a bit uncomfortable asking the players, but felt I should give it a go. At breakfast the next morning I asked Greavsie, "Do you fancy coming along to a bar mitzvah?"

"Is there a bar at the mitzvah?" he joked.

"I'm sure there will be."

"Count me in," he said. By lunchtime, the word had spread and all the touring party had agreed to join us.

When the players arrived at the venue they were clapped and cheered as they got off the team coach and were led to their seats. At each table the host put a case of scotch, one bottle for each of the 14 players in the touring party. It was a costly gesture, as scotch in Israel wasn't easy to come by and very expensive. The players asked me to thank our hosts for the whisky but requested, if possible, that they replace it with a few crates of beer. I put their request to the host and ten minutes later a crate of Goldstar beer was brought to each table. Before long, the 'special guests' were out of their seats and dancing along to the sound of the Beach Boys. They certainly seemed to enjoy the occasion. Before leaving the party, the players raised their glasses and toasted our hosts and our recently departed friend John White. Two days later, Dave Mackay, back in the squad after two broken legs, lifted the John White Cup high in the air following a 3–2 win on a bone-hard pitch in the sweltering sun. Who would have believed that a bar mitzvah would be the best way to prepare for a football match!

Playing Away

When acting as the master of ceremonies at one of my functions, Jimmy Hill stood up and told the guests, "Morris is a lovely man, but you've got to feel sorry for his wife Sylvia. It's taken her five years to realise that a trip to Fulham isn't an overnight stay!" It's true that I was nearly always the last to leave any gathering after a game and one time it resulted in a long spell in the doghouse for me.

I'd spent the early summer of 1968 with my lovely wife on our second honeymoon in Italy. We'd hardly been on holiday together, just the two of us, since our first honeymoon 13 years earlier in rainy Torquay. Sylvia says she really enjoyed our time in Florence and Rome, although she would have preferred it if I'd hadn't dragged her off to watch England play in the Euro '68 Finals! We strolled hand in hand amongst Florence's Renaissance palaces and squares and visited the magnificent domed cathedral, the Santa Maria del Fiore, before watching England lose 1–0 against Yugoslavia. It was the game when Alan Mullery became the first England player ever to be sent off. Nobby Stiles replaced him for the next game in Rome, when England sealed third spot with a 2–0 win over the USSR. The tournament's final was played on the same pitch straight after the England game. Sylvia wasn't too pleased when I insisted that we sat through another 120 minutes of football, in which Italy and Yugoslavia drew 1–1 after extra time. Two days later, when I asked her if she'd like to return to the Stadio Olimpico for the replay, she threatened to throw me into the Trevi Fountain. Nevertheless, we returned home after our romantic getaway feeling very much in love.

Soon after we arrived home, the fixture list for the season ahead was published. To my delight, I discovered that Spurs were to kick off the 1968/69 campaign with a home game against the enemy, Arsenal. In anticipation of the big clash ahead and keen to see how the team were shaping up, I flew to Vienna where Spurs were playing FK Austria Wien in the their final warm-up game before the North London derby. I was hoping for a morale-boosting victory, but the Austrians scored twice in the closing minutes to earn a 2–2 draw. After the match, I tried to persuade Greavsie, Phil Beal and Terry Venables to join me at a nightclub for a couple of beers. However, they wisely declined my offer, saying they didn't want to upset manager Bill Nicholson a few days before the start of the season. I had no other option but to sample the nightlife on my own.

After visiting a few drinking establishments, I soon got the taste for the strong local beer, and by midnight I was propping up the bar of a busy nightclub. To cut a long, embarrassing, story short, one pretty young woman, who I'll call Heidi, although her real name has long been erased from my memory, took pity on me. She introduced herself and I told her that I was with Tottenham Hotspur, who had just played a football match that evening at the Prater Stadium. Over the course of the evening, some of our conversation must have got lost in translation, as she seemed to think that I was either the team's manager or the owner of the club. I could have put her right, but instead I went along with it and spent a pleasant, yet very regretful evening in her company. The following day, I caught my flight home, and to be honest, soon forgot about her and my evening of indiscretion, assuming she would do the same.

Two weeks later, the week after Spurs had suffered a 2–1 defeat against the Gunners, I was sitting in the stands at Goodison Park at half-time, happy with the 1–0 lead Greavsie had just given us, when a message went over the stadium's loud speaker.

"Would Mr Morris Keston of Tottenham Hotspur please contact the nearest steward." My heart skipped a few beats on hearing my name and I feared that something tragic might have happened back home. I made myself known and was taken to the ticket office, where an 'urgent call' was awaiting me.

"Hello. This is Mr Keston speaking."

"Hello. This is the Immigration Office at Harwich. We have a young Austrian woman here by the name of Heidi Feuerstein. Do you know her?" My blood ran cold.

"Er. I did meet a girl called Heidi a couple of weeks ago in Vienna."

"I see. Miss Feuerstein has this morning tried to enter the UK without any money. She says she's here because you are planning to get married."

"What? She must be on drugs!" I exclaimed. "I've already got one wife; I certainly don't want another one." I swear a snigger escaped from the official-sounding voice down the telephone.

"Would you like to explain that to her?"

"I'd rather not. You'd better put her on the next boat back," I said quickly.

"We can't do that. She doesn't have any money. May I suggest you do the decent thing and pay for her trip home." Most people would have told him and his 'decent suggestion' where to go, but at that moment, with Sylvia's stern face flashing through my mind, I would have chewed off my own arm to get her out of the country.

"I'll wire the funds to you straight away." With it being a Saturday afternoon, the banks were closed. It proved a bit problematic, but after a few panic-stricken phone calls the payment was sorted and Heidi was on her way home. On the pitch, Martin Chivers scored in the 81st minute to seal the win over Everton. It was a great victory, but it doesn't compare to my lucky result that day. About ten years later, I decided to come clean to Sylvia. After a few weeks of smoothing things over, all was forgiven.

"What would you have done if Heidi had arrived on the doorstep?" I asked.

"Arranged the wedding and made the sandwiches for the reception," Sylvia replied.

The Stewardesses and the Champagne

On my way home from Tottenham's end-of-season tour to Malta in 1970, I struck up conversation with a British Airways airhostess called Jean Loftus.

"Have you been on holiday?" she asked, as she poured me a coffee.

"No. I've been to watch Tottenham Hotspur play some matches, although I wish I hadn't bothered as we just got beaten by the Maltese."

"Sounds bad," she said. "Even I know Spurs shouldn't get beat by the minnows of Malta."

Jean and I continued to chat during her spare moments on the flight to London. I told her about my obsession with football and how I funded all my trips from the profits I made from my ladies' and gents' fashion business. Her ears pricked up on hearing that I had a warehouse in London's East End.

"Do you sell to the general public?" she asked.

"Yes and usually at trade price."

"I'm looking for an evening gown. I wonder if you'll have something for me?"

"I've a good range of gowns at varying prices. You should drop by and take a look."

Before I disembarked at Heathrow, I gave Jean my work number. A few weeks later she turned up at my showroom with the other trolley dollies from her crew, who were also eyeing a bargain. They all bought something and before long I had what seemed like BA's complete fleet of stewardesses buying from my warehouse. On one subsequent visit during the January sales, Jean asked if I was going to see England's European Nations Cup qualifying match against Malta. She told me that her flight crew had been assigned to take the England team and the British press on their return journey. I couldn't make the trip, but hatched a plan with Jean to impress my photographer mate Monte Fresco, who I knew would be on the flight.

The evening after England's paltry 1–0 win in Malta, which came courtesy of a Martin Peters goal, Monte called me at home. His first words when I answered the phone were, "Now that's what I call style." He then asked how I'd managed to organise the champagne delivery when I wasn't even on the flight.

"Simple. I met Jean, the airhostess, nine months ago when I went to see Spurs on tour in Malta. She told me she was flying the England team to Malta and I knew you'd be on the flight."

"Very clever. You should have seen the press guys' faces when Jean announced over the tannoy, 'Would a Mr Monte Fresco please make himself known to cabin staff. We have a bottle of Bollinger champagne for him, courtesy of Mr Morris Keston.' A few of the players who were sitting behind me quickly jumped up, raised their arms, and tried to claim it! I told them only beating Malta by one goal wasn't a champagne moment and drunk the whole bottle myself."

A few years later, I was also the recipient of a bottle of bubbly handed to me by a British Airways stewardess. I was flying from New York to London on Concorde when a flight attendant asked, "Have you been on holiday?"

"Yes. I've been to Atlantic City."

"Did you have a good time?"

"Yes, but I'm quite pleased to be on my way home as the football season gets underway next week." She asked which team I supported.

"Tottenham Hotspur. I go to the all the matches." She then stared at me and asked, "Are you Morris Keston?" Needless to say, I was surprised that she knew my name and asked her if we'd met before.

"No. We've never met, but your name often crops up around our dinner table. My father is Sidney Wale, the Tottenham Hotspur chairman." She then smiled and walked away. I turned to Sylvia and pulled a face.

"Don't eat the meal, she'll probably poison it," I whispered. A few minutes later, Sidney Wale's daughter returned clutching a bottle of champagne and said, "I'm sure my father would like you to have this with the compliments of Tottenham Hotspur. You've more than earned it being the club's best fan!" Bemused, I thanked her and asked her to pass on my gratitude to her father.

Flip-Flop Spurs

A few weeks after watching England crash out of the 1970 World Cup finals against West Germany in Mexico, I booked a beach holiday for Sylvia and the kids in Spain, where Spurs happened to be playing in a four-team pre-season tournament in Palma, Majorca. I think it was the only time I actually took the kids on a summer holiday, but with Palma's Lluis Sitjar stadium not too far from the beach, I realised I could easily leave them building sandcastles while I watched all four of the tournament's matches: it was an ideal family holiday!

The tournament was played over four days running from Thursday to Sunday, with just one match played each day.

FRIENDLY TRIPS

Before the first game kicked off, my mate Phil Beal, the Spurs defender, found me in the main stand and sat down. "The rest of the team will be over after the stadium announcer has introduced them to the crowd."

"Don't you want to be introduced?" I asked, smiling.

"I'd rather get a good seat for the game," he said.

The stadium announcer spent 15 minutes whipping the crowd up to an excited crescendo, speaking in Spanish and then translating everything into English and then German on his way.

"Is this tournament ever going to get underway?" I asked Phil.

"Looks like I made the right choice. Chivers is bound to be moaning by now at being kept hanging around."

Atlètico Madrid were the first side to be introduced. Being the only Spanish side in the tournament, they received a huge cheer when they walked on to the pitch wearing their tracksuits and looking ready for the first game. Their opponents, CSKA Sofia of Bulgaria, then entered from the opposite corner and took a bow. They too were dressed in their tracksuits and looked the part. Next up were German side FC Cologne, who were due to play Spurs in the second game the next day. They walked on to the pitch wearing smart suits and club ties, and were given an enthusiastic welcoming cheer by the excitable crowd.

"And finally Tottenham Hotspur of England!" With all eyes fixed on the final corner of the ground, the sight that greeted me, and the rest of the 10,000 spectators there, left everyone in fits of laugher. On to the pitch walked Spurs skipper Alan Mullery wearing a multicoloured T-shirt, shorts and flip-flops. Behind him followed Martin Peters, Pat Jennings, Steve Perryman, Alan Gilzean, Mike England, Martin Chivers and the rest of the squad in the same mix-match assortment of beachwear. A few of them were even wearing swimming trunks!

"What do they look like?"

"Now you know why I was so keen to sit with you!" said Phil, laughing. The team smiled and waved to the hysterical crowd before quickly flip-flopping away from the embarrassing scene. Five minutes later, the players came and sat down next to us in the main stand.

"We didn't know we were going to be introduced to the crowd," protested Mullery.

"Typical of the Germans to upstage us like that," said Peters, who was probably still smarting after being dumped out of the World Cup two months earlier.

"I can't wait to stuff 'em tomorrow," he added.

The opening match between Atlètico Madrid and CSKA Sofia ended in a 2–0 victory for the Bulgarians, with the Spaniards having a man sent off in the second half. At the time, I probably thought that seeing a player dismissed in a friendly was unusual. The next day though, I saw two more, and both of them were flip-flop wearers!

FC Cologne had midfielder Wolfgang Overath in their ranks, who was probably one of the best midfielders in the world at the time. He really took the mickey that day with Spurs spending most of the game chasing shadows after going one behind. It was all too much for left back Cyril Knowles, who received his marching orders after one wild tackle. Martin Peters followed soon afterwards, scything down playmaker Overath with a reckless challenge. The Germans coasted for the remainder of the match and booked their place in the tournament's final. After the game, I called my sports writer mate Reg Drury in London and told him about Tottenham's double sending-off. Back in the seventies, pre-season friend-lies rarely stirred up any interest in Fleet Street. You'd be lucky to find any sports reporters bothering to register one being played abroad, but I guessed that Martin Peters's sending off against the Germans, so soon after he'd played in England's 3–2 defeat, was a story worth reporting. Reg certainly agreed with me and ran an exclusive in the *News of the World* the next day.

Despite their dismissals, Peters and Knowles still played in Tottenham's tussle with Atlètico Madrid in the following match. However, their appearance wasn't enough to prevent Spurs taking home the wooden spoon, with the Spaniards winning 1–0. The tournament's X-rated certificate was confirmed in the final, when the Bulgarians and Germans went to war resulting in four players receiving red cards as both teams finished the game with nine men. CSKA Sofia edged the final 2–1, but I think Cologne dished out the nastier tackles. I was just glad that I hadn't taken the family along to see it!

Elton John in Italy

Although not a friendly trip with Spurs, I can't let this story go unheard as it's one of my favourites. In June 1976, my great friend Ted Croker, the FA Secretary, organised for me to travel with the British Press pack to Italy for a World Cup qualifying game. It was during Don Revie's short reign as England manager. On arriving at Rome Airport, I boarded a coach that Ted had arranged to take me, and Fleet Street's finest, to the Stadio Olimpico. As I worked my way down the coach, I spotted a familiar figure lying across the back seats.

"Bloody hell, it's Elton John," said Monte Fresco, my travelling campanion.

"Budge up Elton, we want to sit down," I said.

"Can't you sit somewhere else? I don't want any fans to spot me through the window."

"All the seats are taken," replied Monte.

"Yeah. Come on Captain Fantastic. Shift your bum," I added, laughing.

"If I get mobbed then it's your fault," replied the Rocket Man.

"If you don't want to be noticed, why are you wearing those ridiculous glasses?" asked Monte.

"And those multicoloured trousers and floppy hat," I added.

Elton smiled.

"Good point gentlemen."

Elton John was a big star back then in 1976, as big as he is today. He'd had six number-one albums in America and a few months earlier had just had his first number-one single in the UK – *Don't Go Breaking My Heart* with Kiki Dee. The song had been a huge hit all over the world, including in Italy, where he'd also had a number-one album. As the coach got nearer the stadium, Elton sunk further and further into his seat, and then suddenly he yelled out, "Shit! I've been spotted."

"By who?" said Monte.

"Over there," replied Elton, pointing out of the window.

"By that old lady! Don't be daft, She's too old to know who you are," laughed Monte.

"You're paranoid Elton. No one's gonna expect to see you at a football match. Stop fretting," I added. As I said that, the driver slammed on the brakes and the coach came to a sudden halt. He then yelled,

"All out! You'll have to walk the last half mile – the road's blocked." With that, Elton shouted back, "I can't walk! I'll never make it to the ground alive!" Everyone laughed. Monte and I grabbed Elton's arm and told him to walk in between us.

"You'll be alright, just keep your head down," I said. We then proceeded to walk at a normal pace towards the stadium. We passed hundreds of Italians during the ten-minute stroll to the ground and even more on the way back to the coach after England's 2–0 defeat – not one person batted an eyelid. He didn't even sign one autograph!

"THE KING OF VEGAS"

"Dear Sylvia. I saw Morris here, but where were you?"
Frank Sinatra (1915–98, legendary singer and Oscar winner)

"I was so excited before meeting Frank Sinatra, but when I finally did I wished the ground had just swallowed me up."
Sylvia Keston

I have always had the capacity to make long-lasting friendships wherever I've been, whether it's been in football, business and even on my annual summer holiday. One such friendship that I made in America even opened the doors to a celebrity world I'd never imagined possible for an ordinary Londoner like me.

I will never forget the time on one such summer holiday when a concierge staff member from Caesars Palace greeted me in the arrivals lounge at Los Angeles International Airport with the words, "Welcome to America Mr Keston. We've borrowed Frank Sinatra's plane to fly you to Vegas. Come with me and I'll take you to Lady Barbara." He grabbed my suitcase and I eagerly followed him to a secluded area off the main airstrip. I hate flying, so ordinarily the prospect of taking a trip on a small plane would have made me feel quite queasy, but instead my heart was pounding with excitement at the thought of meeting Frank Sinatra's wife, Barbara. Upon approaching the $2 million Learjet the penny finally dropped and I realised Mrs Sinatra wouldn't be accompanying me on the flight that day. The plane was called *Lady Barbara*!

I nervously laughed off the disappointment and started to hum the words to *Come Fly With Me* to calm my nerves.

"It's just you and the pilot Mr Keston. Make yourself at home. You'll find some of Mr Sinatra's favourite whiskies in the drinks cabinet. Enjoy the flight."

I sat back in one of the eight cream leather chairs and poured myself a Seagrams VO, before excitedly bursting into song as the pilot taxied to the runway.

"Come fly with me, let's fly, let's fly away. If you can use some exotic booze, there's a bar in far Bombay." It was the only time in all my years of flying that I didn't feel the urge to run to the nearest exit just before take-off. Once in the air, I looked around the cabin and tried to guess which A-list celebrities 'the Chairman of the Board' might have entertained in the plane's cabin. Dean Martin? Sammy Davis Jr? Liza Minnelli? Tom Jones? Elvis Presley? The list was endless. I chuckled at the thought of what my friends might say if they could see me with my feet up clearing out Sinatra's drinks cabinet. Bobby Moore had called me 'the King of Vegas', after experiencing one of the luxurious trips laid on for me, and my friends, one summer. I certainly felt like Hollywood royalty on that flight and wondered whether Sylvia would ever forgive me for asking her to stay at home and look after our teenage children who were about to take their exams.

It was all a far cry from my first trip to the entertainment capital of the world, when Sylvia and I couldn't wait to leave: we stayed for just two days! The thing is, back then there was no such thing as the Internet and no way of booking tickets for shows in advance. On arriving at the Strip during that ill-fated first visit in 1967, I headed straight for the Sands Hotel. At the time, it was the only hotel I'd heard of in Vegas, having read in my newspaper during the journey that philanthropist Howard Hughes had just paid $14m for it. I discovered that every one of its 700 rooms were already taken and we subsequently spent the first day of our holiday trying to find somewhere else to stay, eventually settling for the last bed available at the Riviera. I spent the next day trying to book tickets for a top show, but couldn't get a ticket for Andy Williams or Sinatra for love nor money. In the end, we had to settle for one night in the company of country singer Patti Page, and even then we were sat behind a pillar at the back of the theatre.

We left Vegas the very next morning. I remember telling Sylvia on the flight home, "I'd rather spend two weeks at Margate than go back there." A few months after our disappointing holiday, motorcycle daredevil Evil Knievel crashed attempting to jump the fountains at Caesars Palace. He crushed his pelvis and femur, fractured his hip, wrist and both ankles and put himself in a coma for 28 days. I'm sure that after that, Evil Knievel was the only man who hated Vegas more than me!

My feelings towards the place changed two years later, when a friend of mine persuaded me to give the resort another go. He was a Vegas regular, and told me that he'd become friends with Mr William Weinberger, who was the new president of Caesars Palace. I did the sensible thing this time, and booked a room in advance, but Sylvia didn't have any faith in my contact coming up trumps and chose to stay at home instead of joining me on the trip. After booking into Caesars, I sought out Weinberger and arranged to meet him for a few drinks in the casino; it wasn't unusual for Billy, as I came to know him, to have one-to-ones with his guests. He was famous for his personal touch – something that kept the gamblers coming back. Billy was almost 20 years older than me, yet we struck up an instant friendship that became much deeper than the usual, fairly superficial, business relationships he had with the majority of his regular visitors. After a couple of whiskies, we had even made plans for him and his wife, Jean, to visit me and Sylvia in London that autumn. We had clicked instantly, and as a result he gave me the royal treatment on that holiday, and would continue to do so over the next 15 years, as I became a regular on the Vegas scene and one of Billy's closest friends.

During the seventies, Caesars was the favoured gambling spot for high rollers and Billy was without doubt the best casino host around. He worked 14-hour days six days a week, knew all of the big gamblers by name and would make sure they enjoyed their stay. Billy insisted that I got treated to the same luxuries freely given to the millionaires who thought nothing of losing $50,000 in one afternoon at the tables. Not only that, but Billy was happy for me to invite my own friends to join me on my trips. We rarely paid for anything during our stays at Caesars.

The first of my friends to come to Vegas was racing driver

Stirling Moss, who joined us for a few days in July 1975. Stirling was in LA testing the new Cadillac Seville for a motor magazine, when I rang him up and asked if he fancied ending his trip to the States with a few nights at Caesars. Frank Sinatra was due to perform that weekend and Stirling raced over in time for the show. On his arrival, I introduced the British racing legend to Billy, who revealed that Frank Sinatra wanted to meet us for drinks that evening.

"Frank's a big fan of motor sport, and I believe Stirling's his favourite driver!"

"That's nice to know. I'm now doubly pleased you called me up Morris," said Stirling with a broad smile.

As you can imagine, Sylvia was beyond herself with excitement when I told her that we were going to meet Ol' Blues Eyes for drinks. She spent the entire afternoon in our hotel room getting ready and wore her best dress for the occasion. I remember the glamourous little number had over 20 buttons going down the middle of it. Sylvia was so excited that when she put the dress on she did the buttons up in the wrong order, so it looked lop-sided. When the buttons were finally in the correct holes, we made our way down to an area of the bar that Billy had roped off just for Sinatra and a few of his friends. He didn't like being constantly bothered by fans, but that didn't stop Sylvia.

"Hurry up you lot. Let's go and join Frank Sinatra for a drink."

"Hang on Sylvia," I said. "It may be roped off for a reason. There are a few heavies either side of him and they are probably carrying guns. Let's wait for Billy to introduce us."

"I can't wait for Billy and those big chaps wouldn't dare touch me." With that she lifted the ropes, blew the guards a kiss and made a beeline for Sinatra. I covered my eyes, before walking away in embarrassment in search of Stirling, who I found in a neighbouring bar signing autographs. When he'd finished penning his name to well-wishers, we walked over to the reserved area. In the distance, I could see Sylvia in chatty conversation with the sophisticated swinger.

"It looks like your wife's found a new man," said Stirling, before Billy sauntered over to greet us.

"It seems Sylvia couldn't wait to be introduced," Billy grinned. From behind the ropes I managed to distract my wife's attention. She came rushing over and said, "I've told Frank that Stirling is with you Morris and he really wants to meet him." Stirling stood on tiptoes and tried to get a look over the shoulders of the heavies guarding the ropes. Just as he was doing so, Sylvia launched into a high-pitched shriek across the long table of people sitting with Sinatra.

"Frank, Frank. Look, I told you Stirling Moss was here." The shriek stopped Sinatra and his guests in their tracks, and as one they all looked over at Sylvia and an embarrassed Stirling Moss. Today, she says she looks back at that meeting with Ol' Blue Eyes and wishes the ground had swallowed her up. She says, "Within a few minutes of meeting Frank Sinatra for the first time, I was shouting at him across a busy room." I'm pleased to say for the rest of that evening she conducted herself in a more dignified manner. As Billy introduced me to the King of Swing, I at least tried to act cool. He was the biggest star in the world, and there's just no modern equivalent. Standing around a bar in Vegas, being handed drinks by Frank Sinatra was the stuff dreams were made of. I must confess, I can't remember a word of our initial conversation, although I desperately tried to, as I knew the evening would be a story to dine on for the rest of my life! Sylvia on the other hand remembers the conversation she had with "Frank". She says Barbara Marx, then Sinatra's long-time girlfriend, had told her that Frank was planning to sing at the London Palladium. On hearing the news, Sylvia quizzed Ol' Blues Eyes, asking, "Why are you playing there? It's not a very big venue!"

"I know," he said, "But it will be a nice laid-back evening. They even serve tea at the interval."

"Tea? No they don't serve tea. I think you'll find they only serve coffee," she informed him.

"OK, coffee then, but it's sure to be a good vibe." Sylvia was right about the coffee and the venue. When Sinatra sang at the Palladium in November 1975, 350,000 fans applied for one of only 2,200 tickets available for the show.

From what I remember, Sinatra seemed surprisingly normal, as stars invariably do when you meet them in person. I'd heard rumours that he could be quite abrupt and impatient with people that he didn't know, but with us he was nothing of the sort that night. He was certainly in awe of Stirling Moss and keen to hear stories about his great duels on the track with Juan Manuel Fangio. He also asked Stirling what car he drove back home in England.

"A Jaguar. A great British car," replied Stirling.

"I must get one," he said. (He did get one some months later, when Barbara Marx bought him a green XJS as a wedding present.) At one point, Sinatra raised his crystal whisky glass and offered up the toast: "To Great Britain and great British racing drivers". Just as everyone raised their glasses, I chipped in, "And to our great hosts at Caesars and its great American singer". I touched glasses with Sinatra and he replied, "I'll drink to that."

After just a short time in Sinatra's company, he left us to go and prepare himself for that night's performance. Stirling and I continued our conversation over a lovely meal laid on by Billy for "his special guests", in the newly-opened Caesars' Palace Court Restaurant, which became well known for its stained-glass dome, elegant décor and exquisite food. As we ate, I asked Stirling what he thought of the new Cadillac Seville.

"It's a super car Morris. Handles better than a Rolls-Royce. I'd certainly recommend it." I bought a Cadillac Seville on Stirling's recommendation a few years later. One of the first journeys I made in it was to Stirling's home in Mayfair. The only problem I ever had with it was navigating it up the tight cul-de-sac leading to where he lived.

"I'll never be able to reverse it back up the road without hitting those parked cars," I told him on leaving after dinner there one evening.

"Move over then and let me drive," he said, before reversing at 60mph just a few inches from the parked cars and spinning the big American beast around at the end of the lane to face it the correct way. When my racing heart slowed down and I finally regained my breath, I turned to him and said, "Who do you think you are, Stirling Moss?" He climbed out of the driver's seat gave me a knowing wink and waved me off with a smile.

But back to that night in Vegas. After thanking the chef for our meal, Billy led us out of the restaurant to the Circus Maximus theatre, where we sat at a prominent table close to the stage for Sinatra's performance. He greeted the audience that night with the words, "Welcome to the Palace of the Caesars, wherein resides the noblest Roman of them all – me!" He sang all of my favourite songs, *New York, New York*, *My Way* and *Mack the Knife*. All were note perfect, as you'd expect from the best in the business. On taking his final bow after the third encore, the spotlight fixed on the booth where we were sitting and Sinatra said, "Tonight is a really special night for me. I'd like to introduce you to my hero. He's probably the greatest racing driver there's ever been, please give a big hand to Stirling Moss. Stand up and take a bow Sir." Stirling looked a little embarrassed, but stood up and waved to the audience and mouthed his thanks to Sinatra who ended the concert with the toast, "May you all live to be 1,000 years old, and may the last voice you hear be mine." It was certainly a memorable evening for all of us, but the next day was surprisingly just as memorable.

A heavy rainstorm hit the resort in the afternoon, forcing Stirling and I to abandon our places by the pool and seek refuge from the weather in the casino. My good friend Mickey Duff, the boxing promoter, joined us at the tables and we were happily winning when an ashen-faced Billy came over and asked: "Have you seen the parking lot? We've been hit by a flash flood." We cashed our chips and quickly followed him outside, where we were greeted with the sight of over 200 cars being tossed into the air. It turned out debris had blocked a drained culvert and pushed water levels to 20 feet in the car park. What's more, some owners had returned to their cars and were trying to move them away from the area. The build-up of water in the car park had been sudden and caught many people by surprise. We saw half a dozen cars with people appearing stuck inside and decided to act before a tragedy occurred. The three of us waded into the waist-deep waters and helped pull people from their cars. Luckily, everyone got out OK, although sadly in another part of the Strip, two men were swept away while directing traffic. Later that afternoon, a reporter called John Rimmington interviewed us, and filed stories to a number of newspapers back in England about the incident. My daughter Shelley received a shock the following day after picking up a copy of London's *Evening Standard* and seeing a picture of me on the front cover under the headline 'THE THREE HEROES

OF LAS VEGAS'. The story also made most of the national newspapers, with the *Daily Mirror* using the imaginative head-line 'CLEANED OUT' to describe the terrible flooding in the gambling capital of the world. Remarkably, within 24 hours of the deluge, the bulldozers had moved in and cleared the cars and everything was back to normal.

The following year when Sylvia and I returned to Vegas, Billy insisted that we had the best room at Caesars. It was a huge penthouse apartment, filled with ornate things. There were two super king-size beds and a fully equipped kitchen containing all the latest gadgets, as well as a large dining room where you could entertain guests. It was way too big for our needs, especially after Sylvia told me she certainly wasn't plan-ning to cook any meals during her holiday. Anyway, after our first night in the grand surroundings, Billy knocked at the door and sheepishly asked if we'd mind vacating the room.

"Why's that then Bill?" I asked.

"Frank Sinatra is coming tomorrow and has asked for this room."

"I'm not giving my room up for anyone," I said with a straight face. Billy, being an American, took my words at face value.

"I'm so sorry Morris, but I do have another room almost as good at this one."

"Almost as good as this one," I said with a stern look. "I want one the same or better."

"But, this is the best room," he said. I couldn't keep up the charade any longer and roared with laughter.

"Of course we'll move Bill. It's no problem."

"Ah thanks. You Brits crack me up. I'll arrange for the staff to move all your belongings into the executive suite."

We didn't get to meet Sinatra on that holiday, but we did rub shoulders with sporting legends Johnny Weissmuller, the five-time swimming Olympic gold medallist and man who played Tarzan in 12 movies, and Joe Louis, the world heavy-weight boxing champion from 1937 to 1949, both who of whom worked as greeters at the casino.

A couple of years later I met Sinatra again, only this time in London at a dinner he threw for about 50 guests at the

Ritz after one of his concerts at the Royal Albert Hall. Sinatra had been talking to film actress Jean Simmons for most of the evening, when I seized an opportunity when she left to powder her nose to have a chat with him. I reminded Sinatra that we'd met a few years earlier at Caesars when I was with Stirling Moss.

"Yeah. I remember. How are your Spurs doing?" he asked.

"You've got a good memory," I said, flabbergasted that he'd remembered a conversation we'd had before about Spurs and how they'd only just avoided relegation with victory over Leeds in the last game of the season.

"There's a new basketball team in America called the Spurs. That's why I remember your soccer team," he said. We then chatted about American sports. He told me that he had wanted to be a sportswriter as a teenager.

"I was a copy boy and then a reporter for the *Jersey Observer*," he reminisced. "Then I heard Billie Holiday sing and that was it, I wanted to be a singer. Of course you know soccer's a game for girls back home."

"Well, my Spurs are certainly playing like a bunch of girls at the moment." He laughed and then proceeded to tell me about some of the great boxing bouts he'd seen over the years.

"Did you see 'the Fight of the Century'? he asked, referring to the 1971 bout between Joe Frazier and Muhammad Ali at New York's Madison Square Garden.

"I did on TV," I replied.

"You weren't there?"

"No."

"You missed out. I was at ringside taking photos for *Life* magazine. It was some fight that one. I had it evens until the 11th, when Smokin' Joe started to land some hard shots to Ali's body. It was the left hook that won it for Frazier in the end," he said.

"My mate Monte Fresco was ringside at the fight taking pictures for the *Daily Mirror*. He said you were doing a great job and getting in his way." Sinatra laughed.

"Did you go to the Ali–Frazier rematch? he asked.

"I organised a competition where first prize was tickets for the bout in New York, but I watched it at home on TV."

"You didn't miss much. The fight in ABC's TV studios was better!"

At the end of the meal, Sinatra told me he fancied going to a casino and asked if I knew of one that that he could visit. By coincidence, my friend Philip Isaacs, who ran the Sportsman Club in the West End, which had a casino, was also at the dinner. Philip rushed off to get a table ready to play blackjack and we made our way there an hour later. The gambling rules in Britain at the time prohibited drinking at tables, but Frank was unaware of this.

"Can I have a scotch?" he asked Philip.

"Sorry Mr Sinatra. You're not allowed to drink at the tables."

"Who makes the rules?"

"The British Government," replied Philip. "If you want a drink you can come into my office and have a few there with me, but you can't drink at the tables."

"Are you kidding me?"

"Sadly not," replied Philip.

"I don't care about the British government. I play better with a scotch in my hand. Can't you bend the rules."

"Sorry Mr Sinatra." With that Ol' Blues Eyes, now looking a bit red-eyed, climbed off his seat and declared: "All bets are off. We're outta here." With that, his bodyguards followed him out of the building to a waiting car outside and he was off into the night. I didn't see him again on that visit, but received a telegram from him a little later inviting me to see him perform at Caesars. Unfortunately, Sylvia couldn't make the trip and when I told my superstar pal she'd stayed at home to look after the kids, he asked, "Couldn't the mother-in-law have looked after them?" Nevertheless, he signed a photo of himself and wrote a message to my wife that read, "Dear Sylvia. I saw Morris here, but where were you? Love Frank Sinatra." Thirty years on, the photo still adorns one of the walls of our home. I think Sylvia has put a duster over it and given it a kiss every day since I handed it to her!

As well as a developing a friendship with Sinatra, I also became good pals with his spokesman, adviser and confidant Milton 'Mickey' Rudin. Mickey, who died in 1999, was an attorney to many of Hollywood's top celebrities during a

50-year career as an entertainment lawyer. His clients included Elizabeth Taylor, Liza Minnelli, Lucille Ball, George Burns and Marilyn Monroe. He was a fascinating guy to talk to and full to the brim with interesting stories about the A-list stars that he represented. One summer, Billy Weinberger arranged for Mickey and I to stay at a six-bedroom villa that Caesars owned at a picturesque, coastal resort called La Costa in Southern California. During our stay, Mickey had me captivated with his tales. One that has stuck in my memory was about the death of Marilyn Monroe. He was adamant that Monroe didn't commit suicide. He said that his brother-in-law, Dr Ralph Greenson, had prescribed the sedatives from which Monroe overdosed, but that it was a tragic accident. He said that Greenson was unaware that Monroe had taken a barbiturate prescribed by another doctor, which interacted adversely with the sedative he'd given her and killed her. Mickey told me this as we ate a huge gut-busting greasy breakfast by the pool one morning. I remember it well, as after the waitress had taken our plates away, Mickey's pretty, young wife Mary Carol arrived at the table and asked her overweight husband.

"Have you ordered a low-fat breakfast?"

"I haven't eaten yet, but I'll gladly eat a low-fat one now with you." He did the same each morning and I struggled to stop myself from laughing and giving the game away.

Another trip that Billy arranged for me was a visit to New York. I was his guest at a sportsmen's tribute dinner held in memory of the Israeli athletes murdered at the Munich Games. Howard Cosell, the top sports commentator who had reported live on ABC during the terror attack in 1972, hosted the event at the Hilton that night. Cosell built his reputation around his catchphrase, "I'm telling it like it is", and that night he gave a moving speech on how the tragedy had led him to a deeper recognition and appreciation of his Jewish heritage.

At the dinner, Billy sat me next to a big black guy whose face I didn't recognise amongst the many famous sportsmen present. I shook hands with him as we sat down for the meal, and just before our starter arrived, I thought I'd strike up a conversation with the mystery man. We exchanged some small talk, with me telling him how I was a good friend of Billy

Weinberger's and that I was a mad supporter of English soccer team Tottenham Hotspur. As I chatted away, people began coming over to our table and politely asking "Willie" for his autograph. He was happy to oblige and within a few seconds there was a queue of a dozen people all waiting patiently for his signature. As he happily signed the menu cards, I stood up and walked over to Billy, who was sitting next to Cosell.

"Billy. Help me before I make myself look an idiot. Who's the black guy sitting next to me on my table?"

"You don't know who that is? Are you kidding me? I sit you next to one of the biggest names in sport and you don't know who he is." He turned to Cosell and said, "Can you believe it? Morris doesn't know who he's sitting next to?" Cosell looked over at the hordes of autograph hunters surrounding my table and laughed before revealing, "It's the Say Hey Kid. Willie Mays."

"Willie Who?" I replied.

"Willie Mays!" repeated Billy in disbelief.

"Probably the greatest baseball player of all time!" added Cosell, before reeling off Willie's achievements. "Six hundred sixty home runs, a batting average of 302, more than 300 stolen bases and more than 3,000 hits and a 12-time winner of the golden glove."

"Fancy sitting me next to a baseball player," I said indignantly. "I don't know any baseball players."

"Sorry Morris. Look, if you want a conversation piece just ask him about what it was like to take that catch in 1954," advised Billy.

I returned to my seat, and when the soup arrived I resumed my conversation with the "greatest baseball player of all time", admitting to him that I hadn't known who he was until Cosell enlightened me a few minutes earlier.

"That's OK," he said. "You're English, aren't you?"

"I am indeed. We play cricket, not baseball. Howard says you're the greatest player of all time."

"I think Joe DiMaggio and a few others might have something to say about that," smiled Willie.

"So tell me about that catch in 1954," I said. I wished I hadn't asked. He went on to give me the most intricate description of what must have surmounted to about five seconds of the game. I barely understood a word of it, as Billy and Howard laughed behind me.

"It was the World Series against the Indians. The score was tied 2–2 in the top of the eighth inning. Don Liddle pitched to left-hander Vic Wertz, who worked the count to two balls and a strike before crushing Liddle's fourth 440 feet to deep centre field. In many stadiums it would have been a home run and given the Indians a 5–2 lead, but at the Polo Grounds the hit wasn't far enough. I was playing in shallow centre field and made an on-the-run over-the-shoulder catch on the warning track to make the out. We won the game in the bottom of the 10th." He looked at me expectantly, and I desperately grasped for something to say: "It sounds like a great catch," I murmured, hopefully. He roared with laughter.

That night, after the final sad tribute to the 11 athletes and the one German police officer who had lost their lives, Billy told me we'd been invited to join a group of gamblers making their way to Atlantic City.

"It's a bit late. Besides, isn't Atlantic City a long drive from here?"

"That's right Morris, but Steve Wynn has an 18-seater Sikorsky helicopter waiting to take us. It's leaving at 11, so you'll be playing blackjack by 11.30."

"I won't be. There's absolutely no way you're getting me in a helicopter."

"You'll be alright. It's an experience, you'll love it once it's in the air."

"No way Josè. I'll drive." Billy later told me that Steve Wynn believed the helicopter paid for itself, as the time saved ferrying punters from New York to Atlantic City meant more time at the tables for gamblers to lose their money. Indeed, in the three hours it had taken me to be driven there, one of the helicopter passengers had won and then lost $20,000. However, nothing would have got me in that helicopter, so soon after one near-miss a few months earlier.

In June 1972, I had flown to Paris to watch exciting Argentine boxer Carlos Monzon successfully defend his world middleweight title against Jean Claude Bouttier. The next day I travelled to Brussels for the Euro '72 final between the USSR and West Germany. Two goals by Gerd Muller helped West Germany to a 3–0 victory and after the match I rushed away from the Heysel Stadium to Brussels Airport. I was booked on a British European Airways flight for the trip home and was accompanied by sports reporters Peter Lorenzo and Ken Jones and my mate Philip Isaacs. We waited in the airport lounge for our flight to be called, but nothing was forthcoming. After a while, I searched out the airline staff and asked: "Have we been delayed?"

"Yes, I'm afraid so Sir."

"By how long?" I asked.

"Sorry, I can't say at the moment." After ten minutes, I asked again: "What's the latest on our delay?"

"Sorry Sir. We're still waiting for your plane to arrive. There must have been a delay coming out of London."

"It's getting late. Are we going to get home tonight?" I asked.

"We're doing all we can." I sat down again and within a few minutes photographers began appearing in the airport hall. They were taking pictures of the arrivals board. 'Flight BE548. Delayed.' Rumours soon began to spread amongst passengers and airport staff that a plane had crashed in London. Peter and Ken phoned their newspaper offices in Fleet Street to find out if the rumours were fact.

"It's true. A Trident airliner crashed near Staines a few minutes after taking off from Heathrow. No survivors expected," said Ken solemnly.

"118 on board," added Peter. The hairs on the back of my neck stood up and I broke out into a cold sweat. A replacement plane was commandeered from somewhere at short notice and we flew home very late that evening. It was eerily silent on the entire flight home. Everyone knew just how lucky we'd been. On walking through my front door, I hugged my wife and my kids like I'd never hugged them before. I kept the ticket for that British European Airways flight from Brussels to London. It reminds me not to take life for granted.

An investigation into the disaster found that the plane, known as *Papa India*, crashed due to pilot and crew errors. A pathologist found that the captain was suffering from a heart condition immediately prior to the crash, which may have been a contributing factor. Today, it's still the worst air accident involving a British jet, and until the Lockerbie disaster of 1988, was the worst aviation disaster to have occurred on British soil.

The next time casino resort developer Steve Wynn offered me a lift a few years later, even a terrified flier like myself couldn't turn down his invitation. It was in the early-eighties and I was on holiday in Atlantic City, where Billy was now running Bally's Park Place. Willie Mays was also there at the time, having been handed a ten-year contract by Billy to work as the casino's celebrity greeter. Having spent a few days with Billy, I was keen to go to Vegas to meet up with some friends who were staying at Caesars.

"Why don't you get a lift from Steve Wynn? He flies to Vegas every Friday on his Boeing 707." I jumped at the chance when Steve did indeed offer me a free ride on his plane. Before taking off from Newark Airport, Steve and his brother Kenneth showed me around the customised jet, which actually only had six seats. The rest had been ripped out to make way for bespoke rooms including a state-of-the-art kitchen and dining area, a palatial bedroom and lounge and even a games room where Steve and his guests could while away the flight playing pinball.

"I can't believe I'm on a plane. It's like an extravagant penthouse apartment," I told him.

"That's the idea," he said. "I travel between the two Golden Nuggets every week and wanted the trip to be comfortable."

"I can't blame you," I said. "If I had one of these, I think it might cure my fear of flying!" It was no surprise to me a decade later when Steve Wynn spearheaded a resurgence at the Vegas Strip in the nineties, with some more of his wacky ideas. He set a new standard with the construction of lavish themed hotels, like the Mirage, with its artificial volcano that 'erupts' every night and the Bellagio with its amazing dancing water fountain synchronised to music.

I got my own back on Billy for sitting me next to 'Mr Baseball', Willie Mays, at that dinner in New York when the following year I invited Bobby Moore and his wife Tina to join Sylvia and I on holiday at Caesars. Billy was away on business on the day that the Moores arrived, and asked me to apologise on his behalf for not being able to personally welcome them. To 'make up for it', he organised a day out for us 30 miles away at Lake Mead, where Caesars had a luxury boat moored at a marina. Jagged mountains surround the lake and they provide a startling backdrop for what is the largest reservoir in the US. It felt like paradise there and Bobby couldn't believe it when I told him the boat had its own chef on board and it was solely ours for the entire day.

"You're the King of Vegas!" he exclaimed, before asking the captain to sail into the middle of the lake and drop the anchor. We spent a glorious day sunbathing on deck, diving into the blue waters and tucking into a lavishly prepared lunch fit for a king. Today's highly paid footballers probably wouldn't bat an eyelid after experiencing a great day like that. In fact, today's footballers can afford to buy their own yachts and employ their own chefs, but for Bobby, that day living in the lap of luxury was a real treat.

Bobby and Tina were keen to thank Billy for his hospitality, and they got their chance when he joined us for dinner on our last night. Before our meal, Sylvia and I met Billy for a few drinks in the bar and waited for the Moores to join us, as arranged at 9pm. Just before the clock struck nine, Bobby and Tina walked into the bar and sat down at a table just a few feet away. Bobby's entrance caused a stir amongst some of the English clientele, and one star-struck gentleman asked Bobby for his autograph.

"Who's that guy? whispered Billy, watching the crowd round Bobby grow.

"You don't know?" I said, before roaring with laughter. "Are you telling me you don't recognise one of the most famous sportsmen on the planet?"

"Are you kidding me?" said Billy.

"That's the captain of the 1966 World Cup-winning side. That man has won a record 108 England caps and is one of the greatest players of all-time. It's my mate Bobby Moore and you're sitting next to him at dinner!"

"You never told me Bobby Moore was a famous footballer," protested Billy.

"You never asked," I replied with glee and added, "If you get stuck for conversation, why don't you ask him about that tackle against Jairzinho in 1970?"

"Jar ... who?" Billy stuttered, pulling the same face I imagine graced mine when Willie Mays was detailing that catch to me.

From then on, every time I invited friends to join me on holiday, Billy insisted I told him before they arrived if they were "famous English soccer men". One summer, when I warned him that Terry Venables was coming, Billy insisted I provide him with an A4 sheet containing details of Terry's career, as well as a glossary of "soccer lingo".

Terry loved our trips to Vegas, and we had some great laughs. I remember one year we got a call from our friend John Hollins, a former Chelsea teammate of Terry's. John was on holiday with his wife in Los Angeles and asked if we could arrange for them to spend a few nights with us in Vegas.

"The wife's not too keen on coming, but I've bribed her with the promise of an amazing room at Caesars. Can Morris sort it for me?" he asked Terry.

"No problem John," Terry assured him. "I'm sure Morris can arrange it. When you arrive go to reception and ask for the hotel manager, tell them your name and they'll have a deluxe room waiting for you. When you've booked yourself in, come and join us for cocktails by the pool."

"Great! Thanks very much. See you tomorrow," replied John, before hanging up the phone. Terry and I formulated a small plan to wind John up on his arrival the next day, and when he and Linda landed at reception, they didn't get the reaction they were expecting from the manager,

"Sorry Mr Hollins. We have no room booked in your name."

"There must be a mistake. Mr Morris Keston has arranged a deluxe room for five nights."

"I'm the hotel manager and I don't even know anyone called Morris Keston."

"How about Mr Venables? He's also staying here."

"No. Sorry. There's nothing I can do."

Terry and I were watching the scene unfold in our hiding

place behind a large statue, giggling at the little joke we'd organised with the manager. We were just about to leap out and come clean, when, to our surprise, the normally mild-mannered John started to turn red, and began berating the manager, who quickly explained that a mistake had been made and offered over the keys to a deluxe room.

Terry and I scuttled out to the pool, and John joined us half an hour later.

"I'm so embarrassed. The manager made a mistake with our booking and I ended up having a right go at him," he immediately confessed. "I feel terrible; I even swore at the poor guy."

"You didn't!" I exclaimed, feigning surprise; in actual fact I had, of course, been witness to John's tirade. He turned red: he was such a nice bloke and was clearly horrified by his rare loss of control after a long day travelling. Terry's eyes gleamed as he saw an opportunity unfold.

"I'm a bit worried there may be repercussions," he said. "John, you really can't talk to people at Caesars like that. This is Mafia territory. They don't take kindly to threats." The colour immediately drained out of John's face.

"I'd better go and apologise," he said.

"It's probably too late for that," I said. "The manager's just left for the day."

"I'll apologise tomorrow," replied John, as he worriedly sipped at his piña colada.

"Do you mind not sitting so close to me. I don't want to get caught in any crossfire!" said Terry.

"Don't say that Tel, you're making me nervous," replied John.

"And you're making me nervous, sitting this close. Please move nearer Morris."

"Don't come near me or my wife!" I said, before moving his sun lounger further away. "I forgot to renew my insurance policy before this holiday!"

"We could keep this joke up for days," Terry whispered to me, struggling to control his laughter.

Terry and I did indeed keep it going for a few days. At one point, Terry even told John he thought he'd seen a man crouching on a balcony and aiming a rifle in our direction.

"Stop mucking about," said John.

"I'm not," replied Terry, who was so convincing even I started to believe him! By coincidence, an incident at dinner that night contributed to John's fears. Sitting on a table behind us in the Palace Court Restaurant were a large group of shifty looking men in suits. I called over the Head Waiter, George, who I knew very well and had filled in on the joke.

"What's going on? I asked. "We were here way before that mob sitting behind us, but the waiters are only interested in serving them." George leaned over and with his back to the table behind replied: "They're the Mafia."

"That's OK. They're nice guys. We haven't got a problem with them," said Terry.

"Someone will be over shortly," said George. I looked at Terry and said: "What are you talking about? You don't even know those guys behind. How can you say they're good guys?"

"I know," he replied. "But they might be able to lip read!"

"They asked to be sat behind your party, actually," whispered George, conspiratorally. "We thought that maybe you guys were friends." It was the last straw for John, who by now was a nervous wreck.

"We're not hanging around here much longer. I came to Caesars to relax, not to wake up with a horse's head in my bed," he said. We roared with laughter, and Terry then finally put him out of his misery by revealing he'd been set up. I won't repeat what he called us.

Looking back, I certainly spent some great holidays in Vegas, and it was all down to my friendship with Billy Weinberger. If I'd never made that second trip in 1969 and sought him out, I'd have missed out on mixing in the company of, and indeed becoming friends with, many of the show-business stars who topped the bill at Caesars, like Alan King, Harry Belafonte and Petula Clark.

I would often end my evenings smoking a cigar with Alan King, the late Jewish comedian, known for his biting wit and humorous angry rants. Our drinking sessions would often last until 3am, and he'd have me in stitches with the jokes he deemed too risqué for the Caesars audience. On a couple of occasions in 1977, George Best, who at the time was playing for the Los

Angeles Aztecs, also joined me for a few late drinks. George and I were never best mates or anything, but whenever our paths crossed I always enjoyed his company. He certainly had a great sense of humour. I remember one time in LA when I wandered into the Aztecs' dressing room before a match – you could do that sort of thing in the seventies! – I sat inbetween Bestie and my mate Phil Beal as they got changed.

"Don't just sit there, put a kit on," urged Bestie, smiling as he patted my beer belly.

"Good joke George. As you can see, I'm not exactly in great shape!"

"That may be so, but you're probably as good as the Yanks in this side." Even his American teammates laughed at that one!

Most afternoons at Caesars, I'd leave Sylvia by the pool and go off to chat to Harry Belafonte, the 'King of Calypso', at the health club. He told me he preferred it when Caesars only charged punters a few dollars to see his act. "As soon as they put the ticket price up to $15, people expected me to put on a show." He said, "I came to Caesars to retire, not to work my butt off."

One afternoon, as we lifted some weights in the gym, Harry, a strong advocate for civil rights, told me how Petula Clark inadvertently made television history when she touched his arm as they sang a duet. He said the sponsors of Petula Clark's show feared the 'incident' would offend Southern viewers at a time of racial tension following the assassination of Martin Luther King Jr in 1968. Harry said despite pressure from TV executives, Petula refused to cut the scene. As a result, it marked the first time a man and woman of different races had made physical contact on American television.

"The press carried a lot of stories on the subject, but Petula's show survived the publicity and her ratings went up," he said. "It was a brave decision." He was right: Petula's stance provided a significant moment in the struggle for black equality.

Sylvia's a big fan of Petula Clark. She often sings her big hit *Downtown* above the drone of the hoover. One time, I got myself into Sylvia's good books for the whole week when I arranged for Sidney Gathrid, the man responsible in the seventies for booking all the acts at Caesars, to take her to see Petula Clark in concert. After the show, Sidney introduced Sylvia to her idol and later on we managed to get some signed Liverpool pictures for Petula's son Patrick.

My own favourite backstage encounter was when Billy took me to meet the actress Shirley MacLaine. She'd only just stepped out of the shower after entertaining the masses at Circus Maximus, when Billy pushed me through her dressing-room door. My mouth opened and my jaw hit the floor, as I drooled over the beautiful woman wearing just a dressing gown in front of me.

"Hello Miss MacLaine. I'm a big fan of yours," I said, watching the steam rise from her wet, curly, red locks. *The Apartment* is one of my favourite movies, and I really enjoyed your performance in *The Turning Point*."

"How sweet of you," she replied, as my eyes popped out of my head, like cartoon character Roger Rabbit.

Billy would stop at nothing and do anything and everything to ensure our stays at Caesars were enjoyable. One time, he even organised for film producer Robert Evans to take us on a private tour of Paramount Studios. This was in the days before the film studios were open to the public. We met James T Kirk, captain of the starship *USS Enterprise*, aka actor William Shatner, and Richard Kiel, who played *Jaws* in the James Bond movies *The Spy Who Loved Me* and *Moonraker*, during a break in filming their American TV series *Barbary Coast*. On another occasion, Billy even got me an invite to actress and socialite Zsa Zsa Gabor's wedding reception, where I sipped champagne with her sixth husband, Jack Ryan, the man credited with creating the popular image of the Barbie doll for toy company Mattel.

With Billy pulling the strings, I was welcomed into a celebrity world that most ordinary people, like me, could only dream of experiencing. When he passed away in 1996, aged 83, I lost more than a friend and I will never forget those great times we shared. To my friends back home, I might have been known as the 'King of Vegas', but in reality, Billy Weinberger was the real deal.

BOBBY MOORE'S SHIRT AND BOBBY CHARLTON'S BOOTS

"Morris Keston's Bobby Moore shirt and Bobby Charlton boots stories are amazing!"
Graham Budd (sporting memorabila auctioneer)

"The players reckon Morris owns more caps than me!"
Bobby Moore OBE (1941–93, West Ham and England, World Cup-winning captain 1966)

The whereabouts of the shirt that Bobby Moore wore during England's finest hour is one of football's great mysteries. Bobby's first wife Tina was thought to have been in possession of the iconic red number-six jersey, but that myth was dispelled in 2000 when auctioneer David Convery sold all of the 1966 World Cup-related items that Bobby had to West Ham United for their museum. His winner's medal and England cap were included in the sale, but the shirt wasn't, and Tina admitted she had no idea who had it. It certainly got me thinking, and since then I've often wondered whether Bobby actually gave it to me!

Not long after I'd arranged Bobby's testimonial season in 1970, he turned up at my home carrying a plastic bag. "What's in there?" I asked nosily, as he walked through the hallway into the living room.

"Wouldn't you like to know?" he said, teasingly.

"Don't tell me then," I said, pretending not to be interested.

"Actually, it's something for you."

"Well, hand it over," I replied, impatiently, and with that he pulled out a red football shirt. I instantly recognised it as being the same strip worn in the 1966 World Cup final, and wondered whether it was the actual shirt that Bobby had lifted the Jules Rimet trophy in. It had a crew neck collar and long sleeves and on the chest was an embroidered Three Lions cloth badge. I held it up in front of me with both hands.

"Thanks for being a great mate. I want you to have it."

"What? Are you sure?" I asked, praying he wouldn't suddenly change his mind.

"Yes. It's yours. Now put the kettle on."

That night, we chatted about football and our families like any normal visit by the England captain. When he got up to leave I thanked him again for the present. I never did ask him whether it was the actual match-worn shirt, and in all the years we were friends, it was never mentioned again. It was a fantastic gesture and I thought it could have seemed a bit ungrateful if I'd quizzed him over the gift's provenance. The shirt lived in my bottom drawer for many years. I tried it on for a laugh once, but it wouldn't go past my expanding waistline. "You're certainly no Bobby Moore," said Sylvia, who laughed hysterically at the sight of my belly button protruding from it. I occasionally gave it an airing when friends came round and on one occasion, a photographer called at my home and took a photo of me holding it up. The picture was used to accompany a story about me in a Norwegian newspaper in 1975. Apparently, Hunter Davies's book *The Glory Game* had sold very well in Norway, and as I'd featured in the bestseller, a reporter tracked me down for an interview. The article in *Dagbladet* stated that as well as being a Spurs supporter, I was also "England's number-one fan". Another picture of Sylvia and me holding two engraved whiskey decanters was also printed in the paper. Bobby had given me those, along with a silver plated table cigarette lighter, as presents for organising his testimonial dinner in 1970. I still have the decanters on display at home, but sadly I can't say the same about the shirt, as somehow I've managed to lose it! I've lost so much sleep over the years trying to fathom what could have happened to that shirt. The only explanation can be that it was mistakenly thrown out during one of the three times that I've moved home since Bobby gave me it. I've tried to forget about my misfortune, but with every passing anniversary of that famous win over the Germans, the media never fails to remind me.

In 2006, before the World Cup in Germany, a TV series called *The Shirts of '66* told the story of comedian Ricky Tomlinson's bid to trace the jerseys worn on the day of England's greatest ever sporting achievement. Annoyingly, the only jersey he couldn't find was Bobby Moore's! Tomlinson's research discovered that four players, Gordon Banks, George Cohen, Bobby Charlton and Roger Hunt, swapped their shirts after the match with Hans Tilkowski, Lothar Emmerich, Uwe Seeler and Wolfgang Weber respectively. Two players, Alan Ball and Nobby Stiles, swapped with each other and the remaining four, Ray Wilson, Jack Charlton, Geoff Hurst and Martin Peters, all kept their own strips. It's believed that Bobby also kept his, but Tomlinson couldn't find anyone who knew of its whereabouts. I thought about getting in touch with the programme makers, but in the end decided against it, as I no longer had the shirt anyway!

I'm not actually surprised that Tina Moore couldn't find her late ex-husband's shirt. The fact is, Bobby was a generous man and gave many of his England jerseys away to friends or people that had helped him in some way. He parted with the shirt he wore against Argentina in 1966, giving it to a man who was carrying out building work at his home. The doctor who delivered one of his children was also presented with a white England shirt. Bobby's West Ham teammate Bertie Lutton was another recipient of an England jersey. Before England met Northern Ireland at Wembley in 1973, Bobby promised Lutton that he'd swap shirts. However, on the day, Lutton failed to make it off the subs' bench and Bobby ended up swapping with another Irish player. The ever-honourable Mooro turned up on the first day of pre-season training and handed Lutton the shirt he'd worn against Romania in the 1970 World Cup finals! It was typical of the man, although I wonder if he'd have been quite so generous if he'd known just how valuable his shirts would later become.

BOBBY MOORE'S SHIRT AND BOBBY CHARLTON'S BOOTS

The arrival in recent years of the more affluent middle classes into the working man's game has seen the value of football memorabilia rocket, with rarer items, like shirts, caps and medals belonging to the game's great players, fetching huge sums at auction. Alan Ball's 1966 World Cup winner's medal sold for £164,800 at Christie's in May 2005 and his England cap for the tournament fetched £43,200 at the same auction. German footballers Lothar Emmerich and Wolfgang Weber have both sold the shirts they gained as swaps in 1966, with George Cohen's number-two shirt making £38,400 at Christie's in June 2006 and Roger Hunt's number 21 fetching £17,250 at Sotheby's in February 1999. Those figures are dwarfed though by the sum a private collector paid for Geoff Hurst's shirt in September 2000. Auctioneer David Convery slammed his gavel down that day at a mind-boggling £91,750! The guy that bought it already owned Roger Hunt's, although he has since sold both of the shirts to a group of private international investors. They have insured England's hat-trick hero's shirt for £1million!

I've often wondered what the shirt Bobby gave me might be worth today and writing this book gave me a reason to find out. Using the picture taken from the Norwegian newspaper in 1975, experts that I've consulted believe it's almost certainly identical to the one Bobby wore in the World Cup final. Glen Isherwood from the website EnglandFootballOnline.com confirmed that the number six on the jersey was the same font used by England's 1966 kit suppliers Umbro, who replaced Bukta early in the 1965/66 season. There are apparently distinct differences between Umbro and Bukta numbers of that era. Although it's not an exact science when looking at photos, the number six is one of the better examples to distinguish the shirt makers. Bobby Moore wore Umbro's red, long-sleeved, number-six England jersey on seven occasions, including the final. Interestingly, Bobby was issued with two shirts for the final and gave his unworn spare to trainer Harold Shepherdson after the match. Thirty-three years later, Shepherdson's widow Peggy sold it at a Mullock Madeley auction for £44,000. Auctioneer Graham Budd told me that if Bobby Moore's World Cup-winning shirt ever found its way to auction he'd expect it to fetch between £150,000 and £250,000. The current world record price for a match-worn shirt is the £157,750 paid for Pele's 1970 World Cup final jersey at Christie's in March 2002. That fact is, even if I were still in possession of Bobby's shirt, I have no proof that he wore it on 30th July 1966. This seriously affects its value and would probably mean auctioneers could only regard it as being one of the six shirts identical to the one Bobby donned in the 4–2 win over West Germany. Today, David Convery estimates that any of those six would fetch around £5,000 to £10,000. It may not be the quarter of a million, but ten grand would certainly help this pensioner!

During the seventies, I'd often buy the international caps or shirts donated by players at auctions held for charity or to help boost the coffers during a player's testimonial season. The players used to joke that I had more caps than Bobby Moore! I didn't actually have a hundred, but I had a few. I bought one that belonged to Martin Peters at auction and Terry Medwin, Alan Mullery and Bobby Smith all gave me one of theirs. At one of those auctions I bought a pair of Bobby Charlton's football boots. To be honest, I didn't really want them as I didn't collect boots, and my winning bid was actually only aimed at getting the price moving. I can't remember exactly how much money I parted with, but probably no more than £150. The boots came with a letter from England's record goalscorer, confirming that he'd worn them in the 1970 World Cup. I don't know how many boots Charlton took to Mexico, but they could have been the last pair he wore when playing for his country. His last game for England was the 3–2 quarter-final defeat against West Germany in Leon. I kept them in different cupboards over a 20-year period and in 1989 when I heard that Christie's were to hold their first football memorabilia auction in Glasgow, I thought I'd get them valued. I looked high and low, but couldn't find them anywhere. Seeing me in a panic and with sweat pouring from my forehead, Sylvia asked what I was looking for.

"Have you seen that old pair of football boots that I've kept in the cupboard for years?"

"Were they in an old blue bag?"

"That's right."

"Shelley said they were probably an old pair of Paul's, so I threw them in the dustbin."

"You didn't?"

"I did."

"They were Bobby Charlton's!"

I tried to laugh it off to make Sylvia feel better, but inside I felt sick to the pit of my stomach. I recently asked David Convery what they might fetch at auction today. He told me boots are generally pretty poor sellers, but he'd expect those ones to go for as much as £3,000!

That memorabilia mishap isn't the only time that the women in my family have managed to lose me a small fortune. Back in the early nineties my daughter Shelley threw out a dozen match-worn shirts. Today, that collection would probably make about £3,000 at auction, but to her they were just "dirty, smelly old rags". Into the dustman's cart on that occasion went a Northern Ireland goalkeeper's jersey that Pat Jennings gave me, plus many of the swaps that Paul Miller gained when playing for Spurs in Europe in the early eighties. Barcelona, Real Madrid, Bayern Munich and Ajax jerseys were all amongst those lost treasures, as was the shirt Paul wore in the famous 1–0 win over Liverpool at Anfield in 1985. Premier League players are today handed at least two shirts before each game, but in those days the players were only issued with a couple of shirts each season. To mark the occasion of Tottenham's first win at Liverpool for 73 years, the club allowed the players to take their shirts home. After the match, Liverpool's then chief executive Peter Robinson and chairman John Smith came to find me to shake my hand.

"Congratulations Morris. I'm disappointed we lost, but you've been coming here for many years and it's great that you've finally got a victory to celebrate." I thanked them both for their hospitality and replied, "If I were you I'd steer clear of cruise ships this summer. The last time Spurs beat you here the *Titanic* sank!"

Not long after that victory over Liverpool in 1985, I sold my entire football programme collection. At the time, it was probably the best collection of Spurs match programmes in the world. I had every home programme from 1930 onwards, including all of the wartime ones, plus every away one since the War, except Burnley versus Spurs in 1946/47. I also had a few of the programmes from Tottenham's days in the Southern League, the earliest dated 1898. Add to that, every FA Cup final programme since 1921 and a whole load of England ones going as far back as the wartime internationals. When my daughter left home, I had a huge bookcase built in her old room to house the collection. The father of the then Crystal Palace midfielder Barry Silkman did it for me. When he'd finished making it, I spent ages putting each programme inside a plastic wallet and then cataloguing each one, noting down the game and the score for each.

I used to travel all over the country visiting programme fairs and would only ever buy ones in near mint condition. For the games that I went to see, I'd always buy two programmes before entering the ground and then return to my car where I'd lock them away for safety. I was totally obsessed with keeping them crease-free and in immaculate condition. My programme collection meant everything to me. One time, I even swapped my Martin Peters England cap for a pre-War Manchester United versus Spurs programme! The rarer the programme the more I wanted it for my collection. For example, during the big freeze of 1963 a friendly match was arranged between Spurs and Arsenal at White Hart Lane. As it was played at short notice there was not enough time to produce the normal match programme. On the day, the press were given a white single-sheet typescript which also covered a reserves fixture between the two sides played earlier in the afternoon. As it's the nearest thing to a match programme that exists, it's extremely sought after by collectors. I was at that game and was given two of the sheets by the club's programme editor Les Yates. There were probably less than 100 available on the day. They rarely come up for auction, but when they do they go for big money. Christie's sold one for £2,990 in June 1999 and Graham Budd sold another in June 2004 for £2,600.

In 1985, I got my hands on another rare programme, although this time I was even luckier. In March that year, Peter Shreeve took the team to the Middle East to play a friendly against the Kuwait National XI. I didn't go to the game, which was actually played in Jordan, but said to Paul before he left, "Whatever you do, make sure you get me a programme." It's usual practice for the hosts to place a few programmes in the dressing rooms, but on this occasion they didn't. Paul searched for a programme seller outside the stadium, but couldn't find one and came to the conclusion that no programmes had been printed. However, a week or so after the game I was chatting to assistant manager John Pratt in the car park at White Hart Lane when I spotted a sheet of paper with Arabic writing on it lying on the back seat of his car.

"Is that a programme from the Middle East?" I asked hopefully.

"Yeah. It's a bit screwed up, but do you want it?" I doubt there are many people today who have that programme in their collection!

My favourite programmes were the two produced for the 1923 FA Cup tie against minnows Worksop Town. The Tigers held Tottenham 0–0 in the first game at White Hart Lane, but lost the replay 9–0 two days later. That second match caused a bit of controversy as Worksop asked Tottenham to host the replay for financial reasons. I don't know of another occasion when that's happened. The decision alienated Worksop's fans, who refused to attend subsequent home matches and put their club into deeper financial crisis. Thankfully, they survived.

I wouldn't like to guess how much money I spent on my collection, but probably not much more than the £9,000 I sold it for in 1985. Back in the seventies and early eighties when I was a collector, programmes were relatively cheap to buy and even the rare ones were easily within the budgets of most people. Since then, prices have gone through the roof. If someone had told me in 1985 that my collection would be worth one hundred times more in 25 years time, I would have thought they had a screw loose. I remember once thinking long and hard about parting with ten shillings for a 1901 Southampton versus Spurs programme. In the end, the lure of having something with the brilliant all-round amateur sportsmen C.B. Fry in the line-up proved too hard to resist. Even the seller called me 'mad' when I handed over the coins!

I'd need to hand over a huge wad of £50 notes if the same transaction took place today! Back in 1980, I couldn't even give away a complete set, 240 issues, of Charles Buchan's *Football Monthly*. Thirty years on, bids on eBay for the first issue regularly reach three figures!

It feels like the world's gone mad and I'm sure the players who graced the game before the booming wages of the nineties would agree. However, those willing to part with the souvenirs they gained during their careers, at least have a chance to secure a late decent financial reward. In recent years, many former Spurs players, including Dave Mackay, Cliff Jones, Alan Mullery and Maurice Norman, have sold the medals they won during their time at the club. Mackay's double-winning medals fetched £21,150 at Sotheby's in September 2001 and Jonesie's 1963 European Cup Winners' Cup medal sold for £10,575 at Bonhams in March 2006. The medal that Mullers took home when Spurs won the UEFA Cup in 1972 went for £5,520 at Sotheby's in July 2000 and Maurice Norman's 1962 FA Cup medal fetched £13,800 at Graham Budd Auctions in May 2008. Sadly, the same can't be said for Bobby Smith's 1961 Championship medal. He parted with it for just a few hundred quid many years before the memorabilia boom kicked off. Sometime in the seventies, Bobby gave me the medal for safe keeping after borrowing some money from me to pay off some gambling debts. A little while later, he asked me if I wanted to buy the medal for not much more money than what he owed me. I didn't want to take the treasure off him in those circumstances, so he paid me back the money and I returned the medal for him to sell. Smithy deserved a good payday as much as anyone for his dedication to Tottenham, but for him it wasn't to be.

The timing proved better for the daughter of one of Smithy's teammates. Gayle Blanchflower, the daughter of Danny, contacted me asking if I could help find a buyer for a watch that belonged to her father. The timepiece, a Longines Flagship Automatic, was bought by the club at Harrods and inscribed on the reverse with the words "Presented to R.D. Blanchflower (captain) by Tottenham Hotspur FC on winning the Football League and the FA Cup 1961". I firstly asked the Spurs chairman Daniel Levy if the club would be interested, but it wasn't an item they wished to put aside for the club's museum. However, I did find someone willing to pay a good price and the fact that the buyer was a fanatical Spurs fan pleased Gayle.

Whether it's Bobby Charlton's boots or Danny Blanchflower's commemorative watch, until England win the World Cup again or Spurs secure a Premier League title it's likely that the treasures associated with the legends of yesteryear will continue to be highly sought after and command incredible sums. And who knows? Maybe someone out there will find that red England shirt that Bobby Moore wore in 1966, and if they do, I hope they remember me, and the one that got away.

THE TESTIMONIAL ORGANISER

10

"In the world of football, Morris can only be described as a huge, huge man; one who is loved and respected by an army of friends. Morris is dedicated and loyal, and never changes his attitude towards people, whether a regular friend or a passing acquaintance. He is also extremely knowledgeable, a man who doesn't need to impress. His overwhelming personality, principles and warmth of character do that for him!"
John Hollins MBE (Chelsea and England, FA Cup winner 1970)

"In the 40-odd years that I've known the man, including his part in my own testimonial, he always supported the 11 men who wore the lilywhite shirt regardless of status or reputation. A genuinely lovable character."
John Pratt (Spurs, 1972 UEFA Cup winner)

Before top players could demand £100,000 a week, the stars of yesteryear would usually hit the panic button when their playing days looked numbered. It was understandable, as after all Tottenham's 1972 UEFA Cup-winning side were 'doing well' if they found more than £100 in their weekly pay packet. Of course, this was still a bit more than the average wage, but couldn't buy anything like the luxury lifestyles of modern footballers, and certainly didn't leave much money each month to put aside for the day when they landed on the game's scrapheap. Add to this the short career span, and retirement really was a daunting prospect.

Mixing as I did in their company, it was obvious to me that before hanging up their boots my friends had to make the most of any moneymaking opportunities that came their way. For the long-serving Spurs players of the seventies and eighties 'lucky' enough to be granted a testimonial match, it was an opportunity to finally get a decent payday and I was only too happy to help them. Indeed, it was a privilege and I can honestly say that I never earned a penny from them.

Jimmy Greaves was the first Spurs legend to approach me for help after the board had relented under supporter pressure to grant him a testimonial. Before Greavsie, the previous club policy had seen players handed a bonus of £750 and £1,000 before tax after five and ten years' service. The board also awarded free transfers to some players when their time came to move on, thus enabling them to negotiate better deals with their new club as no transfer fee was involved.

I got the call from Greavsie one afternoon.

"Hi Morris. Believe it or not, good old Sidney Wale has granted me a testimonial."

"Bloody hell Jim. How did you pull that one off? There hasn't been a benefit game at the club since John White died."

"I know. I played in it back in '64! Apparently Peter Spall and John Bairstow have been putting pressure on Sidney to grant me one, and he's caved in."

"Good show."

"I know you've got some experience in this field. You organised Geoff's and Mooro's didn't you?"

He was right. By that point, I had not only played a part in Geoff Hurst and Bobby Moore's testimonials, but also George Cohen's. I'd also organised a successful fund-raising function for England cricketer Colin Milburn, who had lost an eye in a car accident, as well as sat on the testimonial committee for Millwall's Harry Cripps. I explained this to Greavsie.

"Funny that. Geoff was telling me about Cripps's game just the other day. He said he'd scored a hat-trick but no one had seen it as the Millwall and West Ham fans were fighting on the terraces."

"That's right. I missed the game, thank God. Reg Drury had invited me along to the football writers' awards on the same night. There was a good turnout though. I was told over 10,000 showed up." By now, I had guessed where this conversation was going.

"Would you mind being chairman of my testimonial committee?" "Mind?" I thought. Greavsie was Tottenham's record goal-scorer – still is – and I was salivating at the prospect of being a part of something that would go down in the club's history.

"It would be an honour. But you'd better not tell Sidney Wale that I'm organising it for you. You know he doesn't like me and I wouldn't put it past him to cancel it if he knows I'm involved."

"Mum's the word Morris."

"Who do you fancy playing?" I asked. Greavsie thought for a moment.

"I'd love to get a top European side to come over for the occasion. It gives the supporters something different and I'm sure Bill Nick will see it as good preparation for the UEFA Cup."

"Leave it to me Jim."

I wrote to no fewer than eight top European clubs, including the likes of Ajax, Benfica and Inter Milan, asking them if they'd be interested in providing the opposition for the game. Sadly, only two clubs replied. AC Milan said they couldn't make it, but luckily the other, Dutch side Feyenoord, agreed to come if we paid their expenses. The committee, chaired by football-kit firm owner Peter Spall, agreed. The expenses ended up amounting to £3,500, a fair sum in those days. We advertised it as the 'Goodbye Greaves Match' and interest from fans was immense, eager to say a belated farewell to Jim. He had left Spurs for West Ham somewhat abruptly on transfer deadline day in March 1970 in a £200,000 part-exchange deal that saw Martin Peters come the other way. Greavsie lasted just 14 months at Upton Park, before deciding to retire altogether in May 1971, aged 31. It was way too early.

A bumper crowd of 45,799 crammed into White Hart Lane on a Tuesday night in October 1972, paying 70 pence for a seat or 40 pence to stand on the terraces. The size of the gate surprised everyone, especially me, as I'd only ordered 20,000 match programmes and they sold out. Each ten pence programme contained a draw number and gave the holder the chance to win a new Ford Consul car. It was a great idea and one I used in many other testimonials. The match itself was an entertaining and keenly contested encounter, against the side that had just gone top of the Dutch league. Who else but Greavsie netted the opener after just three minutes, although he admits today it shouldn't have counted, as he was about five yards offside. Full back Ray Evans scored a rare goal that night and it proved to be the winner as Spurs won 2–1. After all the expenses were paid, the committee handed Jimmy a cheque for £22,000. I believe he put the money to good use by becoming a Lloyd's underwriter and his lovely wife Irene spent the rest on home improvements. Greavsie gave the players and testimonial committee members an inscribed pewter tankard. It's one of the few items of memorabilia that I haven't given away to charity auctions. In fact, somehow I ended up with two of them and can't bear to part even with my spare one!

The following season, Phil Beal, who played in Jimmy's testimonial, became the first active Spurs player to be granted one of his own. Unfortunately though, the match itself was an unmitigated disaster. Due to a number of factors, many of which were beyond our control, Phil lost at least £1,000 on the night.

The fact that the match even went ahead was a minor miracle. Unrest amongst coal miners had led to a work-to-rule policy that was seriously denting coal production and affecting electricity supply. All this meant there was a real possibility that we'd lose power to the floodlights on the night of the game and we were worried. There were potentially 30,000 fans turning up to see Spurs play the stars of Bayern Munich and no lights would have been a catastrophe. As usual, my bulging address book saved us: a chap called Sid Gray, who was my mate's father, worked for the City of London Corporation. He loaned us the spare generator used to open Tower Bridge. It weighed 30 tonnes and needed a police escort to move it to White Hart Lane, but at least it ensured we had floodlights for the evening.

We really did pour blood into that game. A publicity-grabbing interview on *The Big Match* was booked for Bayern's best-known players, Franz Beckenbauer and Uli Hoeness, and I even arranged for someone to pick them up from the airport to chauffer them over to ITV's studios for it. We also organised a post-game dance at London's Lyceum, and spent hours on the phone to journalist friends trying to crank up as much interest in the match as possible. I made sure that catering for the night was top-notch and spent a lot of time liaising with the club over other aspects of the evening, such as programmes, police, turnstile operators and merchandising.

The extortionate £14,000 we had agreed to pay the Germans for the match put extra pressure on us to ensure the evening was a success and that Phil didn't end up out of pocket. I was against caving into their unreasonable financial demands; after all, the fee was four times higher than that paid to Feyenoord for Greavsie's match a year earlier. But the majority of the testimonial committee members, who included Bobby Moore, thought they'd be worth the expense as they'd pull in a bumper crowd. Ordinarily they would have done, what with big names like Beckenbauer, Hoeness, Paul Breitner and Gerd Müller in their ranks, but once again, the tumultuous political situation at the time, both at home and abroad, worked against us. In that December of 1973, Britain had been gripped in a global oil crisis after Arab nations refused to sell to the US and other countries that supported Israel in the Yom Kippur War. It resulted in petrol rationing all over London, making it difficult for people to get to the match, and an accompanying rail strike didn't help matters! Just 19,150 came through the turnstiles on the night, when we'd hoped for a sell-out. At least the game was an entertaining one, ending 2–2 against a Bayern side that were to go on and win the European Cup that season. Phil certainly felt honoured that so many fans had turned out in such difficult circumstances to see it. Despite losing money, he still maintains that the evening is a great memory of his time at Spurs.

In truth, everyone on Phil's testimonial committee was gutted for him and we decided amongst ourselves to organise an auction at the Sportsman Club to help recoup some of his losses. All sorts of items, ranging from match-worn shirts to international caps, were donated by Phil's Spurs teammates and other professionals in the game like Dave Webb and Bobby Moore. Jimmy Hill always acted as chief auctioneer at such events and boxing commentator Reg Gutteridge assisted him.

You could always guarantee that if no bids were forthcoming, Jimmy would end up putting in a bid himself. Many times he ended up winning an item that I'm sure he never wanted in the first place! The best prize available on the night of Phil's auction was a night out with former Bond Girl Julie Ege. Jimmy knew the Norwegian actress quite well and she'd agreed to be wined and dined by the highest bidder. There was some frantic bidding for the honour and I almost secured a date with her. Sadly, my pockets weren't quite deep enough and a £600 bid secured the Scandinavian beauty on the night. I was disappointed to lose out, but happy in the knowledge that Phil had benefitted. It was typical of Phil's luck though when the winner's cheque bounced and the prize ended up unclaimed! A few days after the auction I told my wife about how I'd almost won a date with Miss Norway. She laughed at first and then steam came out of her ears when I told her I'd bid £550. I knew there and then there was no chance of me stepping in when Julie said she was happy to accept a reserve.

My wife Sylvia seemed to take a more of an interest in my testimonial productions from then on, although maybe that's just my imagination. She took an active role in many of the meetings, which were usually held at my home, preparing lavish finger buffets fit for a king. Alan Mullery still says today that he'd wished more of the meetings for his testimonial had taken place at my home, as he loved Sylvia's spreads.

I certainly learnt some lessons from the Phil Beal disaster, and from then on I advised the players to choose a local rival to play. Cyril Knowles picked Arsenal in 1975, as did Pat Jennings in 1976. Pat's testimonial went especially well and he cleared £25,000 after deductions, probably about £10,000 more than he earned all season! Greavsie, then aged 36 and playing semi-pro for Chelmsford City, donned a Spurs shirt on the night and conjured up all the old magic around the penalty box, scoring twice in a 3–2 win. I watched his magical display sitting in the first row behind the directors' box, even though Pat had given me tickets to sit with them. However, I couldn't bear to sit near the directors, having tolerated so many years of their 'nose in the air' attitude towards me every time I was in the players' company. In the bar after the game,

Jimmy walked over to Pat and I with a big grin covering his face. I laughed.

"You've still got the old magic then Jim."

"Thanks me old son. Bill Nick and Keith think the same. They've been trying to talk me into making a comeback at Spurs!"

It didn't surprise me. I had always thought he'd retired too early and had often told him so.

" If I were you Jim, I'd give it some serious thought. You've still got a lot to offer."

I was desperate for Jim to play for the club again and we certainly needed him. Keith Burkinshaw hadn't made the best of starts to his managerial career since taking charge after Terry Neill had walked out and joined Arsenal. Pat had conceded eight goals up at Derby a few weeks before his testimonial and I was sure a Greavsie return would provide a welcome boost. He certainly thought long and hard about it and talked it over with Professional Footballers' Association chairman Derek Dougan, but in the end decided against it. Unknown to me, Jim actually had a serious drink problem at the time, one that was beginning to rule his life. Knowing that now, it makes sense why he passed on the comeback idea. He certainly wouldn't have wanted to become a liability or an embarrassment to the club. It was a very dark time for him as well as Spurs, who were relegated at the end of that season.

As well as organising fund-raising events for Spurs players, I've also helped the star players of other London clubs. My friendship in the seventies with Chelsea chairman Brian Mears and the Blues club secretary Chris Matthews resulted in me filling the role of testimonial chairman for three of their 1970 FA Cup winning side. Left back Eddie McCreadie, striker Ian Hutchinson and midfielder John Hollins were all rewarded for their loyalty to the Blues with benefit games. For John's match in November 1974, Arsenal provided the opposition on what was a terrible night weather-wise. It rained heavily in the days leading up to the game as well as on the night itself. The weather always played a big part in the financial success of testimonial matches and I warned John beforehand not to expect a big gate. My prediction was right: only a few thousand showed up at Stamford Bridge that evening. As was customary, I went into the dressing rooms after the game armed with envelopes containing £25 for every player who had taken part. In the visitors' dressing room I spotted Arsenal skipper Alan Ball and headed over to him to hand over the envelopes.

"What's this for?" Alan asked.

"John insists that every man gets £25 expenses as appreciation for turning out for him tonight."

"We can't take it. The weather's been atrocious and the gate looked poor to me. I'll be thanking John for the offer, but please give them back."

It said a lot for Alan's standing as captain in that Gunners side, as £25 was a decent amount in those days. It was equivalent to about a quarter of their weekly wage, yet not one of Alan's teammates questioned it.

At the end of that 1974/75 season, John left Chelsea for QPR, where he spent four good seasons, helping them to runners-up spot in the First Division in 1975/76. In 1979, QPR were relegated and John found himself forced to look for another club. My involvement in his testimonial had led to us becoming very good friends and he called me up that summer seeking my advice.

"Luton are interested in buying me. What do you reckon?"

"They only just avoided relegation to the Third Division. I reckon you can do better John; you're only 33. If I were you, I'd sit tight and wait for the big guns to come in." He did just that, and a week later Arsenal manager Terry Neill came knocking and John put pen to paper. The move was an excellent one for him and brought a new lease of life to his career. He played over 120 league games for the Gunners, but sadly for him didn't win any medals during his time there. The closest he came was in the European Cup Winners' Cup final in 1980, but the Gunners were beaten 5–4 on penalties. John scored his spot kick, but Liam Brady and Graham Rix missed and Valencia snatched the trophy.

John's teammates during his spell at QPR included midfielder Mick Leach and fullbacks Ian Gillard and Dave Clement, all three of whom benefitted from my expertise after Rangers chairman Jim Gregory asked me to help out in their testimonial seasons. Dave Sexton had moved on to manage Manchester United by 1978, when I arranged Clement's match and I asked him to bring a team to Loftus Road for the game. Unfortunately, once again, the weather played havoc with a testimonial's preparations and two days of solid rain put the game in jeopardy. In the end, despite the terrible state of the pitch, Jim Gregory allowed it to go ahead. The small crowd that showed up witnessed a farcical encounter that QPR won 4–2, with the ball holding up in huge puddles throughout the 90 minutes of play. I was sorry for the spectators, but unlike John Hollins's match, the payday was not entirely dependent on the gate receipts, as Jim Gregory had guaranteed me that Dave would earn £10,000 out of the game. Aside from the football match, I had, with the help of promoter Beryl Cameron-Gibbons, also organised a fully licensed boxing night at the Royal Garden Hotel in Kensington and it was a knockout success. The day after the event I went to tell Jim the good news and collect the £10,000 cheque he'd promised for Dave.

"We managed to raise six grand from that boxing night," I gleefully told him.

"That's great Morris. Obviously the game didn't bring in anything like that, but I'll give you a cheque for four grand that'll take the total pot up to the ten grand as I promised."

"Hang on a minute. The boxing night was a separate fundraising event. Surely, you're not counting that towards the ten grand you promised for the match."

"I never promised ten grand for the match!"

"You did."

"No. You obviously got the wrong end of the stick. I guaranteed that Dave's testimonial would bring in ten grand and that included all events associated with it."

I wasn't happy with the outcome, but it seemed we had been talking at crossed purposes a few weeks before. Jim handed over a cheque for ten grand and Dave was delighted.

The following year, QPR were relegated to the Second Division and Dave was sold to Bolton for £170,000. He stayed there for one season before moving to Wimbledon and then on to Fulham. He then broke his leg quite badly and became depressed at the thought of his career coming to an end.

Although testimonials were a great way to provide players with a cash boost for their lives after football, they couldn't fill the void keenly felt by many when their days on the pitch were over. Tragically, Dave took his own life in 1982. He was just 34 and left a wife, Pat, and two young boys, Paul and Neil, both of whom have since made a name for themselves in the game. Neil has made over 250 appearances for West Brom and Paul has coached the Republic of Ireland under-21 side, as well as the Chelsea reserve team in recent years.

Six weeks after Dave's death, I organised a memorial game at Loftus Road to help raise funds for his young family. The QPR first team played a side made up of Dave's former team-mates that included Phil Parkes, Frank McLintock, Stan Bowles, Ian Gillard and Don Givens. In the boardroom after the match, Jim Gregory took me aside and handed me a cheque.

"Here's £10,000 for the memorial fund. You can have it on one condition, that you never tell the press or anyone else that I gave it to you."

Jim passed away in 1998 and until now I hadn't revealed the secret, but I feel it's right that people should know his generosity. It was typical of him. He was a real tough nut to crack and a man who stood by his own principles. He'd been adamant four years earlier that the takings from the boxing night should be included in the £10,000 he'd guaranteed, and now here he was donating £10,000 to the memorial fund.

Almost 10 years after Dave's memorial match, I had the sad duty of having to organise another one, this time in honour of Cyril Knowles who died of brain cancer in August 1991. I was at Carrow Road with Terry Venables, then Tottenham chief executive, watching Spurs play Norwich when the news filtered through to us that Cyril had passed away, aged just 47.

"We've got to do something for his family," I said to Terry, who had been a teammate of Cyril's from 1966 to 1969.

"Morris, I'll leave it with you. I'll give you full use of White Hart Lane and the staff. I know you'll do Tottenham proud."

I decided to make the occasion a really fun day out for the family, one that would reflect Cyril's own personality. I organised not one, but two matches and decided it would be fitting for Arsenal to provide the opposition for one as Cyril had enjoyed many great tussles against them as a player. One of the best, although at the same time most disappointing for Spurs fans, had been the night in May 1971 when the Gunners won the league title at White Hart Lane. With George Graham's help, who at the time was the Arsenal manager and had been a member of that '71 side, we organised a match against Cyril's old teammates, who had won the League Cup that same year. Terry made the first team available for the second game, although rather than ask another club to provide the opposition, I delved into my contacts book and with the help of my daughter Shelley, who made many of the phone calls, we reformed Tottenham's 1981 FA Cup-winning side.

The day's events on Remembrance Sunday began at 2pm, when I'd organised for all three domestic trophies to be paraded around White Hart Lane. Arsenal provided the championship trophy and Spurs the FA Cup. The famous three-handled League Cup, a trophy Cyril had won twice in his time at Spurs, was provided by Sheffield Wednesday. I must admit, I was disappointed when Wednesday later charged the Memorial Fund the £200 it cost them to employ a security firm to bus it down from Sheffield for the day. They were a top-flight club then and I'm sure they could have done it without charging. Celebrity boxer Frank Bruno showed up to sign autographs and start the kick-off. He was a great sport on the day, although he refused to come onto the pitch wearing a Spurs shirt. He is a West Ham fan, although his diplomatic answer was that he didn't want to upset the Arsenal fans in the crowd. I certainly wasn't going to argue with him about it!

It was a marvellous day's entertainment, with Glenn Hoddle especially wowing the 13,000 spectators with a mesmerising display. Terry Gibson also got them off their seats, scoring one of the sweetest volleys I'd ever seen at the Lane. Both matches were played in a great spirit and warmed the hearts of a crowd that laughed when Tottenham's reserve-team manager Ray Clemence conceded a bizarre own goal by throwing the ball into his own net and booed George Graham's every touch. George took it well though, and it was a testament to him and Arsenal that despite going out of the League and European Cups that week, they still laced up their boots for the occasion. All the ex-pros who turned out gave their time for free and refused to take any travel expenses. For some, like Arsenal's Eddie Kelly who journeyed up from Torquay, it was a sizeable gesture. Alan Gilzean, who wrote to me saying he couldn't make the game, still did his bit for the cause by sending me one of his Scotland international jerseys to raffle off. It made over £2,000 for the fund. Terry Venables also made sure that a video entitled *Nice One Cyril* was made available to the fans and many happily parted with 12 quid to watch the day's highlights with commentary provided by the legendary Kenneth Wolstenholme. A few weeks later, I was able to hand over a cheque for £120,000 to Cyril's widow, Betty, and her three children, Tracey, Julian and Matthew. It was the least we could do to honour a lovely man.

Former Spurs player Graeme Souness was very disappointed when commitments he had as Liverpool manager prevented him from playing a part in Cyril's memorial. I told him not to be too hard on himself, as he'd helped me out on many other occasions, including my son-in-law Paul Miller's testimonial game in August 1986. When Tottenham granted Paul the honour, the youngest player ever at 26, I warned him that he'd struggle to get a good crowd, as the public were turning their backs on football at the time due to widespread hooliganism.

"If a player like Glenn Hoddle can only pull in 13,000, you'll be lucky to get 5,000," I told him. A few days later on 5th April,1986, Paul travelled to Scotland with Tottenham to play a friendly match against Rangers. Spurs won 2–0 and it proved to be Jock Wallace's last game in charge of the Scottish giants. Two days later, I met up with Paul at Kenilworth Road where he was playing for an England XI in a testimonial for Luton's Ricky Hill.

"Did you hear that Graeme Souness got the Rangers job?" I asked him.

"No, I didn't."

"Shall we ask him if he'll bring Rangers to Tottenham for your testimonial?"

"I reckon it's worth a go."

A couple of weeks later, Paul and I drove over to St Albans where Graeme, as captain of Scotland, was preparing for the

Rous Cup clash against England at Wembley that weekend. At the end of the training session, Paul strode over to Graeme and asked if Rangers could make it on 2nd August, the date Spurs manager Peter Shreeve had made free for his testimonial. Graeme wasted no time and got straight on the phone to the Rangers club secretary. After a short call he said, "We've got a friendly over in Germany a few days before, but I'll cancel our return flight to Scotland and stop in London on the Thursday so we can play Spurs on the Saturday. Don't worry about expenses, Rangers will cover the cost."

By the time the match came around, David Pleat, who I'd known for many years during his time in charge of Luton Town, had replaced Peter Shreeve in the Spurs hot seat. Soon after taking the reins, David told me of his desire to make Ipswich and England central defender Terry Butcher his first big signing at the club. It didn't sound good news for Paul, who played in that position alongside Graham Roberts. However, the day before his big day, Graeme Souness beat David to Butcher's signature and Paul breathed a temporary sigh of relief.

As we'd hoped, thousands of Rangers fans crossed the border, many probably hoping to get a glimpse of their new English recruit in action. Butcher didn't play, and instead watched from the stands. It didn't stop the Scots singing his name for almost the entire 90 minutes of a 1–1 draw. After the match, I congratulated Paul on a good performance and joked, "I think there were 16,000 Rangers fans out there today and about half a dozen Spurs!" I believe Paul and Shelley took Graeme out for a meal that evening and gave him a nice watch to say thank you. Another Scot, former Manchester United boss Tommy Docherty, also boosted Paul's testimonial coffers by refusing to collect a fee as the after-dinner speaker at another fund-raising event that I helped organise for my son-in-law.

A few weeks later, the writing was on the wall for Paul at Spurs. David Pleat may have failed to capture Terry Butcher, but he beat Chelsea to the signature of Dundee United and Scotland defender Richard Gough. Paul played just two more league games before joining Charlton halfway through the season. Graham Roberts also left Tottenham about the same time, becoming another one of the 'Souness Revolution' of English signings at Rangers.

Following the success of Paul's match against Scottish opposition, Irish international Chris Hughton was tempted to bring Celtic to London for his testimonial. Tottenham, though, discouraged the idea, pointing out that a small minority of Rangers fans had caused some damage to White Hart Lane and they'd rather not risk the same happening with the arrival of another Glasgow giant. Chris instead chose Arsenal, which seemed logical to me. In fact, ten years earlier I had wanted to sign a testimonial pact with our North London rivals. The idea being that when a player from either club was due a fund-raising game that Arsenal or Spurs, depending who they played for, would provide the opposition. That way, I'd be able to keep the expenses down and the players would end up with a bigger payday. It made sense to me, and would have eradicated another Bayern Munich/Phil Beal scenario, but the pact idea was never sanctioned when I sounded out the Gunners.

Looking back, of the 25 testimonials I've been involved with over the last 40 years, the four I'm most proud of are the ones for World Cup winners Bobby Moore, Geoff Hurst, Gordon Banks and George Cohen. As well as enjoying the kudos that comes with being associated with the Boys from '66, I also got great satisfaction from going the extra mile to ensure they were successful. When George asked me to sit on his committee in 1969, his 13-year career at Fulham had just come to a premature end following a bad knee injury. I was determined that a man who had dedicated his entire career to one club should get a good send off – and he did. The committee agreed to the suggestion that England's 1966 World Cup winners should be asked to play a team of international all-stars at Craven Cottage. Sadly, George was just getting over pneumonia so couldn't take his usual spot at right back, but the game was a big success and ended with England's World Cup XI winning the game 10-7! More importantly, it raised £8,000 for George's retirement fund. It may not have been enough to set him up for life, but it did allow him to take the first rungs up the ladder of a successful property business.

In 1970, West Ham granted Bobby Moore a testimonial,

and for that I planned a number of fund-raising events over the course of the season. A ladies' night at the Hilton was a huge success, with over 1,000 guests paying good money for their dinner-and-dance ticket. Top entertainers of the day, including Ronnie Corbett, Jimmy Tarbuck, Kenny Lynch and Danny La Rue performed for free and, as you'd expect, they went down a storm. Drag artist La Rue wasn't too happy with me when he arrived in his dressing room and discovered that I hadn't supplied a dressing rail long enough to hold the extravagant dresses he wore during his act. He threw a tantrum and called me "incompetent", before storming off like a spoilt diva. I guess he was just playing the part! The loudest laugh of the night didn't come from one of the acts I'd booked, but from a joke told by Bobby himself. Just a few weeks after being accused of stealing a £625 diamond and emerald-encrusted bracelet from a hotel jewellery shop in Bogotá when away with the England team. He stood up and said: "I'd like to thank all the ladies for coming tonight. I would have liked to have given you all a bracelet, but I could only get the one." As you can imagine, everyone roared with laughter. It was typical of Mooro to make a joke out of something as serious as being accused of theft. When the news broke about his arrest, I got straight on the phone to his wife Tina and told her, "Get yourself on the next flight to Bogotá. I'll pay." She thanked me for the offer, but said the Foreign Office had told her Bobby would soon be released. "I don't want to get on a plane and miss him altogether," she said. As it turned out, Bobby's ordeal lasted longer than Tina or anyone expected. He was kept under house arrest for four days before eventually being freed after signing a declaration that he'd make himself available for questioning if neccessary. After his ordeal Bobby flew to Mexico, where he was reunited with his England teammates who were preparing for the World Cup. Tina eventually met up with her husband in Guadalajara, as they'd originally planned before the nonsense about the bracelet. It wasn't until 1975 that the Colombian authorities officially closed the case, even though it was obvious to everyone that the entire episode was a plot to frame the England captain. Bobby Moore wouldn't even steal a crisp without asking first!

The 1970 World Cup saw Bobby produce possibly his best ever performance in an England shirt. In fact, I wasn't even planning to go to the finals in Mexico, but changed my mind after watching him make one brilliant tackle after another against Brazil in the group stages. That match is also remembered for the so-called 'Save of the Century' by Gordon Banks from Pele's powerful header. England lost 1–0, but deserved a draw and I was convinced that the two sides would meet again in the final. My mate Philip Isaacs agreed and we hastily booked a flight to Mexico City with the aim of seeing England in the knockout stages. The problem was, our flight was due to leave a few hours after England's final group game against Czechoslovakia and Ramsey's men still needed a point to progress to the quarter-finals. We spent a nervous evening watching the match at the Sportsman Club in central London with one hand on our suitcases ready for a mad dash to the airport. Allan Clarke's second-half penalty confirmed England's place in the last eight and our seat on the plane!

The match against West Germany in León was a terrible let down, with England throwing away a two-goal lead and striker Gerd Müller bagging the winner for the Germans in extra time. After the game, Philip and I met up with some of the England players at their hotel, including Martin Peters and goalkeeper Peter Bonetti, who had replaced stomach-virus victim Gordon Banks in goal. Bonetti had been a fault for the first German goal, allowing a relatively tame shot by Franz Beckenbauer to creep under his body. Banks would have saved it for sure, and so too would Bonetti 99 times out of 100. I sought out England's stand-in goalie at the hotel directly after the match to offer my condolences.

"Bad luck Peter. The Germans never know when they're beaten."

"I wish they bloody did. I can't believe we're out," he replied.

"I certainly didn't expect to be going on my summer holiday quite so soon," added Martin Peters, who was standing with Bonetti and like him looked utterly crestfallen.

"Are you flying back to London?" I asked.

"No. We're going to Guadalajara to meet up with our wives before going on to Acapulco for a holiday."

"How are you getting to Guadalajara?"

"No idea," replied Martin.

"You can't get a flight from León, I've checked. You can fly from Mexico City though. You're both welcome to jump in our taxi to the capital tomorrow."

"That would be great. I'm itching to see my wife again," said Peter.

That evening at the team hotel, I grilled Bobby Moore about England's exit.

"What happened?" I asked.

"It doesn't seem real. I can't believe it. I thought we were home and dry at 2–0. I can't remember the last time we conceded three goals in one game."

"It was three years ago against Scotland at Wembley," I replied. Bobby forced a smile.

"Oh yeah, that's when they won the World Cup! Anyway, to be honest, I think Peter's got to be disappointed with their first goal. It wasn't a great shot, was it?"

"Nah. Losing Banksie like that has cost us."

"I know. Between you and me, I don't think Peter's been properly focused. He's been too worried about what the wives are getting up to."

Alf Ramsey had been against the players' wives travelling to Mexico, but a few went along nevertheless, including Tina Moore and Frances Bonetti. Their prescence in Mexico certainly proved a distraction, especially to the gentlemen of the press who had something other than football to write about. Tina even penned her own World Cup diary for the *Daily Sketch* in 1970! I suppose you could call Tina and the three other ladies in Mexico that summer, the original WAGs. Personally, I don't understand the media's fascination with WAGs, and most of today's crop just seem to be publicity-seeking, shopaholic empty-heads. During his time as manager of Sunderland, Roy Keane condemned the WAGs for allegedly making his players "weak and soft" and claimed that he had missed out on signing star players because the WAGs weren't impressed with the shopping opportunities in the working-class city. In my opinion, footballers' wives and girlfriends should stay firmly in the background and out of the newspapers. My daughter Shelley certainly never attempted to claim any limelight when married to a top professional footballer. She always stayed in the background and provided great support to her husband, as did the other wives and girlfriends of the Spurs players in the eighties.

I guess only Peter Bonetti knows whether he was mentally prepared for the biggest game of his life. All I can say is during the long drive to Mexico City the next day, the man they called 'the Cat' didn't seem too troubled by the defeat or his own performance. He happily cracked jokes and whistled merrily for much of the 200-mile trip, while those around him were deep in thought of what might have been. In fact, after stopping for a bite to eat, Martin Peters turned to me when the Cat was out of earshot, scowled and said, "I can't believe Bonetti's taken it so well. We're out of the bloody World Cup and he doesn't seem bothered in the slightest!" I guess the defeat hit Martin harder. He'd scored the second goal in England's defeat and had been substituted by Alf Ramsey with England 2–1 up. He may have already been the owner of a World Cup winner's medal, but Martin was bitterly disappointed not to be lining up against Italy in the semi-final and playing for a probable place against the Brazilians in the final. For Peter Bonetti, the likelihood is that Banks would have replaced him in the side for the next match. He probably viewed the fact that he even played in Mexico as a bonus, having been a non-playing member of the 1966 squad.

After dropping Martin and Peter in Mexico City, I caught a plane to Miami for a few days of relaxation and to try and get the England disappointment out of my system, although I wished I hadn't. On arriving at Miami Airport, US customs officials swooped on me and before I knew it they were accusing me of being a Mexican drug-runner!

"Empty out your pockets," asked one burly officer as I walked through the customs hall still wearing the sombrero I'd worn during England's defeat. I pulled out a handful of white breath-freshening sweets from my jacket pocket and was instantly pounced upon by two guys. Tic tacs had only been available in British sweet shops since 1969, but it seemed they hadn't found their way on to candy store shelves in Miami.

"You're coming with us," said one of the two officers checking me over and before I knew it, I was lifted up off my feet and carried away to an interrogation room. Once there I suffered a humiliating strip-search.

"Are you a Mexican drug-runner?" asked one of my inter-rogators, as I stood there naked. I had long, thick sideburns at the time and coupled with my tanned skin from time spent sunning myself by the hotel pool, I could understand why they'd asked if I was Mexican.

"No. I'm an English soccer fan and they're tic tacs, not drugs!" Thankfully, one of the officers settled the argument by placing the sweets in a test tube and adding some liquid to them.

"It's come back negative. Sorry about that Sir. You can put your clothes back on now."

It was the last thing I needed, as I struggled to come to terms with the fact that England had relinquished their grip on the Jules Rimet trophy. After a couple of solemn days in Miami I got bored and flew back home. I never even considered returning to Mexico to see the final between Brazil and Italy. It's a decision I've regretted for the last 40 years! I should have put England's defeat behind me and been in the Azteca Stadium to see Brazil claim a third world title with a 4–1 victory, but instead I watched it on my new colour TV at home. I jumped off the sofa and roared my appreciation when Carlos Alberto sealed the win with a perfect goal in the 86th minute. I never tire of watching that strike, considered by many as the greatest goal ever scored. A total of eight outfield players passed the ball before Brazil's captain hammered it into the corner of the goal following Pele's inch-perfect pass across the 18-yard box. It's the one game I wished I'd never missed.

A few weeks after the World Cup final, I organised a gentlemen's evening as part of Bobby Moore's testimonial season. Bobby invited many of his personal friends and fellow professionals in the game to come along.

"Who's Freddie Starr?" asked Bobby, when I showed him the tickets I'd had printed for the occasion.

"He's a young comedian that I saw at the Cabaret Club in Manchester."

"Never heard of him. He'd better be good or the lads will slate you and him."

"Don't worry Bob, he'll have everyone in stitches."

I don't think Freddie Starr had ever performed in the capital before, and was understandably a little apprehensive. "It'll get you noticed," I told him. That night, Freddie had Bobby and the boys rolling in the aisles. He was absolutely brilliant. Some months later, the week before Bobby's testimonial match against Celtic, Freddie performed at the Royal Variety Performance in the presence of Her Majesty the Queen Mother. Also on the bill at the London Palladium that night were singers Andy Williams, Max Bygraves and Dionne Warwick and comic actors Marty Feldman and Tim Brooke-Taylor. It was Freddie though who stole the show, with his impersonation of Mick Jagger. The audience loved it and demanded an encore. He duly obliged, making him the first Royal Variety performer in 47 years to be allowed one!

The job of organising Bobby's match was taken off my hands when he called me up and sheepishly asked whether I'd mind if oil firm Esso took over the running of the game, as they wanted to sponsor the match.

"Are you kidding? Would I mind? I'd love them to take it off my hands. It saves me a job and hopefully you'll earn a lot more out of it." It was typical Bobby and I'm sure he sat at home for ages mulling over how to break the news to me. I had a real laugh winding him up that year. I remember on one occasion he was pictured in a national newspaper standing by a Jaguar car with his wife Tina, their children and an au pair. A caption accompanying the photo read, 'The Moores are off to Paris.' After reading the story, I called him up and bellowed down the phone, "What the hell are you doing being photographed next to a Jag and telling reporters you're off to Paris? I'm sat here slogging my guts out, telling everyone how poor you are and why they should support your testimonial and you're off jet-setting! You're certainly not making my job any easier you know!" He stuttered uneasily and apologised before roaring with laughter on realising that I was just mucking around.

In truth though, despite being the second most recognisable footballer in the world, behind Pele, Bobby never earned megabucks at West Ham and he certainly appreciated the 25,000 fans that dug deep in their pockets to pay tribute to him. Sadly, just six weeks later, West Ham's hierarchy decided Bobby's 13 years of loyal service counted for nothing when they publicly humiliated him a few days after making his 499th appearance for the club – a 4–0 FA Cup defeat at Blackpool. The night before the match, Bobby had made the mistake of going to a nightclub called the 007, owned by former British heavyweight boxer Brian London, where he sunk a few beers with teammates Jimmy Greaves and Brian Dear. Young striker Clyde Best also went along, but only drank Coke. In the players' defence, they were under the impression the game would be cancelled due to an icy pitch and hence wanted to make the most of the New Year's Day evening. All four returned to the team hotel a little after 1am, where they ordered coffees and sandwiches before getting eight hours sleep and joining the team for breakfast at 10am. Unfortunately, one irate West Ham fan took the Cup exit very badly and turned up at manager Ron Greenwood's office on Monday to complain about the players' pre-match preparation. The same supporter then told several Fleet Street newspapers. As a result, the club went public on the matter and decided to suspend Bobby, Greavsie and Dear for two weeks and fine them one week's wages. Best was treated more leniently, as he wasn't amongst the 12 players on duty against Blackpool and no alcohol had passed his lips that night. Bobby was absolutely shattered by the way the club had treated him and couldn't understand why they'd not dealt with the matter behind closed doors. I told him, "You've done your time at Upton Park. Come to Spurs and be treated like a king." I know he gave it some serious thought and he may have made the switch, if he hadn't two years remaining on his contract. "I've got to honour my contract. The fans at least deserve that," he said.

The following year Geoff Hurst completed my hat-trick of testimonials for the Boys of '66. Once again, a ladies' night and gentlemen's evening formed part of the fund-raising events and once again the top celebrities of the day turned up. For one of Geoff's functions, singer Clodagh Rodgers, who sang *Jack in the Box*, the UK's entry to the Eurovision Song Contest that year came along with her husband, as did film director Bryan Forbes, a big Hammers fan who was on Geoff's testimonial committee,

and his wife, the actress Nanette Newman. I have a nice photograph of us all sitting around the top table with Geoff and his
lovely wife Judith.

After much deliberation amongst committee members,
who aside from Forbes, also included Ernest Maxin, the man
responsible for choreographing many of the great musical
comedy routines performed by Eric Morecambe and Ernie
Wise on their TV show, we ended up assembling a squad of
big-name European stars to face West Ham. The big names
included Scotsmen Dave Mackay, Tommy Gemmell, Jimmy
Johnstone and Ted McDougall, Englishmen Rodney Marsh,
John Jackson, Mike Doherty, and Jimmy Greaves, who grew
an impressive handlebar moustache for the occasion, as well
as Portuguese internationals Eusebio and Antonio Simoes,
West Germany's Willi Schulz and Uwe Seeler and Israeli striker
Mordechai Spiegler. Ron Greenwood had tried to sign Spiegler
for West Ham a year earlier, after the Israeli had impressed
during the World Cup finals in Mexico. Spiegler had phoned
me from Greenwood's office to ask my advice.

"Hello Morris. I'm here with Mr Ron Greenwood. He
would like to sign me, but I don't do anything without asking
you first." I was taken aback, as I'd only known Mordechai
for a short while, but here he was asking for my advice on a
life-changing decision. I hesitated at first, but then told him to
put pen to paper and with that he hung up and continued his
discussions with Greenwood. In 1970, the signing of foreign
stars by English clubs was unheard of and almost certainly any
transfer would have involved breaking through masses of red
tape due to its groundbreaking nature. West Ham looked into
it, but Mordechai later told me that obtaining a UK work permit
had proved impossible and a few months later he signed for
Paris FC instead. It took another eight years before Sheffield
United manager Harry Haslam pioneered the signing of foreign
stars, when he put his good contacts in Argentina to use, signing
Alex Sabella and Pedro Verde and tipping off Spurs manager
Keith Burkinshaw about the availability of World Cup winners
Osvaldo Ardiles and Ricardo Villa.

Geoff's match drew a full house to Upton Park and they
were treated to a marvellous game, refereed by Jack Taylor,

who went on take charge of the 1974 World Cup final. Geoff opened the scoring for the Hammers on his big night but McDougall equalised before half-time. After the break, the Europeans played some lovely football and went 4–1 up with two goals from Rodney Marsh and one from Greavsie who scored within five minutes of replacing Eusebio. West Ham's then record £120,000 signing, Bryan 'Pop' Robson, scored twice in two minutes and Clyde Best added another minutes later; the game ended 4–4. Now that's entertainment!

A late-night call from Stoke manager Tony Waddington in 1973 put the wheels in motion for Gordon Banks's testimonial.

"We want to organise a game for Banksy, but I haven't got a clue where to start. The chairman suggested I 'speak to our good friend Morris Keston.'"

"You know me. I'd love to help out if I can. In fact it would be an honour."

"Our Gordon deserves the best, especially after what's happened. Is there anything we can do to guarantee the fans turn out on a December evening?" I had done enough testimonials to know you couldn't take anything for granted, and told Tony so.

"Even though it's a game to honour a national hero, a few drops of rain or a freezing night and we'd struggle to get 10,000. Firstly, let's ask Tommy Docherty to bring Manchester United along and I'll find out if Eusebio will be free. Give me a few days and I'll come up with an idea of how we can persuade fans to buy tickets in advance."

I tossed and turned in bed most of that night, trying to think of something to pull in the punters, and then an idea came to me as quick as a Muhammad Ali left jab: a competition where the winner had their picture taken with 'the Greatest'. I'd heard that boxing promoter Mickey Duff was selling tickets through his Anglo-American Boxing Club to see Ali's first heavyweight rematch with Joe Frazier in New York. The fight was due to take place six weeks after Gordon's testimonial and Duff was selling tickets, which included return flights, for about £250. I knew that my good friend, sports photographer Monte Fresco, would be covering the follow-up to boxing's 'Fight of the Century' for the *Daily Mirror,* and so

I asked him if he'd be able to arrange for my competition winner to have his photograph taken with Ali. "No problem," he said, and the competition to beat all competitions was born. All you had to do to enter was a buy a ticket for Gordon's testimonial in advance, which I arranged with the help of the club and the local Stoke-on-Trent newspaper *The Sentinel,* who publicised the competition.

Come the Wednesday night of the match, I was at White Hart Lane watching Spurs beat Dinamo Tbilisi 5–1 in a UEFA Cup tie. Gordon understood that despite being the vice-chairman of his testimonial committee, I couldn't miss a Spurs game for him. I believe the committee chairman, the Lord Mayor, picked out the winning ticket from 9,000 at half-time. The next day I called the winner, a guy from Stoke.

"Don't worry. It's all sorted. The fight is scheduled for 28th January at Madison Square Garden and we'll fly you out five days before it. We'll put you up in a hotel and Monte Fresco will take your picture with Ali sometime during your stay, probably before one of Ali's training sessions." Every other day for the next three weeks it seemed the competition winner was on the phone to me, asking when his tickets would arrive. I must admit, I was sweating myself when, ten days before the fight, the tickets still hadn't turned up from Duff. Then, that afternoon they arrived, and I called the competition winner with the news. He was beside himself with excitement by then; the build-up to the fight was immense and he had just seen Frazier and Ali brawling in a TV studio!

"Thanks so much, Morris. Buying a ticket to that testimonial was the best decision I've made in my life!" Everything worked out brilliantly and he got his trip and his photo. What an experience!

Calls for help with testimonials started to dry up later in the eighties, with fewer players showing the loyalty to their clubs that warranted them. In 1993, Spurs legend Eddie Baily contacted me for a moan about the fact that he'd never been offered one by the club, despite giving ten years service on the field between 1946 and 1956 and assisting Bill Nicholson with the team between 1963 and 1974. He felt that Bill Nicholson should have done more to push the club into awarding him a testimonial at White Hart Lane. Instead, I organised a game against Enfield FC at their Southbury Road home, for which the current Spurs squad were made available. That was pretty much the last of my testimonial matches, with the exception of the one that I hold close to my heart – Bill Nicholson's in 2001. I had also sat on Bill's first testimonial committee in 1983, along with sports journalist Ken Jones, for a match against West Ham. The game against Fiorentina was an emotional day, and I had a lump in my throat seeing 82-year-old Bill being led on to the pitch by Martin Chivers. I will never forget the feeling of love and respect that came from the fans in the packed stadium that day.

Testimonials have become a thing of the past, really. These days, the few players at the top level who do give more than ten years' service to a team, tend to have their matches organised by their clubs, with the proceeds going to charity. Like everything else associated with the modern game, figures are astronomical; Alan Shearer's Newcastle honour in 2006 raised £1.64 million for 14 worthy causes and Manchester United's Ole Gunnar Solskjaer gave the £2 million proceeds from his in 2008 to set up a charity to build schools for impoverished children in Africa.

Looking back on all the testimonials I have been a part of has got me thinking: if years of loyalty and dedication to a club is the criteria for being granted the honour of a testimonial match in one's name, surely these days it's the fans who deserve them! With the exception of a few – Ledley King and Ryan Giggs spring to mind – it is certainly no longer players who stick by clubs through thick and thin, through relegation, failure to clinch trophies and the disappointment of losing popular members of the team. Maybe Spurs could start with me – after all, the hours of my life dedicated to the testimonials alone must surely be worth a nod!

FANTASY FOOTBALL

"I've known Morris for many years and have always regarded him as Tottenham's number one supporter. He's always had a finger on the pulse of the game and hence I've always considered him to be an expert. I look forward to reading his thoughts on the greatest Spurs XI."
Roy Hodgson (manager of Fulham)

"Tottenham Hotspur runs thicker through Morris' veins than anyone else I've ever known. He's also a very generous man with a heart of gold."
David Pleat (ex-Spurs manager and former Director of Football)

In his 1984 autobiography *Glory, Glory, My Life With Spurs*, the late Bill Nicholson devoted a chapter to picking a team of the best players to have represented Tottenham Hotspur in the post-War era. He said at the time that he'd always been reluctant to join the 'dream team' debate, as the club had been blessed with so many great players over the years, making it "an impossible choice". The 16 players that made Bill Nick's squad would, he said, "probably win the championship or one of the Cup finals if they were available for the club next season".

People often ask me who, over the 66 years that I have followed Spurs, would make it into my dream team. I agree with Bill: it's a difficult task and one that, for this book, I deliberated on for weeks!

Funnily enough, my squad has ended up being almost identical to Bill's. Only two players are different to his selection, and one of the two was illegible when Bill picked his side as the lad in question was playing youth-team football for Newcastle. Both Nicholson's picks and my own only include players that we've actually seen don the lilywhite shirt. For me, that's all players from 1943 onwards. Like all Spurs aficionados, I've read great things about players who represented the club before I walked through the turnstiles. I can't help but wonder whether a player like 1921 FA Cup-winning captain Arthur Grimsdell, thought by football historians to be one of the best half backs ever, would have made my squad if I'd seen him in action. The same must be said for the likes of Jimmy Dimmock, the Ryan Giggs of the 1920s, and Vivian Woodward, the elegant, skillful amateur, who represented the club between 1900 and 1909.

I guess some people will say it's ridiculous to even compare today's players with those from a bygone age. After all, the game today is unrecognisable from the matches I paid sixpence to see in the 1940s. How can you compare those footballers with the superstars of the 21st century? I reckon if David Beckham could spend his millions on a time machine, and I set the clock at 1943, he'd be in for one hell of a shock. Football back then was played on pitches that would resemble ploughed fields by October, not at all like the bowling green surfaces Beckham plays on all year round. I'd like to see him bend one of those heavy pudding balls 30 yards into the top corner, wearing over-the-ankle boots caked in thick mud! And what about the kit? He may like wearing thick cotton shirts on the catwalk, but could Becks play with a heavy rain-soaked one on his back? Would he even know which position to take up, if you asked him to play at inside right? Come to think of it, would he even be playing the game in his 30s after suffering years of legitimate meaty tackles from behind? I'm convinced that players back then developed a better first touch to avoid those crunching tackles. Now they've been outlawed, today's overpaid players don't seem to have the ball control of yesterday's men. Being a professional footballer was certainly a more hazardous occupation in the good old days, especially if you played in goal. Every season by about December, I'd lose count of the number of goalkeepers that Tottenham's bulldog centre forward Bobby Smith put into the back of the net with his typically robust challenges. Nowadays, you can't so much as breathe on the goalie without conceding a foul!

Bill Nicholson's life at Spurs began in March 1936, when as a 17-year-old he was offered a job on the groundstaff earning £2 a week. He was handed the job of painting every stand in the ground, although manager Jack Tresadern took some pity and asked another young prospect, Ron Burgess, to be Nicholson's paint-pot partner. The two young men soon became best friends at the club and the pair made their first-team debuts in the same season – 1938/39. The outbreak of the Second World War halted their progress, although I regularly watched Burgess play in unofficial matches during the conflict. He was almost always the best player on show and I marvelled at the way the Welshman went past players like they weren't there.

When peace resumed, Burgess was handed the captaincy and he proved to be an inspirational leader. He led Arthur Rowe's 'push and run' side, which included Nicholson at right-half, to the Second Division title in 1950 and the championship the following year. Despite missing Tottenham's title-winning season of 1950/51, due to my Army posting in Egypt, I did see Burgess in action the following season. Aged 34 then, he didn't much look like a footballer, with a slim figure and a premature bald spot, but he was deceptively strong and was the complete player. He was brilliant that season, as Spurs only just failed to clinch back-to-back titles with Manchester United pipping them at the post. I often spent matches focusing mainly on Burgess, trying my best to find a weakness in his game, but couldn't. He possessed a great engine and was constantly on the move facilitating the side's fluid push-and-run style. His distribution, ball control and positional sense were second to none. He also had a great turn of speed, was a great tackler and could hit a powerful shot with either foot. Not only that, but he was also formidable in the air. Ron Burgess was the perfect footballer. I look back today and feel privileged to have seen a player of his calibre. In my mind, Burgess is the best player in the post-War era to have represented Spurs. Bill Nicholson thought the same, naming the great all-rounder as the first player in his dream team line-up, saying his old team-mate was the best midfielder to have played for the club.

The choice for the goalkeeper's position in my dream team

was probably the most difficult decision I had to make. It's a straight decision between Ted Ditchburn and Pat Jennings, as no other keepers, with the exception of maybe Ray Clemence, ever coming close to showing the same level of consistency. Part of the reason it was such a difficult decision is that Ditchburn was my first hero in the game, although I never knew him personally, as I do Big Pat, who is a great friend. Both were excellent keepers, and during their long careers at White Hart Lane, both were known for having huge hands that were as safe as houses. Both men were athletic and extremely brave, with Ditchburn famed for his knack of whipping the ball off the toes of an onrushing centre forward, whereas Jennings, with his superb positional sense, gave strikers little of the goal to aim at. They both commanded their boxes brilliantly, with Pat often claiming crosses one-handed. It was amazing to watch.

My vote goes to Ditchburn. I hope Pat will understand! The only reason I can find for giving him the nod, is that he shone more when playing in weaker sides. For the first four seasons after the War, Spurs were in the Second Division and during that period Ditchburn was superb. He was kept busy by the struggling defenders in front of him, but still kept clean sheets despite his goalmouth being under constant threat. Sorry Pat, but you'll have to make do with a place on the bench.

My vote for right back is an easy one and it goes to Alf Ramsey. 'The General', as he was called due to his ability to command the play and keep calm under pressure, was a key player in Arthur Rowe's 'push and run' side. He was the first real cultured full back in the game and would charge over the halfway line and instigate play down the right flank. His passing was amazingly accurate and I thought he made winger Sonny Walters, an ordinary player, look much better by feeding him some great passes that gave Walters time and space to deliver telling balls. Ramsey's only fault was that he lacked pace, but he could read the game so well that it rarely mattered.

Looking back over the years, the full back berth is one position where Spurs have struggled. Since Ramsey, the club has had a succession of average performers. Double-winners Peter Baker and Ron Henry were decent enough, as were Chris Hughton, Steve Perryman and Danny Thomas in the eighties, but none were in Ramsey's class. However, one full-back who was, is my selection at left back – Cyril Knowles. Cyril was a brilliant player who had a magic wand for a left foot. I loved watching him bomb forward and deliver perfect crosses for the likes of Martin Chivers, Alan Gilzean and Martin Peters to head home. It was a mystery to me why Sir Alf Ramsey didn't pick him for England in the early seventies. In fact, I once questioned Alf over a coffee in the Sportsman Club in Tottenham Court Road. If I remember rightly it was just after he had selected his squad for the 1970 World Cup finals in Mexico.

"Why isn't Cyril Knowles in your squad?" I asked.

"It's a tough call, but I don't think he's as good as Terry Cooper, " he replied. To be fair, Cooper had played really well in the Leeds side that had won the championship in 1969 and finished runners-up to Everton in 1970, but I was having none of it.

"You've got it wrong, Alf. Cooper's a great player, but Cyril's something else. He's the complete package. His crosses are more accurate than Cooper's and he's a better tackler."

"I disagree Morris," Ramsey replied in his typical measured way. "Terry's better defensively and will run all game. I'm not saying Cyril can't run all game, but in the intense heat and high altitude in Mexico, England will need the fittest players in the country and Terry Cooper is certainly one of them. I know he won't let me down in Mexico."

Cyril Knowles only ever won four caps, the final one coming in June 1968 when England lost 1–0 in West Germany, the national team's first ever loss against the Germans. In my mind, he deserved many, many more.

The options available at centre half are limited, as it's a position every manager since Bill Nicholson has struggled to adequately fill. My first choice has to be Nicholson's signing from the summer of '66 – Mike England. His towering presence at the back gave Spurs strength and stability and it paid an instant dividend with the club winning the FA Cup in '67. England certainly wasn't your average centre half, as he possessed a good turn of pace for a big man and controlled the ball as well as any midfielder. His best attribute was undoubtedly his commanding presence in the air, which also made him a potent weapon in attack from corners and free kicks. For a dozen games during the 1968/69 season, Nicholson even paired him up with Jimmy Greaves in attack. England excelled there too, creating a hat-trick for Greavsie and scoring a couple himself. In the early seventies, the club claimed three more trophies thanks in part to the great partnership England struck with Phil Beal at the back. It's no coincidence that when England decided to leave for a stint in US soccer in the spring of '75, Spurs suffered badly and were relegated in 1977.

In my mind, only Maurice Norman gets close to England for the traditional centre-half's role in my starting line-up. Like England, Norman was a strapping six-footer who was deceptively quick, having joined Spurs as a right back from Norwich. I'd say Norman was actually a better tackler than England and just as good at distributing the ball. He was also one of the first centre halves in the game to push forward at set plays, scoring some vital goals during the double-winning season when he was the team's dependable rock at the back. Norman, though, only gets a place on my bench. Other players who came into my reckoning included Graham Roberts and Paul Miller from the FA Cup winning sides of '81 and '82. As a pair they weren't pretty to watch, but they were effective and opposing strikers rarely got the better of them. More recently, Gary Mabbutt was a consistent performer in the nineties, but when you've been spoilt watching Norman and England there's no room for him. Ledley King has also given Tottenham good service, but regular injuries have prevented him from staking a credible claim.

The player I've chosen to partner Mike England at the back is Dave Mackay. Of course, Mackay could quite easily have filled a place in midfield, but with a wealth of talent at my disposal there, he serves my team best at the back. Bill Nicholson gave Mackay the same position in his dream team, with orders to push forward when possible. It's a role Mackay filled brilliantly after fighting back from two broken legs to skipper the side to FA Cup success in '67. Every side needs a competitor like Mackay, but few ever get one half as good as him. He possessed a never-say-die attitude and bulldog spirit that stirred Spurs to great heights, including the 'impossible' double in '61. Mackay was more than just a born leader though: he was also a terrific footballer, a complete all-rounder. He displayed complete mastery over the ball, as well as eagle-eyed vision to pick out teammates with inch-perfect passes. At the heart of my dream-team defence, I doubt many strikers would get up too quickly after feeling the force of one of his crunching tackles! Despite his terrifying presence on the pitch, he was a thoroughly nice bloke who was approachable and easy to chat to at the bar after a match.

The candidates for the three remaining starting positions in midfield with Ron Burgess are: Eddie Baily, Danny Blanchflower, Cliff Jones, Glenn Hoddle, Ossie Ardiles and Paul Gascoigne. I've left out many great players to get to this shortlist, including John White, Alan Mullery, Martin Peters, Tony Galvin, Chris Waddle and David Ginola. Of this group, John White and Alan Mullery probably came closest to making the cut.

John White was actually a good pal of mine in the sixties, often coming to my parties with his teammate and comedy sidekick Cliff Jones. They were a real pair of jokers when they got together and frequently had me in fits of laughter with their antics. I remember once they teamed up for a caper on a train journey back to London after a match up North. I was sitting at a table in the dining carriage with Jimmy Greaves and 'Johnny and Jonesy', when the team's clowns got out off their seats and walked off mid-conversation.

"Where are they going Jim?"

"No idea. Maybe they've got bored waiting for the food to arrive."

Five minutes later Johnny and Jonesy returned wearing the waiters' white jackets, carrying tea towels over their arms and struggling to balance bowls of soup on a rickety trolley.

"Sir, would you like bread with your soup?" One of them handed me a bowl of Scotch broth, before moving on and serving the rest of the carriage!

Aside from being a great joker, John White was also a key player in the double side. He had superb stamina and would run all game, making himself difficult to mark. The press nick-named him 'the Ghost', for the way he'd ghost into space during matches and either score or create a goal for a team-mate. He was an unselfish player and when through on goal would often play a perfectly weighted pass to a teammate if they were in a better position for glory. Terry Venables told me that he'd pick White in his dream team, but as I'm not a technician like Terry, White's contribution to the side often passed me by, and sometimes I believed he went missing in games. Sadly, John was struck by lightning and killed on Crews Hill Golf Course in July 1964. I felt very emotional at his memorial game that November; he was only 26 and an even better player than Martin Peters, who was nicknamed 'the Ghost' a few years later.

Alan Mullery would probably be an automatic inclusion in most clubs' best post-War sides and I'm sure he'll have something to say about it when I tell him I've left him out. We've been great friends for many years and often meet up on match days in the hospitality suites at White Hart Lane. Bill Nicholson bought Mullers in March 1964 to replace the double skipper Danny Blanchflower. It was an impossible task, but after suffering at first from the crowd's weight of expec-tation he turned into one of most consistent performers I've seen in a Spurs shirt. For eight seasons he served the club well, with his non-stop work ethic and ability to inspire those around him. Far from being just a great motivator, Mullers could play a bit too. He was strong on the ball, passed it fluidly and was a fierce tackler who also possessed a powerful shot. He played just as well for England as he did for Spurs and never seemed overawed by the big names in the game, shack-ling Pele brilliantly during the 1970 World Cup finals.

The best winger in my time has without question been Cliff Jones. Forget Ginola and Waddle: they weren't in the same league as Jonesy. In truth, I rate Tony Galvin from the early eighties side above Ginola and Waddle. Former Spurs boss George Graham once told me, "You don't win trophies with players like David Ginola in your side", and I agree with him on that score. Don't get me wrong, Ginola was a great enter-tainer at the Lane when George was the manager, but the Frenchman often saw too much of the ball, making the team one-dimensional and predictable. Spurs did in fact win the

Worthington Cup in 1999 with Ginola in the side, but he was easily marked out of the final by Leicester's Robert Ullathorne. "Robert who?" I hear you cry. I don't recall Cliff Jones being marked out of many matches and especially not by an 'unknown'. Jones could play on either wing, but tended to play better on the left despite being right footed. His extraordinary pace would see him go past a player on the inside, before delivering perfect crosses for the likes of Bobby Smith and Les Allen to score. There was no greater sight during the glory days, than watching Jonesy skimming through the mud at full speed. For a man of average height, he also notched more than his fair share of headed goals. He was totally fearless in the box and never thought twice about putting his head amongst the flying boots and has the scars today to prove it. In the early sixties, the Welsh Wizard was undoubtedly the best winger in the world and I breathed a huge sigh of relief when Spurs snubbed a huge offer from Juventus for him in 1962. I'd play Jones on the left wing in my dream team.

In my lifetime, I've been fortunate to mix in the company of many of the game's top personalities, although none have ever captivated me in conversation the way Danny Blanchflower did. On one occasion, during the Double-winning season, I was staying with some friends in the same hotel as Blanchflower and the rest of the Spurs team. One evening, I was heading out of the hotel when I stumbled upon him sitting in an armchair reading. As I walked by with a couple of friends, he looked up and asked, "Are you off out on the town boys?"

"Yes we are. Do you fancy joining us?"

"Thanks for the offer, but I'm staying in this evening. We've a big game tomorrow."

"How many are we going to win by?" I asked.

"Why don't you take a seat? Not only will I tell you how many we will score tomorrow, but also how we're going to win the championship and the FA Cup this season."

We sat down and three hours later we were still glued to our seats. Our night out ended up being a night in, as we listened intently to Danny's vision on how the game should be played and were privy to his unshakeable belief that Spurs were going to become the first club in the 20th century to achieve the Double. Of course, that's exactly what they did, and I had, as I have the knack of doing, managed to hear it not only from the horse's mouth, but months before it was even to happen.

There's a well-known quote by Blanchflower that reads, "The great fallacy is that the game is first and last about winning. It's nothing of the kind. The game is about glory. It's about doing things in style, with a flourish, about going out and beating the other lot, not waiting for them to die of boredom." I often hear it quoted and whenever I do it always reminds me of that great night spent in his eloquent company.

On the pitch, Blanchflower was as great a player as he was a talker and made everything look so easy. He would impose himself on games, constantly demanding the ball and paralysing the opposition with defence-splitting passes. During his frequent probing forays forward, Dave Mackay would usually have to cover for him as Blanchflower lacked pace and wasn't that great defensively. He got round this by being able to read the game better than anyone else and often changed the team's game plan during matches. He was a born leader and the club's greatest ever captain and would skipper my dream team. Depending on how the game was going, I'd give him authority to change the set-up of my midfield quartet. He could move Jones from the left to the right wing and move himself into the middle and push Burgess out to the left. I'd be confident in him making the right decisions. After all, I'm not a top coach like my mate, Terry Venables. I'm just a fan!

Football is all about opinions and a good case could be made for Eddie Baily, Glenn Hoddle, Ossie Ardiles or Paul Gascoigne to claim the final central slot in midfield. Interestingly though, Bill Nicholson left Hoddle out of his 16-man squad, preferring Ardiles from the 1981 FA Cup-winning side. Paul Gascoigne was only in Newcastle's youth team when Nicholson selected his dream team, although I'd be interested to know what he would have thought of the Geordie genius. I know for sure that Terry Venables rated him highly as he told me he'd pick him in a team of Spurs legends. Gazza reminded me of Eddie Baily from the 1951 Championship side, who also had a brilliant first touch and could open up defences with an accurate pass or a mesmerising dribble. And like Ardiles, they were also masters at shielding the ball before delivering killer passes that unlocked the country's best defences.

My former son-in-law, Paul Miller, introduced me to Ossie Ardiles soon after the World Cup winner arrived with Ricky Villa in 1978. They joined me at the Ritz Club Casino in London's Piccadilly and we had a good evening out with the wives. If I recall correctly, Ossie won a few quid on the tables that night. He had a big beaming smile across his face until we overheard a conversation between my wife Sylvia and his wife Silvia.

"It is much cold [sic] in London, more than Buenos Aries."

"Is it? Don't worry Silvia, your husband's just won some money.

Tomorrow we go out and buy you a fur coat." And they did!

I never saw Glenn Hoddle win on the roulette tables or part with any money for a fur coat, but I did witness him score some of the best goals ever seen at White Hart Lane. One of my favourites was the volley against Nottingham Forest in October 1979. Goalkeeper Milija Aleksic kicked it up field, Chris Jones headed it onwards and Gerry Armstrong headed it towards Hoddle who volleyed it home. From the moment it left Aleksic's hands, the ball did not touch the ground until it was being picked out of the back of Peter Shilton's net. It was just one of many great goals that Hoddle scored during his career, with the Spurs fans recently voting four of his strikes in their top ten. He was certainly the best English player of this generation, an artist supreme with sublime vision, an exquisite touch and a box of tricks the Brazilians would envy. He takes the last spot in my midfield.

Tottenham's record goal scorer, Jimmy Greaves, takes one of the two places in attack, with Bobby Smith, Martin Chivers and Alan Gilzean in the frame for the other. A few others came close to making the cut, including Gary Lineker, Teddy Sheringham and Jurgen Klinsmann. Lineker did brilliantly during his short spell and I never tired of watching him make perfectly timed runs into the box, before stealing a yard of space and scoring. Sheringham was a great link player with a sharp eye for goal and combined excellently with Klinsmann during the 1994/95 season. I thought long and hard about including the German, but it wouldn't really be right to pick a player who only wore the shirt 68 times. After all, what's to stop me then from picking Diego Maradona, who was out of this world in his one appearance at Ossie's benefit match in 1986?

Greavsie had a remarkable career with his best days spent at Tottenham, scoring 306 goals in 420 matches. He is by some distance the best striker I've ever seen at the club. Some days you'd watch him and he'd do very little during the game, but give him half a second and half a chance and the ball would be in the back of the net. He ruled supreme in one-on-one situations, displaying immaculate close control coupled with the poise and balance of a ballerina. I never tire of watching a goal he scored against Manchester United in 1965 on DVD. He received the ball from Dave Mackay 35 yards out with his back to the opposition's goal. He then turned on a sixpence before dancing past the converging tackles of Bill Foulkes, Nobby Stiles and Tony Dunne before drawing 'keeper Pat Dunne and stroking the ball into the gaping net. Pure genius.

Martin Chivers wasn't as consistent a performer as Greavsie, but did have two amazing seasons in the early seventies, when he was rightly regarded as the best striker in Europe. When he was in the mood, there was no stopping him, although some say he lacked aggression and with a better attitude could have scored more. He bagged 202 goals during his nine seasons at the club, making him third in the all-time list at Spurs. When he left the club for Switzerland in 1976, I missed watching his powerful surging runs and asked him to get me some match tickets. I then jumped on a plane and watched him plying his trade for Servette!

One player you couldn't accuse of lacking aggression was Bobby Smith – the human battering ram, who notched 251 goals for the club. He put the fear of God into defenders, but that's not to say he was just all muscle. The burly marksman could also apply a skillful, delicate finish when one was needed. Alan Gilzean's game, on the other hand, overflowed with creative subtle touches from which Greaves and Chivers were chief beneficiaries. Today, ex-Spurs player Dimitar Berbatov is often compared to the Gilzean of 40 years ago, although in my reckoning Gillie was a much better player. He was brilliant in the air, producing deft flicks that Chivers would ram home and also was quicker and more adaptable than Berbatov as well as being a real team player.

I could have chosen any from those three, but in the end opted for the Greaves and Smith partnership, as I believe Smith gelled slightly better with Greavsie in the sixties than the others did. Chivers and Gilzean therefore have to be content with warming my bench along with Pat Jennings, Maurice Norman, Ossie Ardiles, Paul Gascoigne and the very underrated Phil Beal, who gets the nod for his versatility. Now bring on the Arsenal!

My Dream Team:

Ditchburn
Ramsey   England   Mackay   Knowles
Blanchflower   Hoddle   Burgess   Jones
Greaves   Smith

Subs: Jennings, Beal, Norman, Ardiles, Gascoigne, Gilzean and Chivers.

Bill Nicholson's Dream Team:

Jennings
Ramsey   England   Mackay   Knowles
White   Blanchflower   Burgess   Jones
Greaves   Smith

Subs: Ditchburn, Norman, Ardiles, Gilzean and Peters.

FINAL THOUGHTS

12

"Morris has been truly supportive over the years, before and after Tommy's passing. He is a man who never forgets his friends, a man to rely on."
Jean Harmer (wife of Tommy, 1928–2007, Spurs 1949–1960)

"His lovely wife Sylvia said to me, 'Who's going to want to read a book about Morris?' I told her that I couldn't disagree more as everyone's going to want to read about his dedication to football. There's never been a supporter more deserving of having a book written about them"
Betty Knowles (wife of Cyril, 1944–1991, Spurs and England, FA Cup Winner 1967)

Since the formation of the Premier League in 1992, the game has changed more than during any other period that I've been a fan. It's now entirely driven by money and the media, with Sky and other TV firms dictating almost everything – from kick-off times to which teams are actually capable of winning the trophies. There's no denying that as a product the Premier League is second to none, attracting the majority of the world's best players and bringing millions into the coffers of the top clubs through sponsorship and TV rights – but at what cost to the game?

The number of homegrown players has fallen dramatically since the inception of the Premier League. For example, of the starting XIs that played on the first week of the first Premier League season of 1992/93, only ten per cent (23 players) were from outside the UK, whereas on the opening day of the 2009/10 season, 52 per cent (114 players) were foreigners, with Arsenal's side made up entirely of foreign players. What chance do good young British players have of building a career for themselves in the game when their opportunities are being severely limited? Once upon a time, the majority of Tottenham's players came from the youth set-up. In the early eighties, Garry Brooke, Mark Falco, Mickey Hazard, Glenn Hoddle, Chris Hughton, Paul Miller and Steve Perryman were all regulars in the side that had been reared by the youth-team coaches at Tottenham. In the Spurs team today, only Ledley King and Jamie O'Hara have come through the ranks, although Peter Crouch also played for the youth and reserve sides before being sold to QPR for £60,000. I must admit that after watching the 6 ft 7 in striker play for the Reserves in 1999, I told David Pleat, then the Director of Football, that in my opinion Crouch was "useless".

"What's he doing in the side?" I said. "He's a giant, yet he can't even head the ball. Maybe you should tell him to try basketball, because he's never going to be a footballer!" To give David some credit, he reckoned Crouchy had potential and it was with a heavy heart that he allowed him to join Gerry Francis at QPR. Since then Crouch has gone on to play over 30 games for England and scored more than 15 times. I'll admit I was wrong about him! Like Crouch, I'm sure the cream of young British talent will continue to make it through the system today, even though many youth teams at top clubs are as full of foreign players as their senior sides! Exceptional talent, like Wayne Rooney and Jack Wilshire, will always make it, but late developers like Arsenal legend Ian Wright, who signed a professional contract shortly before his 22nd birthday, probably wouldn't get the same opportunity today.

One thing's for certain, the top players today are a world apart from the ones of yesteryear, and the difference isn't just in the astronomical wages they take home each week. Don't get me wrong, I'm not against footballers earning good money. After all I played a small part in helping players earn more through the testimonials I organised in the seventies and eighties. The players today, though, are earning obscene amounts and it's alienating them from the fans. In 1992, the average Premier League player took home £75,000 a year. Today, most top-flight professionals bank over £1million, with the top earners like John Terry and Steven Gerrard reportedly earning over £7million! Today's players have about as much in common with the man on the street as ET – the Extra Terrestrial! Before the Premier League came along, the players were on the same wavelength as the fans that came through the turnstiles each week. Many mixed socially with the supporters and everyone felt like a member of a team. It's ridiculous that clubs are even called clubs today, as that implies that it's a place where people mix! These days the majority of the superstars at Spurs collect their 40 grand each week, play half a game then speed off home in their £100,000 cars. They don't know many, if any, of the fans who turn up to watch them in action and don't seem to want to know them either! There may be better fans than me at Spurs today, but I'm still amongst the club's best-known supporters, yet the current players don't have a clue who I am!

Today's professional footballers have lost touch with the supporters and the power they wield is making fans like me resent them. They sign contracts that aren't worth the paper they're written on, and they only show loyalty if they get paid for it! As soon as they're out of the starting line-up, they're knocking on the manager's door and asking for a transfer. In the old days, players would buckle down on the training field and do everything possible to impress the manager. I can't wait for the day when club chairmen finally make a stand and refuse to release players from their contracts. The players would then have no choice but to show some loyalty! I don't know, maybe I'm being too hard on them and underestimating the power of the players' agents. At the end of the day, I just want players to start showing more loyalty to the fans.

The Premier League's decision to assign TV broadcasting rights to BSkyB in 1992 was a radical move, but it has certainly paid off. At the time, I didn't believe fans would be willing to fix an ugly satellite dish to their homes, and also pay for the privilege of watching live football. I was wrong on both counts, and the Premier League has been coining it in ever since. Deals for UK TV rights have soared from £633,000 per game in 1992 to £4.3million per game for fixtures to be played between 2010 and 2013. In the latest deal, Sky will pay £1.314billionn to show 276 live matches between 2010 and 2013. Foreign TV companies are also forking out £625million over three seasons to show Premier League games, and that figure is expected to increase significantly when the next contract is penned for the seasons 2010/11 onwards. It all adds up to healthy sums in TV revenue, but as a result the fans in England have more chance of predicting the lottery numbers than the kick-off times for games. With matches being beamed live to 600 million homes in over 200 countries, overseas viewers are putting the Premier League under more and more pressure to move kick-off times to suit them. How long before games kick-off at midnight in the UK to enable the fans in New York to watch the match at 7pm?

The biggest problem with top-flight football today is the dominance of the big clubs. Since Blackburn won the Premiership trophy in 1994/95, only three clubs have won it, Arsenal, Chelsea and Manchester United, and if that isn't bad enough, the top four places in the last four seasons to 2008/09 have all been occupied by the 'Big Four' of Arsenal, Chelsea, Liverpool and Manchester United. With the same four teams consistently pocketing the game's rich pickings, the gap between them and everyone else grows wider each season. The sale of Manchester City to members of the ruling family of Abu Dhabi has seen City become the lion in the pack of a new 'Big Five'. Finally, it seems a significant battle is guaranteed for the four lucrative Champions League places. For the rest, survival remains the goal with consistent also-rans Aston Villa, Everton and my beloved Spurs fighting it out for places in the Europa League. It's a sorry state of affairs when you consider the goal for the majority of the teams in the Premier League is a decent Cup run and nothing lower than 17th place in the table. I really miss those days when every fan began a new season believing their club was capable of a top-four finish or a place in the FA Cup final. Being a football supporter back then was so much more interesting when it wasn't the same clubs year after year reaching Cup finals, finishing in the top three or winning the trophies. The fairytale Cup years for Sunderland (1973), Southampton (1976), Ipswich (1978), Norwich (1985), Oxford (1986), Coventry (1987),

Luton (1988) and Wimbledon (1988) are now just distant memories. The only real surprise in recent years was when Harry Redknapp secured the FA Cup for Portsmouth in 2008. I'm hoping Harry can muster a repeat performance, only this time with Spurs!

In recent years, international football has changed almost as much as the English league game. One of the things that bugs me about the national side is just how easily players earn caps. For example, in 1973 I watched Bobby Moore play his 108th and last match for his country. Sadly it ended in defeat when Fabio Capello scored the only goal in a 1–0 win for the Italians at Wembley. How ironic, that it was Capello who handed David Beckham the cap that saw him overtake Bobby Moore's record as England's most capped outfield player. I have nothing against Beckham, but I'll admit that it grates on me that he eclipsed Moore's mark when he'd only actually played 54 full games! Bobby Moore played for the entire match of every one of his 108 England appearances, whereas Beckham had been used as a substitute ten times and withdrawn from play in 43 of the games on his way to breaking the record.

In reality, Beckham is unlikely to accumulate more than 9,000 minutes on the field of play by the time he retires from international football, probably after the 2010 World Cup. It will put him in fifth place in the all-time list, according to englandstats.com. That's way behind the likes of Peter Shilton (10,725 minutes), Bobby Moore (9,780), Billy Wright (9,480) and Bobby Charlton (9,439). I recognise that football today is a squad game, but caps are awarded far too easily for my liking. I'd like to know why man of the match Aaron Lennon was replaced by Beckham in the last ten minutes of England's win over Croatia in September 2009, especially as England were leading 5–1 up at the time! It was Beckham's 114th cap for his country. I don't know why Capello doesn't just throw caps into the crowd and let everyone have one!

With over 120 England games under my belt, I'd certainly be the first to deserve to catch one; when Hunter Davies interviewed me in 1972 for his book *The Glory Game*, I told him that fans never get any credit for their loyalty. Almost 40 years on, I guess the fact that you're reading my story proves me wrong. Finally, a fan gets some recognition! Hopefully, after getting this far you're still thinking my 66-year journey of fanaticism has been a story worth telling. One thing's for sure, it's a been a life filled with as many lows as highs, but I suppose that comes with the territory of being a supporter of both Spurs and England! I never imagined that I'd get the chance to tell my life story, and certainly never dreamed that anyone would part with their hard-earned cash to read it! I guess it shows that, in football, anything's possible, and that's why I'll never lose my appetite for the beautiful game.

Record of Testimonial and Memorial Matches

George Cohen Testimonial
Match: 1966 World Cup XI 10–7 International XI
Date: 10th November 1969
Venue: Craven Cottage
Role: Committee member

Bobby Moore Testimonial
Match: West Ham 3–3 Celtic
Date: 16th November 1970
Venue: Upton Park (24,445)
Role: Chairman

Geoff Hurst Testimonial
Match: West Ham 4–4 European XI
Date: 23rd November 1971
Venue: Upton Park (29,250)
Role: Chairman

Colin Milburn Testimonial
Date: 30th January 1972
Venue: The Hilton Hotel
Role: Chairman

Harry Cripps Testimonial
Match: Millwall 3–5 West Ham
Date: 4th May 1972
Venue: The Den (13,800)
Role: Committee member

RECORD OF TESTIMONIAL AND MEMORIAL MATCHES

Jimmy Greaves Testimonial
Match: Spurs 2–1 Feyenoord
Date: 17th October 1972
Venue: White Hart Lane (45,799)
Role: Committee member

Phil Beal Testimonial
Match: Spurs 2–2 Bayern Munich
Date: 3rd December 1973
Venue: White Hart Lane (19,150)
Role: Chairman

Gordon Banks Testimonial
Match: Stoke 1–2 Manchester United
Date: 12th December 1973
Venue: Victoria Ground (21,000)
Role: Vice-chairman

Eddie McCreadie Testimonial
Match: Chelsea 1–2 Manchester United
Date: 1st May 1974
Venue: Stamford Bridge
Role: Chairman

John Hollins Testimonial
Match: Chelsea 1–1 Arsenal
Date: 6th November 1974
Venue: Stamford Bridge
Role: Chairman

Cyril Knowles Testimonial
Match: Spurs 2–2 Arsenal
Date: 22nd October 1975
Venue: White Hart Lane (17,343)
Role: Committee member

Barry Kitchener Testimonial
Match: Millwall 3–1 Spurs
Date: 27th October 1975
Venue: The Den (7,006)
Role: Committee member

Mick Leach Testimonial
Match: QPR 4–0 Red Star Belgrade
Date: 2nd February 1976
Venue: Loftus Road
Role: Committee member

Alan Mullery Testimonial
Match: Scotland International XI 2–3 Rest of Great Britain
Date: 22nd March 1976
Venue: Craven Cottage
Role: Vice-chairman

Pat Jennings Testimonial
Match: Spurs 3–2 Arsenal
Date: 23rd November 1976
Venue: White Hart Lane (28,924)
Role: Committee member

Dave Clement Testimonial
Match: QPR 4–2 Manchester United
Date: 5th May 1978
Venue: Loftus Road
Role: Chairman

John Pratt Testimonial
Match: Spurs 3–5 Arsenal
Date: 12th May 1978
Venue: White Hart Lane (23,044)
Role: Committee member

RECORD OF TESTIMONIAL AND MEMORIAL MATCHES

Ian Hutchinson Testimonial
Match: Chelsea 2–2 QPR
Date: 27th November 1978
Venue: Stamford Bridge
Role: Chairman

Ian Gillard Testimonial
Match: QPR 1–3 Spurs
Date: 24th April 1979
Venue: Loftus Road (3,937)
Role: Committee member

Steve Perryman Testimonial
Match: Spurs 2–2 West Ham
Date: 30th April 1979
Venue: White Hart Lane (17,702)
Role: Committee member

Terry Naylor Testimonial
Match: Spurs 0–2 Crystal Palace
Date: 29th April 1980
Venue: White Hart Lane (6,363)
Role: Committee member

Dave Clement Memorial
Match: QPR 6–2 Dave Clements XI
Date: 17th May 1982
Venue: Loftus Road
Role: Chairman

Bill Nicholson Testimonial
Match: Spurs 1–1 West Ham
Date: 21st August 1983
Venue: White Hart Lane (20,101)
Role: Committee member

Paul Miller Testimonial
Match: Spurs 1–1 Rangers
Date: 2nd August 1986
Venue: White Hart Lane (16,365)
Role: Chairman

Chris Hughton Testimonial
Match: Spurs 3–1 Arsenal
Date: 10th August 1987
Venue: White Hart Lane (17,826)
Role: Committee member

Cyril Knowles Memorial
Matches: Spurs 1971 0–0 Arsenal 1971
Spurs 1981 2–2 Spurs 1991
Date: 10th November 1991
Venue: White Hart Lane (12,732)
Role: Chairman

Eddie Baily Testimonial
Match: Enfield 1–5 Spurs
Date: 14th May 1993
Venue: Southbury Road (2,700)
Role: Chairman

Bill Nicholson Testimonial
Match: Spurs 3–0 Fiorentina
Date: 8th August 2001
Venue: White Hart Lane (35,877)
Role: Committee member

MY MATCH JOURNALS 1952–2010

Match Records

Season-by-Season Breakdown

Season	Spurs	Others	England	Total
1952/53	32	29	0	61
1953/54	28	15	2	45
1954/55	31	20	3	54
1955/56	37	14	1	52
1956/57	44	27	4	75
1957/58	38	56	7	101
1958/59	37	50	4	91
1959/60	39	46	2	87
1960/61	35	42	4	81
1961/62	56	39	6	101
1962/63	54	36	3	93
1963/64	46	16	4	66
1964/65	53	17	5	75
1965/66	50	27	13	90
1966/67	58	13	4	75
1967/68	48	11	9	68
1968/69	48	10	5	63
1969/70	52	21	7	80
1970/71	53	23	6	82
1971/72	70	29	7	106
1972/73	73	39	6	118
1973/74	55	35	4	94
1974/75	49	38	7	94
1975/76	60	44	4	108
1976/77	51	58	8	117

1977/78	46	37	6	89
1978/79	54	60	5	119
1979/80	68	56	7	131
1980/81	64	51	6	121
1981/82	65	27	4	96
1982/83	54	28	4	86
1983/84	63	32	3	98
1984/85	59	27	3	89
1985/86	66	24	4	94
1986/87	68	27	4	99
1987/88	50	26	5	81
1988/89	54	14	1	69
1989/90	49	12	1	62
1990/91	48	33	5	86
1991/92	62	19	0	81
1992/93	55	19	1	75
1993/94	45	20	0	65
1994/95	41	21	3	65
1995/96	35	8	4	47
1996/97	32	26	0	58
1997/98	34	22	2	58
1998/99	40	10	1	51
1999/00	31	14	2	47
2000/01	41	5	0	46
2001/02	43	6	1	50
2002/03	38	11	0	49
2003/04	38	8	0	46
2004/05	31	5	0	36
2005/06	28	3	1	32
2006/07	38	3	2	43
2007/08	34	2	1	37
2008/09	31	0	1	32
2009/10*	16	0	0	16
	2,718	1,411	202	4,331

* To 26/01/2010

Note: I don't have any record of the matches I watched between 1943 and 1951, but I'd estimate that I went to about 300, with at least 200 of those Spurs games.

Also by Vision Sports Publishing

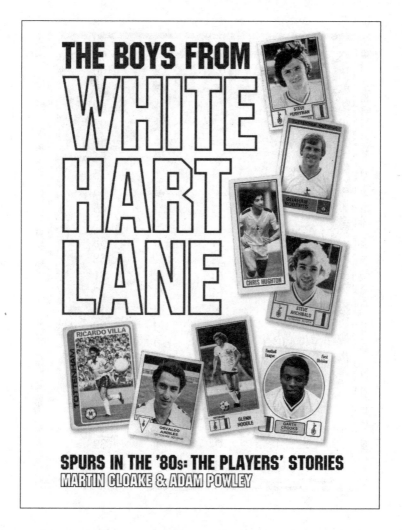

THE BOYS FROM WHITE HART LANE

SPURS IN THE '80s: THE PLAYERS' STORIES
MARTIN CLOAKE & ADAM POWLEY

www.visionsp.co.uk

Also by Vision Sports Publishing

www.visionsp.co.uk

Also by Vision Sports Publishing

BIG CHIV **MY GOALS IN LIFE**

by **MARTIN CHIVERS** with PAOLO HEWITT

www.visionsp.co.uk

Also by Vision Sports Publishing

THE

SPURS

MISCELLANY

BY ADAM POWLEY & MARTIN CLOAKE

FOREWORD BY **STEVE PERRYMAN**

www.visionsp.co.uk

Coming Autumn 2010

The Spurs Double:
The official 50th anniversary book

www.visionsp.co.uk

Coming Autumn 2010

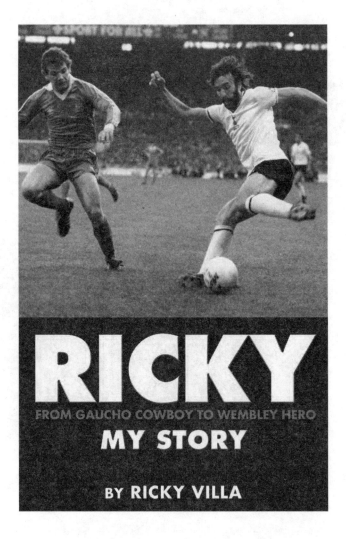

RICKY

FROM GAUCHO COWBOY TO WEMBLEY HERO

MY STORY

BY RICKY VILLA

www.visionsp.co.uk